# COMPULSIVE ACTS:

## ESSAYS, INTERVIEWS, REFLECTIONS ON THE WORKS OF SKY GILBERT

# ESSENTIAL WRITERS SERIES 37

**Canada Council    Conseil des Arts
for the Arts       du Canada**

**ONTARIO ARTS COUNCIL
CONSEIL DES ARTS DE L'ONTARIO**

an Ontario government agency
un organisme du gouvernement de l'Ontario

Guernica Editions Inc. acknowledges the support of
the Canada Council for the Arts and the Ontario Arts Council.
The Ontario Arts Council is an agency of the Government of Ontario

We acknowledge the financial support of the Government of Canada
through the Canada Book Fund (CBF) for our publishing activities.

# COMPULSIVE ACTS:

## ESSAYS, INTERVIEWS, REFLECTIONS ON THE WORKS OF SKY GILBERT

*Edited by*
## David Bateman

**GUERNICA**
TORONTO—BUFFALO—BERKELEY—LANCASTER (U.K.)
2014

David Bateman, editor
Michael Mirolla, general editor
Joseph Pivato, series editor
Book Design by Jill Ronsley
Guernica Editions Inc.
P.O. Box 76080, Abbey Market, Oakville, (ON), Canada L6M 3H5
2250 Military Road, Tonawanda, N.Y. 14150-6000 U.S.A.
Distributors:
University of Toronto Press Distribution,
5201 Dufferin Street, Toronto (ON), Canada M3H 5T8
Gazelle Book Services, White Cross Mills, High Town, Lancaster LA1
4XS U.K.

First edition.
Printed in Canada.

Legal Deposit—First Quarter
Library of Congress Catalog Card Number: 2014934847
Library and Archives Canada Cataloguing in Publication

Compulsive Acts: Essays, Interviews, Reflections on the Works of Sky
Gilbert / David Bateman, editor.

(Essential writers series ; 37)
Includes bibliographical references.
Issued in print and electronic formats.
ISBN 978-1-55071-720-4 (pbk.).--ISBN 978-1-55071-721-1 (epub).--
ISBN 978-1-55071-722-8 (mobi)

1. Gilbert, Sky--Criticism and interpretation. I. Bateman,
David, 1956-, editor of compilation II. Series: Writers series
(Toronto, Ont.) ; 37

PS8563.I4743Z84 2014      C812'.54      C2014-900249-1
                                        C2014-900250-5

# CONTENTS

## INTERVIEWS

# CONCLUSIONS

# Introductions

# Compulsive Acts & Everyday Revulsions

## David Bateman

I HAVE A LONG HISTORY OF RESPONDING to the prolific output and the cultural generosity of Sky Gilbert. In the 1980s I was introduced to his work through his play *The Dressing Gown*. As a young writer testing my wings in a gay publication (RITES), I felt compelled to respond to Gilbert's play with my own set of liberationist politics and my mistrust of stereotypes firmly planted within a critical view of gay representation, both onstage and off. A brief exchange in RITES revealed differences that Gilbert and I had regarding queer representation. As RM Vaughan states in his *National Post* article on Gilbert's status as a quintessentially Canadian "freak" and "patron saint," those differences of opinion are never the stuff of which a bad professional relationship is made when it comes to the generosity and encouragement Sky has shown to other queer artists over the past four decades.

> "And unlike many intellectual leaders, he has never asked us to agree with his prolific opinions—only to be equally forthright and unashamed in ours."
> —RM Vaughan

Before the initial RITES review appeared I met Gilbert for the first time in the lobby of the Poor Alex theatre. I introduced myself and had the audacity to let him know that a less than positive review was about to appear, one that I had written. He responded by telling me to let my review speak for itself and we parted company. We were not off to what one might call a good start. Not long after this period, in the late eighties, I sent an autobiographical monologue to him, on the recommendation of a mutual friend, David Ramsden. Given our first meeting, I was hesitant, but gave it a go. I was a young queer artist embarking on a career as a performance artist. I was very pleasantly surprised by Gilbert's quick and positive response to my submission. He invited me to be part of the annual Queerculture festival. My performance was programmed into the 1st Annual Avant-Garde Drag Performance component (there was no second) of the week-long series of queer entertainment that attracted the attention of right wing city hall aficionados, and culminated in a public protest that a number of queer artists attended. Gilbert gave me my first opportunity in Toronto theatre and I went on to perform in two Queerculture festivals at the George Street venue, and over ten Rhubarbs at both George Street and Alexander. In the intervening years I had a solo show as part of the Alexander Street season and most recently I sang a dirty little happy birthday ditty to Gilbert at his 60th on stage in Talulah's Cabaret with Gilbert dressed as Jane (his drag alter ego) sitting not far away from me, in a glamourous wheelchair that eased the pain of arthritis. We have come a long way, and we're still rolling along.

As editor of this collection I see my role in much the same way I have always viewed Gilbert's work: as someone interested in finding the impulse, the compulsion, the motivating factors, and a handful of the high points in a prolific career that cannot be fully served in a single collection of essays. The incredibly prolific nature of a fin de siècle playwright moving into the 21st century with a body of work that continues to excite on a variety of complex levels, makes Gilbert a foremost queer Canadian theatre artist. This volume can by no means represent all of his work. What it can represent is a selection of responses to specific works that locate him within a pantheon of acutely queer, political writers whose primary impulse strikes me as being a kind of compulsion, and what some readers, and city councillors, might describe as revulsion. I have constructed my revisionist title from Gloria Steinem's formative collection of feminist essays *Outrageous Acts and Everyday Rebellions* because I feel that the work being examined here possesses a fine commingling of both compulsion and revulsion, both close cousins to the inbred notions of outrage and rebellion. Gilbert sees cultural injustice, writes a play about it, and reveals all of the outrage, revulsion, rebellion, and compulsion that these everyday narratives possess. To put it not so mildly, by doing so he liberates audiences, in a theatrical manner, whether they like it or not, from the tyranny of political and cultural oppression.

The titillating and intentionally misleading intimacy of a line like "It seemed enough, inside my mind, that Sky Gilbert was coming home to me" reveals, in Hope Thompson's piece, the effects Gilbert's work had on a young woman, Thompson herself, whose boyfriend at the time rode his skateboard to see an early Gilbert play with her. Thompson's emergence as an acclaimed lesbian playwright, and Gilbert's later support of her work, skillfully configure the kind of performative promise that a queer play and a queer playwright can make to their audience when that audience is young, about to come out, and hungry for provocative representations of sexual and sensual identity. Thompson places herself at the apex of this queer coming out story and, following her preface, utilizes the work of another queer playwright, Tennessee Williams, in order to further exemplify the profound effect Gilbert had on her emergence as an artist and an astute theatre practitioner who continues to use forms of inter-textual nostalgia in her work to great parodic effect.

Thompson's contribution unconsciously reflects later work in this collection including Carl Wilson's blog entry about a Bob Wiseman lyric that pays homage to performer Tracy Wright. Wilson reflects upon Wiseman's ambivalent yet changing response to Gilbert through the refracted gaze of an artist being affected by ways in which Gilbert can performatively create common ground, among diverse individuals, through his words—words that ultimately have the power to change the spectators mind.

Closer to the end of the book we have a poolside email from Palm Springs where Gilbert sustains his career long compulsion for observing the social and sexual environments surrounding him. Indirectly reflective of Hope Thompson's insights into his work, Gilbert offers up some of his own radical and insightful observations about generational differences and behaviour among individuals immersed within an ever evolving queer environment marked by significant issues ranging from drug use, AIDS, and the empowering evolution of HIV identity. Ultimately, Thompson, Wiseman, Wilson—and Gilbert himself—attest to the ways in which the artist, as observer, can evolve through a myriad of experiences by way of diverse, intimate, and complex personal journeys.

From the interview between Mike Hoolboom and Hillar Liitoja, we may glean a sense of Gilbert's reputation as a frequently misjudged artist whose impulse to write write write write write can sometimes get him into hot water with artists and audiences. So be it. At the end of the day he has a body of work that he has, to some degree, lost track of. But this volume possesses the especial luxury of being able to include the thoughts of those closest to him during a long career that has not let up, despite lovers and detractors, and continues to evolve.

There are so many plays out there it is hard to keep them all accounted for. And that is part of the point around his compulsive artistic nature. In an interview conducted for this collection, Gilbert said he felt that "a lot of artists are compulsive." He went on to say that this quality "makes his work more immediate." As we chatted about a variety of ideas around his work, we went back and forth from this notion of compulsion and various strains trickled in. When he said that his "need for approval is a bit compulsive, a bit neurotic," I was struck by an especially honest admission concerning the why and the how of his immense artistic output. What better way than an endless stream of plays to gain the approval of a community of actors and spectators all scrambling to find work and to be successful in a small explosive queer community over a thirty- to forty-year period.

While artist/designer Wendy White's whimsical poem celebrates Gilbert's drag persona, and musician Bob Wiseman's lyric reveals an evolution of both positive and negative thought regarding Gilbert's work, Paul Halferty's essay articulates the specific period and politics that began to inspire Gilbert to write immediately and directly about the very queer events unfolding around him. And yet his acute attention to detail, as I discuss in the closing essay on *The AIDS Plays*, comes full circle and reveals that Gilbert's body of work consistently possesses a broad, in a sense timeless awareness of the many components that comprise queer politics. It has never been about just one thing. Gilbert's most successful scripts—from *Drag Queens In Outer Space* and *Drag Queens on Trial*, to *The Birth of Casper G. Schmidt* and *Rope Enough*,[1] and *I Have AIDS*—all possess a sense of a somewhat universalized queer theme that can be applied to many identities within many seemingly disparate communities. Lana from *Drag Queens on Trial* and Ron from *I Have AIDS* exemplify this dramaturgical tendency to locate similar pleas within very different personalities. These diverse personalities take us on a journey through the degrees of glamour found in the world of drag to "the ugliest little small town on earth" to the glam/grimy city lights of Toronto and the historicized sites of AIDS celebrities, dead philosophers, transsexual identity, and the infatuated, measured anecdotes of a lover/muse who co-celebrates non-monogamy with Gilbert in his work and in his bedroom. A personal response to Gilbert's quirky and delightfully dirty play *Heliogabalus* reveals one of Gilbert's many muses and how he can pick up an idea from the reading list of an immediate source—his lover of many years, Ian Jarvis—and turn it into a wild historicized ride through the life of a Roman Emperor's lustful philosophies and erotic encounters.

Moynan King, as an actor/writer located firmly within the community of artists that have moved through Buddies In Bad Times Theatre and into their own artistic spheres, gives a meta-theatrical take on what it was like to inhabit a role written specifically for her. As a lesbian woman 'playing it straight' she finds a variety of well-documented academic sites to visit and to apply to her experience. King's spare and eloquently personalized use of Lionel Abel's formative work on meta-theatre reveals the ways in which it applies to Gilbert's frequently meta-theatrical view of the world onstage and off. The diversity of Gilbert's political trajectory in any given play lands him in the unenviable writerly position of having to make sense of a chaotic social sphere. Including more than one focus in his work, as he did in *Drag Queens in Outer Space*, by coupling drag identity and AIDS identity, he problematizes a political site in a complex manner that radiates outward from the playing space meta-theatrically and into and immediate political sphere. Gay men and drag queens are already marginalized. When we are dying of AIDS, and/or living with HIV, the marginalization becomes even more acute. When King negotiates her own place within this queer drama, she is able to discover the complex ways in which playing it straight problematizes her own identity, as well as the identity of the other characters within Gilbert's overall body of work.

Like Abel's definitive take on meta-theatre, Gilbert's work represents an obstinate, unyielding "unwillingness to regard any image of the world as ultimate." Abel points to the meta-theatrical text as a phenomenon that "glorifies" this unwilling nature. King, as an actor and researcher, locates this in a specific play, *The Birth of Casper G. Schmidt*, and indirectly articulates the ways in which these "destabilizing point[s] of view" connect the experience to my general point regarding compulsion when she includes Gilbert's admission that he always experiences a "general anxiety about not getting it right" as a playwright. By trying to always get it right Gilbert makes a consistent attempt to establish this "destabilizing point of view" rather than the perspective of the "omnipotent narrator." Abel's assertion that "[t]ragedy glorifies the structures of the world" places Gilbert's body of work within a kind of postmodern theatrics committed to fracturing the monolith, to look inside, and to see all of the messy parts—the decidedly non-glorious aspects of tragedy that turn his plays into nothing of the kind—in all their sordid glory, and frequently fabulous because fabulous is never glorious—it is just fabulous and fabulous is messy—and fabulous is verbose …

Gilbert masters and re-masters the "dramedy" over and over in his plays, never stooping so low as to suggest that he would allow a stabilized version of Oedipus to wander through one of his works and end up in some contemporary version of Colonus. If Gilbert were to write a play of such Greek-ish proportions, undoubtedly Jocasta's jewellery as visual weaponry would play an essential drag role, and the incestuous impulse for all of Oedipus' whiny meanderings would be full blown, onstage, and not hidden behind the mask of the very tragic non meta-theatrical heritage that much of mainstream theatre has been prone to. Let's fuck onstage is what so many characters in Gilbert's plays insist upon. Let's see the pity and fear enacted rather than a cast of wailing characters responding to it. Whether they do it or not in a Sky Gilbert play, we are always on the edge of our seats anticipating how and when the playwright might decide to just go ahead and fuck us all up with an infuriating idea or an irresistible theatrical ploy.

Keith Cole's sly anecdotal response to working with Gilbert in a variety of capacities over the years provided the initial impulse to investigate the idea of compulsion in Gilbert's works. In early talks with Cole, where I repeatedly asked him when he was going to re-mount my favourite performance piece of all time, *The Dildo Ballet*, he focused his attention away from my preoccupation with classically trained cock and committed himself to a no holds barred discussion of Gilbert's ongoing compulsion to find everything everywhere every time he looks at a new situation and a new idea that interests him. Cole asks important anecdotal questions that provide fascinating clues for anyone involved in finding all of the plays and poring over them for instances of grand insight, quirky misidentification, ponderous at times revealing stereotypes, and explosive and highly politicized critiques of all the bullshit we queers have had to endure. Among Cole's many queries lie significant inroads into questions as open ended and as soul-searching as: "Where does this world exist and what does it reveal to the viewer and the reader?" Cole becomes interested in how Gilbert has consistently played with himself, as a complex character writing complex characters, and the ways in which femininity in particular has both entered and exited Gilbert's own body and the bodies he writes in diverse ways:

Sky and his characters have been passing on information and the theatrical baton of stage magic for several years now. Information and the value of it is a concern for Sky and his otherworld creations. All those relevant are located theatrically through their deeds, situations and words and this allows Sky and his merry gang to extend their points of view, passions and mad musing to the great outwards and beyond without losing their imperative message— written history must and will change and the future must also enjoy the same fate in the hands of Sky and his many beloved or much maligned characters.

With an eloquent conclusion, positing "Sky as woman. Sky as mother. Two absurd sentences. Sky is a biological off shoot of a woman, his mother" Cole goes on to state:

Sky has re-generated his woman-mother as the object and a highly characterized, desirable product who lives generously in a community of Sky's work. The female spectre character looms large in Sky's work: either as oral and aural confrontational visions or as oral and aural haunting woman who is plaintive, incoherent and pleading who needs to be released from their mental fog and sexual recession and repression before they fade into the void known as the past.

And finally, Cole claims a meta-theatrical space as someone who has witnessed this plethora of problematized identity when he simply states that "Sky's characters are monumental often reflecting back onto the people who play them—more than the sum of all their parts."

The sum and substance of an overview of a playwright's work—an overview that can only account for a half dozen or so plays—is generously and critically configured in Mike Hoolboom's interview with Hillar Liitoja. Liitoja's especial love for Gilbert and his work, and the rigourous ways in which they tackled a non-collaborative collaboration, giving Liitoja free rein with one of Gilbert's novels as he adapted it to the stage of his very own kitchen, shows the magnanimous quality of someone hell bent on gaining approval—Gilbert—and the theatrical depths to which this magnanimity can go. The haunting and embracing ambience of the actual production Liitoja created was a very unique and enduring experience for me. The interview with Hoolboom reveals Liitoja's fascination with Gilbert as a person and an artist, and moves into some enlightening details regarding Gilbert's insistence on the immediacy of the play writing act, and his stubbornness to resist editing. Gilbert places this impulse within his self-assured desire to create juicily and prolifically, and with an acute sense of the here and now. Liitoja's extended meditation on the ways in which he adapted *Wit in Love* to the meta-theatrical stage of his own home shows a strong bond between two somewhat disparate artists connecting in a single and satisfying moment of theatre and theatricality, as well as providing an in depth look at another artist's very intriguing meta-theatrical process. In his adaptation Liitoja inhabits the psyche of a complex character from history translated through the necessary distortions of any retrospective dramaturgy in general, and the interiority of Gilbert's novel based on an aspect of Wittgenstein's life as a homosexual philosopher of closeted proportions.[2]

In examining Gilbert's work in film, RM Vaughan takes us on a journey that lands us back within the realm of theatre by astutely observing the ways in which Gilbert "shows a scene, allows the viewer to recognize the inherently manipulative strategy of 'showing,' presents dilemmas to be unpacked (and one does unpack them, one does take sides, has moments of illusive 'identification' with particular characters) and then moves on to the next scene, repeating the passive/active game play." Vaughan's interview harkens back to the meta-theatrical idea of destabilization when he discusses some of Gilbert's critics as individuals intent upon discrediting his films because they were "just like plays."

Giving power to his characters and then taking it away, and perhaps re-gifting that same power back to them in another scene, another play, works the notion of meta-theatricality in the films and the plays in an evocative and challenging way. Vaughan's interview further examines the general lens of Gilbert's work and how it has been consistently committed to a worldview that simply never stays the same.

Moynan King's interview with Ellen-Ray Hennessy and Ann Holloway's personal/academic essay on women's comedy of resistance gives us further fuel for Gilbert's compulsive commitment to his characters and the people who have played them. Loyalty is at times a strained relationship that actors, writers and directors must endure within the ever ephemeral and close-knit world of theatre. There are many views of many identities in a Gilbert character before it leaves the page. When an actor steps in manifold identities join the crowd and battle it out for a place in the proverbial sun.

As a former artistic director of Buddies In Bad Times Theatre, just after Gilbert's reign, Sarah Garton Stanley provides us with enlightening anecdotes regarding the ways in which his work has moved out into the world,

affecting a whole new generation of performers and spectators, and how she has come to view her own theatrical
journey as a part of the recent fascination with queer
failure theory outlined in Judith (Jack) Halberstam's
formative text *The Queer Art of Failure.*

Two selections from my review blog give a glimpse
of the ways in which I have chosen to locate Gilbert's
work within a larger political sphere, while an email from
Gilbert during a winter vacation reveals his ongoing
compulsion to keenly observe and comment upon everything around him, even while he's sipping a cocktail by a
pool in Palm Springs trying to relax with his lover. Sky's
2013 play *To My 28-Year-Old Self* provides this collection
with a glimpse of how the playwright takes a step back
in a long career to look closely at his past aspirations
within both social and sexual spheres. The full script
of Gilbert's two hander, where he plays himself with
another actor playing his younger self (Spencer Charles
Smith played the young Gilbert in the original production), gives readers a balanced self-professed framework
to the overall meta-theatrical tone that both directly and
indirectly marks all of the essays, interviews, and medita-
tions in this collection. There are many more plays and
many more reviews that this slim volume cannot hope to
encounter. In the meantime, I continue my fascination
with Gilbert's proliferation of characters and ideas as they
continue to act, to revile, to react, to be compulsive, to
outrage and to rebel. What will he come up with next
in his ongoing compulsion to say what he thinks about
everything under the queer explosive sun.

# Endnotes

1. The play *Rope Enough* is based on the Hitchcock film
   *Compulsion.*
2. *The Professions in Contemporary Drama* pp. 124-125
   by Daniel Meyer-Dinkgräfe, ch. 9 Wittgenstein and
   Morality.

# Ode To Jane: Une Poème of my Owen

## Wendy White

**S.B.,**

'Ello, Bonjour, Bienvenue, Welcome, Salut, Ça va? Moi?

Je suis 'appee parce que aujourd'hui ees la fête de ma belle coquette amie:

La Jane! Et voilà, pour elle, une poème of my owen:

Oh Jane
Oh Jane
Oh la la, La Jane
We are so veree much ze same
Lovink to Love ees our claim to fame
Sometimes our 'earts are beegerrr zen our brain
But we are not completelee to blame
For driveenk so many eensane
So many, we cannot rememberrr ze name!
Eet ees only natural we eegnite beaucoup a-flame
Parce que—amourrr, to us, ees a funny leetle game
When ze arrow de Coopid takes eets aim
Somsing sweetches eenside our brain
We flush our een'ibitions down ze drain,

And next sing you know,
We run stark-ed nake-ed, gaylee in ze rain
Ah oui, we are creatures of eternal pass-ione
Eet ees een our blood, not simply fass-ione
To be deep een amourrr
To feel love troo every poorrr
We embrass la vie
Wheech eese veree much like ze sea
We can plunge deep down, or onlee to ze knee
Sometimes, zere ees pain
But la reesk-taking ees never een vain
Thees ees la leçon we gain
When we embrass l'esprit de La Jane
I raise my imaginaire glass of champagne
Bon fête, Oh Jane
Oh Jane, je t'aime!

Note: "S.B." is the abbreviation for Wendy's drag name "Solita Bleu"—a chanteuse and poet coquette. Solita recited this poem for Sky Gilbert's fortieth birthday in 1992, at Buddies on George Street. There were ten Janes—ten people dressed as Jane including Daniel Brooks, Greg Campbell, Bruno Miguel (baby Jane in a diaper), Darren O'Donnell, Grant Ramsay, David Roche, Edward Roy, and Wendy White.

# Sky Gilbert: National Post Article

## RM Vaughan

Note from the paper: *The National Post is conducting a search to find Canada's most important "public intellectual." In today's installment, RM Vaughan profiles playwright and author Sky Gilbert. For Canadian "freaks," a patron saint.*

Until recently, Canada's literary establishment (particularly the more cautious, closeted members of its lavender mafia) liked to pretend that Sky Gilbert didn't exist. When it did speak his name it was always modified with a "too"—Gilbert was too radical, too open, too confrontational, too sexy, too outrageous. In other words, he was—and is still—everything Can-Lit is not.

Gilbert's career as a playwright is the stuff of Canadian theatre legend. Beginning in the late 1970s, back when "gay" meant happy in polite society, Gilbert founded Buddies in Bad Times—a theatre company dedicated to poetic, sexual, queer liberationist productions. He ran the company for 18 years, from 1979 to 1997, and managed to excite, illuminate and piss off just about every critic and culture commentator in the country.

The plays Gilbert produced—his own and the works of others—drop-kicked a snore-inducing theatre scene that was better known for polite parlour-room comedies. His plays focused on unmentionable subjects—sexual deviance, class conflict, artistic excess—and approached them with a poetic panache that had more in common with watering-hole drag shows than the tea cups and crinolines of mainstream theatre.

Gilbert's tenure at Buddies opened up theatre practice to a generation of misfits and restless souls who would otherwise have had to ply their trade in New York or London, or not at all. I am proud to say that I am one such artist.

Gilbert has never been one to hide behind the curtains. Along with running Buddies and writing an astonishing number of plays (42 at last count), he has penned countless fiery articles for magazines, always arguing for sexual freedom and against prudery; authored 15 books in every genre from fiction to memoir; and made a point of supporting, often at the front of the picket line, causes as diverse as sex-workers' rights, arts funding and police accountability.

Who can forget Gilbert's legendary 1993 fight with the *Toronto Sun*, prompted by the newspaper's foolish attempts to have public funding taken away from the "smut mongers" at Buddies? Arguing that art that offends the general public is actually *more* vital than art that merely flatters the public, Gilbert raced to the *Sun*'s offices in glorious drag—all the rage, big blond wig, and smart skirt set.

In more recent years, Gilbert has taken on the 19th century hangovers that fuel our vice laws, the conservative gay backlash of the late 1990s (which threatened to turn all queer people into lawn-mowing suburban homeowners in matching sweaters) and, most recently, the pitfalls of the gay marriage debate.

The effect of Gilbert's public intellectualizing has been twofold. First, his frank—and, at times, unabashedly lurid—art helped break the stranglehold of "good taste" and Anglican decorum-choking English Canadian writing. As Gilbert explained in his memoir, Canadian art can easily be divided into two camps: the charming and the ejaculatory. The charming—think *The Hatbox Letters*, Freeman Patterson photographs, or practically anything generated by the CBC—gently reaffirms the status quo with comforting homilies. The ejaculatory—Riopelle's paintings, Peaches CDs or the novels of Michael Turner—asks more questions than it answers, favours blunt talk over discretion and is not afraid to be messy and inconclusive. Gilbert, always ready with an impertinent response, is patron saint of the ejaculatory.

Second, all of us who scribble for a living owe thanks to Gilbert for helping to create a more inclusive and far more honest public dialogue around sexuality issues. Gilbert pushed open the door and the rest of us freaks poured in behind him. And, unlike many intellectual leaders, he has never asked us to agree with his prolific opinions—only to be equally forthright and unashamed in ours.

Canada is a less shy and socially backward nation thanks to Gilbert's bluntness. He has taught us that change only comes when there is somebody willing to stand at the front of the line with a pike—or, just as powerful, a gorgeous wig and spectacular falsies.

# Crises and Community: Sky Gilbert, *Drag Queens on Trial*, and the Development of Gay Theatre and Community in Toronto 1975-1985

## J. Paul Halferty

*LANA: Perhaps I have made choices many would not agree with but I followed my heart [...] I have not been afraid to look inside myself, to live on the edge of morality, society, of the world itself and if I must die for it, so be it. And to all the little boys out there who don't want to wear their blue booties but pick out pink ones, to all the little girls who would rather wear army boots than spike heels, to anyone who has ever challenged authority because they lived by their own lights I say don't turn back. Don't give up. It was worth it. (78–79)*

On 17 October 1985 a seminal event in the cultural history of gay men and theatre in Toronto occurred at a porn cinema on Bloor Street: Sky Gilbert did drag for the first time. The occasion was the opening night of his play *Drag Queens on Trial: A Courtroom Melodrama*. In his memoirs, Gilbert recalls:

> I arrived with [my friend] David Pond as my escort. It was my first experience with drag, and I must have

looked a treat. I didn't even apply any foundation (I wouldn't leave the house in drag without foundation these days, but of course I'm much older now!). With David Pond's help, I applied a little rouge and made up my eyes, and plopped a punkish fright wig on my head. It was lovely having my little skinhead boy on my arm and sitting down right in front of the critics. 'Well, this is the end of my career,' I thought. 'But, fuck, this is a funny play. And I'm going to go down in all my flaming glory.' (*Ejaculations* 92)

Gilbert was convinced that with *Drag Queens*, an "outrageous, filthy, frank slice of gay life," (*Ejaculations* 87) whose "subject matter was sure to offend" (*Ejaculations* 85), he was "sabotaging [his] career" (*Ejaculations* 87). "I was afraid that critics would be offended by my foul-mouthed piece, but I believed in what it had to say—that the outcast position was, in effect, sacred and holy" (*Ejaculations* 87). Thankfully, these grim predictions were not true. In fact, the very opposite: *Drag Queens* would be Gilbert's greatest success; the critics would rave, though they misinterpreted the play and its politics; and it would lay the political and aesthetic foundation of the rest of his career. Like his drag queens Gilbert would embrace a marginal position *vis-à-vis* Toronto's gay community and its theatre industry. Gilbert's first foray into drag would also eventually beget his now legendary alter-ego "Jane," whose performances onstage and off would blur the line between reality and theatricality in productive and political ways.

No other theatre artist has had a greater influence on Toronto gay theatre than Gilbert. Buddies in Bad Times Theatre, the company he founded in 1979, was by 1994 the largest gay and lesbian theatre in North America. In a variety of genres, but none more than drama, he is a prolific writer. He has written more than thirty plays, five novels, several books of poetry, and a number of films. In its thirty-four-year storied history Buddies has produced hundreds of plays by almost as many playwrights. In Gilbert's theatrical career, gay identity, community and politics intersected with *avant-garde* theatrical perform-ance in ways that are both rich and complex.

Although Gilbert had been staging plays that con-cerned gay love, sex, and culture from the time that he came out as a gay man in 1980, *Drag Queens on Trial* stands out as a watershed: it expresses the political and social currents of its time, and its production determined the course of his career, and the politics of his theatre, Buddies in Bad Times. *Drag Queens* intervened in debates about the purpose of gay community: a radical force for revolution and liberation, or a group of individuals entitled to equality and integration within existing social and political frameworks. Its critique of society's liberal institutions responded to the backlash Toronto's gay community suffered in the late-1970s and early-1980s, and challenged its increasing desire to be included within the nation's legal frameworks. Its parody of the legal justice system in particular reacted to the raids on *The Body Politic* and, more spectacularly, "Operation Soap," the raids of four Toronto bathhouses by Toronto Police in February 1981, resulting in hundreds of arrests and which galvanized the gay community. Its parody of the medical establishment intervened into the politics of the AIDS crisis, specifically the politics of promiscuity in gay male community formation, and the dangers of gay men being re-pathologized by the AIDS pandemic. Its camp deployment of drag indicted society, including the gay community, for its marginalization of non-traditional expressions of gender. Privileging a self-conscious theatricality, *Drag Queens* combined meta-theatrical and parodic form with its political content to humorously but critically demonstrate how non-normative gender identities were regularly delegitimated, anticipating the performative critique of gender, queer theory, and politics articulated by theorists such as Judith Butler at the end of the decade.

One of his greatest successes, and a play anthologized with significant contemporary Canadian works, *Drag Queens* is also pivotal in Gilbert's career.[1] In it his iconoclastically pro-sexual politics, his voice as a political gay playwright, and his use of drag and parody come to maturity. It was a departure in form, content, and politics from his early "poet-and-his-boys" plays, and reacted against his greatest success to date, *The Dressing Gown*. *Drag Queens* was, in Gilbert's own words, "an act of theatrical rebellion [...] against *The Dressing Gown*. [...] And everything else I identified as mainstream" (*Ejaculations* 85). When read in the context of his biography, the early years of both Buddies' history, and Gilbert's own artistic development, *Drag Queens* stands out as a radical dramaturgical and political turn in Gilbert's career and gay theatre in Toronto.

Gilbert's biggest box-office and critical hit, this play is, I argue, the most important gay play produced in Toronto in the 1980s. It firmly entrenched Buddies in its anti-assimilationist position *vis-à-vis* the city's mainstream gay and lesbian politics; it espoused a constructivist/performative conception of gender and identity that laid the foundation for the queer politics that the company would espouse toward the end of the decade; it is the first play produced in Toronto to deal with the AIDS epidemic, which it does through a radical, defiant, and, most importantly, pro-sexual politic. Like Lana Lust suggests in the excerpt that opens this essay, Gilbert now embraced politics that were aggressively iconoclastic, ironic, coalitional, and rousing. He also regularly deployed camp and drag as a performative form of political and social critique in his stage plays, and in performances offstage as Jane. Since *Drag Queens* Gilbert has continually railed against conformity within the gay community and its increasing embrace of liberal integration. He has asserted the inviolate importance of personal choice, and encouraged solidarity amongst those at society's maltreated margins, what the play characterizes as its "sexual outlaws." Directly preceding both Buddies inaugural Four-Play festival, the company's first explicitly gay *and* lesbian programming, and its first independent Rhubarb! festival since 1980, *Drag Queens* announced the company's place as Toronto's and Canada's gay and lesbian theatre.

## Backlash and Transformation: Gay Politics, Activism and AIDS in Toronto, 1976 to 1985

Toronto's gay community underwent significant growth and change between in the late-1970s and early 1980s. Paradoxically, this period saw a decline in the currency of the revolutionary gay liberation politics, which had encouraged the civil rights model and gay identity politics as a *strategy* to transform political consciousness and which had encouraged its growth. The community suffered a severe and multi-pronged backlash, waged primarily by an emerging Christian Right and the

Metropolitan Toronto Police Force.[2] By the mid-1980s, fuelled by the backlash and other factors, a gay identity politics wed to gay civil rights activism became the *raison d'être* of a larger, more politically liberal and mainstream gay community. In this period, the community was transformed from a disparate set of discrete groups at the margins of society, represented by a small but vocal contingent of gay liberation activists—mostly associated with *The Body Politic*—into a complex and "institutionally complete,"[3] "minority" community, associated with Ward 6, and viewed as a cohesive voting block within the city's municipal politics.[4] Suddenly, a deadly epidemic appeared in this already changing and fraught context; HIV/AIDS came to public consciousness in June 1981, when the Centre for Disease Control and Prevention in the United States noted a cluster of deaths among gay men in Los Angeles ("Pneumocystis Pneumonia—Los Angeles"). It threw the traditional pro-sexual tenets of gay liberation into further dispute, and forced paradigmatic changes in gay consciousness, sexual practice, and community organization.

The backlash against gay community organizing of the early 1970s begins with Anita Bryant's "Save our Children," campaign, which was launched in 1977 to repeal an anti-discrimination ordinance in Dade County, Florida. The American country singer's organization aimed at fostering "traditional" role models in schools by prohibiting employment of gay and lesbian educators. She waged her battle across the United States and was successful in repealing anti-discrimination legislation in five of the six jurisdictions that she and her organization targeted.[5] Bryant also undertook a national tour of Canada, organized by Ken Campbell, Christian minister and founder of Renaissance International, an anti-gay rights organization based in Milton, Ontario. In response to her campaign, the Coalition to Stop Anita Bryant (CSAB) was formed in Toronto in June 1977. On 14 January 1978, the day before Bryant spoke at the People's Church in Scarborough, the CSAB organized a protest that saw more than 800 people march loud and proud along Yonge Street, the largest gay and lesbian rally in Canadian history to date (Warner Never Going Back: A History of Queer Activism in Canada 136).[6] Bryant's visit is particularly important because the size of the protest it provoked signalled a shift in gay politics in Canada: what had been a relatively small number of gay liberation activists working at the fringes was becoming an organized, politicized, and popular social movement.

The six months leading up to Bryant's Canadian tour were tumultuous ones for Toronto's gay community for several reasons. Toronto's gay liberationists had pursued civil rights as a strategy to create a politicized and visible gay community. Their efforts seemed to be working. After years of pursuing human rights legislation in Ontario, a report by the Ontario Human Rights Code Review Committee, entitled *Life Together,* called for the inclusion of "sexual orientation." There was substantial evidence that gay liberationists were successfully changing gay consciousness and making progress toward greater civil inclusions for gay people. A shocking series of events, however, would change the course of gay political culture, philosophy and organizing only a few short days after its release.[7] The first of these was the murder of shoe-shine boy, Emanuel Jaques. Sexually assaulted and killed by four men on 28 July 1977, Jaques' body was discovered on the roof of a heterosexual sex shop on Yonge Street two days

later. As historian Gary Kinsman suggests, the incident
quickly turned from a grisly and tragic death into "moral
panic" (336-38). It provoked a barrage of homophobic
coverage in the press, which called it a "homosexual
murder," among other equally dubious designations.
On the day of Jaques' funeral, 4 August 1977, protestors
held a rally at city hall and demanded the "eradication of
homosexuals," "more power to the police," and the return
of the death penalty (Lynch "Media" 1).

In Toronto of the early 1970s, gay liberationists
employed a civil rights strategy, not as valuable in and of
itself, but primarily as a means to foster gay community by mobilizing unpoliticized gay men and lesbians.
Toronto gay activists appealed to discourses of civil rights
to raise awareness of gay issues, change consciousness
and build a gay community. Their identity politics were
part of a broader and much more radical gay liberationist
project that was dedicated to sweeping sexual liberation,
and refused any form of sexual regulation or censorship.
At its heart, this form of gay liberation was not interested
in equality within society's social, legal and cultural structures: it was a utopian movement dedicated to a sexual
revolution, the aim of which was to fundamentally alter
society. True sexual liberation for all would emerge, they
believed, when "sex stigma" (what we would now call
homophobia), along with sexism, patriarchy, and racism
were eliminated and new forms of bisexuality and an an-
drogynous gender identification would become the norm.

The backlash forced the gay community to organize in new ways, encouraged spokespeople to come
forward, and prompted political positions and alliances
to form, especially within the city's municipal politics.
For example, Coordinator of the Coalition for Gay

Rights in Ontario (CGRO), Tom Warner, Director of the Community Homophile Association of Toronto (CHAT), George Hislop, acted as spokespeople for the provincial and municipal gay organizations. In response to the media's handling of the Jaques' murder, they called a press conference in which they expressed their discontent over the media's treatment of the story. They charged the press with transferring guilt for Jaques' murder onto Toronto's gay community. They called for assurances, particularly from Mayor David Crombie, that the city's plans to "clean up" Yonge Street would not include actions against gay businesses, people, or the community generally (Lynch "Media" 1). This was among the first time individuals came forward as leaders within the community and, though they intended to present a formal response on its behalf, it was not received as such by the media. The *Sun*'s general editor Peter Worthington dismissed the news conference, calling it "bizarre" and "ill-conceived," but was nevertheless threatened by it. His editorial cautioned that the city be "weary" of homosexual activists. Quite undemocratically, he characterized their participation in civic life as a thirst for political power, their investment in community as a "sick" hunger for "new recruits," and the defence of gay men and lesbians as a recipe for a new form of normality.

On 30 December 1977, Toronto Police raided *The Body Politic,* the locally published and internationally recognized gay liberation journal, quickly changing the issue from the mainstream press' responsibility not to incite hatred against the gay community, to the gay press' right to freedom of expression. This event was the catalyst that facilitated then Mayor John Sewell's first open support of the community, which he recognized as being under attack. The raid was undertaken in reaction to an article written by Gerald Hannon entitled "Men Loving Boys Loving Men," published in the November 1977 edition of the paper ("Men Loving Boys Loving Men"). Given the rhetoric that lesbians and gay men were a danger to children—propagated by Bryant's "Save our Children" campaign and the rhetoric swirling around Jaques' murder—the article's investigation of consensual sexual relationships between adult men and young boys was politically gutsy and expressed the more sexually radical aspects of gay liberation politics.[8] Member of *The Body Politic* collective, Rick Bébout, characterizes the decision to publish Hannon's article by saying: "So long as kids & sex, however linked, remained a hot button issue (forever, maybe?), the time would never be right, never perfectly safe. But, we realized, we'd never been into playing it safe" (Bébout "Promiscuous Affectations"). When then Mayor Sewell spoke at *The Body Politic*'s "Free the Press" rally early in 1979, the controversy quickly spread to municipal politics. In his address, this young, progressive, and famously bike-riding mayor (those were the days!), took up the minority model of gay community, suggesting that it, like other "ethnic" communities, "contribute[d] significantly to the vitality and versatility of the city" (Hannon "Sewell: Unleashing the Whirlwind" 8). The Mayor also emphasized the importance of the alternative press:

> The trial now going on in regard to *The Body Politic* is seen by many as an attack on the freedom of the press. I wrote the Attorney-General some months ago. Following the seizure of documents from *The Body Politic*, stressing that very concern [...]. I hope that my attendance here tonight can help ensure that an attack on the alternative press in Toronto

> must not be countenanced and that we all must
> act strongly when any kind of attack is suggested.
> (Hannon "Sewell" 10)

Although Sewell intended his appearance to "help calm the political atmosphere so that issues c[ould] be clarified," his presence and his remarks had the exact opposite effect (Hannon "Sewell" 8). Following his appearance at the rally, evangelical minister Ken Campbell appeared on the Christian television program *100 Huntley Street* and, in a highly melodramatic performance, while the telephone number of the mayor's office flashed regularly across the screen, he cried as he recounted his experiences as a witness for the Crown in *The Body Politic* trials. The following day the mayor was met with a barrage of hateful callers, and Sewell would eventually have to leave his office under police protection, having "believable and detailed" death threats (Hannon "Sewell" 8).

Despite this negative attention, Sewell made alliances with members of the gay community, greatly impacting the 1980 election. On 3 September, he announced his endorsement of George Hislop, the first openly gay man to run for city council. Hislop competed in Ward 6, the municipal district that includes the intersection of Church and Wellesley Streets and that portion of Yonge street between Charles and Carlton, the geographic area where most gay businesses were located and where many gays and lesbians lived. His candidacy was established with the support of the Association of Gay Electors (AGE). Formed in the summer of 1979, AGE's mandate was to foster visible gay and lesbian involvement in municipal politics (Nash 238). Sewell's primary rival in the race, Art Eggleton, stoked the flames of homophobic fear in the city by accusing Sewell and Hislop of pushing their way into city hall and "facilitating San Francisco-style gay power politics in Toronto" (Jackson 9). Both Sewell and Hislop lost their bids with popular hostility toward "the rise of 'gay power'" in Toronto being widely cited in the media as the primary reason for their defeat (Warner *Never Going Back: A History of Queer Activism in Canada* 139). Despite this loss, however, the large-scale media attention cast on the gay community by the Sewell and Hislop campaigns helped to establish it as a "minority" within the city's municipal politics, and within popular consciousness (Nash).[9] Among gay men and lesbians, the municipal election of 1980 confirmed the efficacy and possibilities of a liberal politics of participation and inclusion.

Seeing these comparatively conservative movements take shape, some old school gay liberationists argued that the civil rights strategy was beginning to have negative effects on their more utopian gay project. They feared that the civil right strategy, combined with a gay identity politic, was in danger of making the community too liberal, and too easily contented with equality with heterosexuals, at the expense of their radical sexual project. Michael Lynch supports this view in an article entitled "The End of the 'Human Rights Decade.'" He insisted that, with the advent of vibrant, visible, and politically active gay and lesbian communities in Toronto and elsewhere, the civil rights strategy had served its purpose. Lynch published his article in July 1979. In it he cites the recent political turmoil into which San Francisco was plunged when Harvey Milk, the first openly gay man elected to public office in the U.S., was shot and murdered by fellow city supervisor, Dan White. On the evening of Milk's murder, 27 November 1978, San Francisco's gay community mourned with a massive candle-light vigil, attended by tens of thousands, marching from Castro Street to city hall. But on 21 May 1979, when White received the lightest sentence possible for his crime, "voluntary manslaughter," the community rioted, burning police cars, and vandalizing city hall. In contradistinction to the gay rights activists involved in what Lynch calls the "human rights lobby," he encouraged gays to embrace the San Francisco riots as "our own," likening them to the Stonewall riots and arguing that a new strategy for revolutionary politics be similarly born in their wake. The riots for Lynch marked a time for retrospection and radical renewal: "Looking back on ten years of Canadian gay politics we can see that the human rights strategy has in fact been *so successful that it is no longer necessary*" (emphasis in original). Lynch argues that the civil rights strategy was reducing the revolutionary potential of gay liberation by transforming the community into a rights-orientated, liberal movement that "seeks assimilation, legislation, and isolation—the isolation of this one issue from all the rest that concern us." Writing after the 1977 raid of *The Body Politic* but before Operation Soap, Lynch suggests that a new central focus might be the "containment of totalitarian power, particularly that of police." He advocates for such a focus because it would encourage coalition among "women, gays, nonwhite and poor [people]," and curtail the power of the police as "the strongest arm of racism and patriarchy." In the article, Lynch augurs that if gays continue on the civil rights path, they "risk the fate of the abolitionist movement after Emancipation, the feminist movement after the franchise, [and] the black movement after the Civil Rights Act of 1964." He feared that gay liberation's utopian goal of society-wide sexual liberation would evaporate if the movement equated success with legal recognition and civil rights. Indeed, Lynch suggested that "the greatest danger in continuing to seek human rights above all is that we might get them."

Similarly, Ken Popert, stalwart gay liberationist and important member of *The Body Politic*'s editorial collective, wrote an article called "The Dangers of the Minority Game," in 1982. In it he outlines the various ways that homosexuals have been viewed historically, as a "third sex," as a "life style," and now as a "minority community." As one of the most outspoken advocates of gay liberation politics, he argues that gays should not struggle to fit themselves into the world but that they should conversely work toward "reshap[ing] the world, so that *it* will fit *us*" (Popert "Dangers of the Minority Game" 139).

> Looking at ourselves as a minority community has definite survival value. But it is a precarious shelter which can be demolished at any time, for it is easy to show that gays are not just another tile in the multicultural mosaic. And the analogy can blind us to our own realities. But it cannot cancel them out. (Popert "Dangers" 139)

Popert recognizes the "strength-in-numbers" afforded by identity politics, which appeals to an easily understandable and efficacious framework through which community, visibility, and political organizing is effected. He also concedes that its rhetoric fits well within civil rights discourses, and the broader system of governance designed to accommodate difference: the multicultural paradigm that had been gaining currency since it was passed by Pierre Trudeau's federal government in 1971. But Popert also emphasizes the historicity of the minority model. In his article he cautions against a view of identity politics that casts gay and lesbian community as analogous to other "ethnic minorities," suggesting that its place within a multicultural framework can be easily disputed. For Popert, such a view of identity politics, one that fits the gay and lesbian community within existing frameworks, impedes the gay community's ability to see the problems inherent in its own formation, diminishing its ability to address such problems directly. It is not the case that Lynch and Popert were against "identity politics" when deployed to form gay community. But, they opposed the ways that it combined with civil rights discourses to foster inward looking politics, and the ways it encouraged gay men and lesbians to adopt heterosexual paradigms, that mitigated society-wide change.

Shortly after the 1980 election, which did so much to reify the gay and lesbian community within the city's political culture, come the Toronto Bathhouse raids. Operation Soap was executed late in the evening of 5 February 1981. Toronto Police launched simultaneous raids on four area bathhouses, arresting 304 "found-ins" and twenty others as "keepers of a common bawdy house."10 The raids caused more than $35,000 in damage, as the police used hammers, crowbars and shears to break open lockers and doors, and to intimidate bathhouse workers and patrons (Warner *Never* 110). The raids were the largest attack ever faced by Toronto's gay community and were met with a massive revolt. Over 3,000 gay men and lesbians marched down Yonge Street on the evening of 6 February, and diverted to 52 Division's headquarters on Dundas, where they chanted "No More Shit" and "No More Raids." Met at the station by hundreds of police officers, the crowd of angry gay men and lesbians very nearly rioted before taking their protest and their anger to Queen's Park, where the most radical among them broke into the legislature. The raids were interpreted in the press and on the street as a stunning attack on a minority community by the State. The number of arrests was only rivaled by the October Crisis of 1971.

The sinister and scary enormity of the raids galvanized Toronto's gay community, politicizing many who had not historically participated in the gay liberation movement. Despite the dissenting voices of people like Lynch and Popert, the events of the backlash strengthened the agenda of gay rights activists by making gay civil rights an even greater priority. These activists began to enter existing structures of power and to position themselves as leaders of a disenfranchised minority community that demanded equal treatment, access, and recognition, socially and legally. Before the raids, the gay community was somewhat fractured and isolated. It was comprised of activists, who mostly congregated around *The Body Politic* and the Gay Alliance Toward Equality, and gay men who frequented bars and baths, but were unpoliticized (Knegt 20). "What the bathhouse raids did," in the view of gay activist Tim McCaskell, "was bring those groups together" (Knegt 21). One of the "found ins," John Burt, describes his experience of gay identity before and after the raids as follows:

> For the first time I started conceiving of myself being a member of a gay community. Prior to that, I mean, when I heard people talk about a gay community I always laughed, because we were basically a group of strangers who only knew each other from the waist down, and that's it. I mean I have nothing in common with these individuals except sex, a very casual sexual encounter. But now I realize that there

were forces afoot in the world that were now picking on us as a minority, and whether we liked it or not, whether we thought of ourselves as a minority, we were a minority through adversity.

The raids forced gay men and lesbians from all walks of life to realize their need to collectively organize and fight back against malevolent social forces, including agencies of the State.[11] The raids made the need for civil rights that much more urgent as the gay community began to understand legal protections and civil rights as the only real defense against discrimination and attack, ultimately diminishing the currency of gay liberation's more lofty and radical goals.

It may seem surprising today that raiding bathhouses would elicit such varied and widespread outrage from both inside and outside the gay and lesbian community. But it must be remembered that the community, while it had grown significantly in the 1970s, was still fledgling in 1981. The foundations of its keystone organizations were either just being laid or were subject to the same sort of oolice harassment, including established collectives like *The Body Politic*. Among the community's most important organizations, the Lesbian and Gay Community Appeal had only just been founded (1980), Gay Pride was a small-scale community picnic held in different parks, and Buddies was 24 months old and just beginning to identify itself as a gay theatre.[12]

The raids were an affront to gay liberationists, closeted gay men, and to liberal assimilationists, an increasingly large demographic of the gay community which held that equal civil rights should be the primary goal of gay activism. Gay liberation was first and foremost a sexual politics. From this perspective, to attack the bathhouses was to attack the institutional, philosophical, and corporal foundations of gay community in Toronto. Gay liberationists viewed gay sex and male intimacy as means through which gay men could change their consciousness, a view we saw enacted in *No Deposit, No Return*. They understood gay sex as a form of lived political praxis with "Bars and baths," as Ken Popert would later suggest, "[being] to the gay movement what factories are to the labour movement: the context in which masses of people acquire a shared sense of identity and ability to act together for the common good" (Popert "Public Sexuality and Social Space" 29). For closeted gay men, the raids curtailed one of the few places where they could meet, fraternize, and have sex. As Burt suggests, for many gay men who were not politically engaged, the raids were the catalyst that forced them to re-evaluate their understanding of their sexual practices and identity with many concluding that their interests were wed to those of other gay men and the gay community. For liberal assimilationists, the raids were an overt attack by the State on a minority group whose civil rights were not being observed. How could broader acceptance in the mainstream of society be achieved for gay people, couples, and families, when sex in the subaltern world of the bathhouse was subject to such severe social degradation and censure?

In the years that followed the bathhouse raids, the gay and lesbian community deeply distrusted the Toronto Police force, the legal establishment, and the criminal justice system, which they viewed as agents of a conservative heterosexual morality that sought to control its constituents—a concern taken up in *Drag Queens on Trial*. The police attempted to justify their extreme actions by associating gay bathhouses with other "criminal" activities, specifically prostitution, offenses against minors, and organized crime. They brought no evidence to support these accusations, however, and were unable to convincingly make this case in court (Kinsman 314). As many argued in this period, parts of the legal and political establishment in Toronto and Canada, especially the police, continued to associate gay men with criminality, despite the fact that social attitudes toward homosexuality had improved and some legal battles had been won.

Established in 1978, the Right to Privacy Committee (RTPC) represented found-ins and bathhouse owners, fundraised, and defrayed legal costs for those arrested in bathhouse raids (M.C. Smith 68). As a result of Operation Soap, the RTPC became the largest gay and lesbian organization in the country, with a mailing and volunteer list of over 1200 names (Smith 68). Within a year of the raids, it helped organize five large demonstrations and ran publicity campaigns aimed at found-ins, urging them to plead not guilty (Spalding 12-13). The arrests and many trials that followed the raids, including those of *The Body Politic* and the Glad Day bookshop, perpetrated by both the Toronto Police and Canada Customs, were viewed as agents of the State trying to break the political power of the gay community on two fronts: by intimidation and fear of public humiliation through exposure; and by taxing its limited human and financial resources with multiple and costly legal battles.[13] Through its "Court Watch" program, which began in 1982, and which sent volunteers to observe gay-related trials and then report their details in *The Body Politic* and *Xtra!*, the RTPC continued to keep legal issues current in the gay and lesbian community, and to rally support against the malevolent actions of agents of the State (Krawczyk).[14]

The raids and the trials that followed prompted gay liberationists to once again speak out against the liberal assimilationist trend they saw emerging in what was quickly becoming gay rights activism, rather than gay liberation.[15] Once again, Popert was a loud and radical voice. In an article titled "Public sexuality and social space," published as in July 1982, Popert took issue with the way "privacy" was being deployed in the trials that followed the bathhouse raids. For Popert the issue of "so-called public sex" was so important that it threatened to divide gay men from supportive straights, lesbians, and from other gay men. As Popert saw it, sex in public spaces, and the gay promiscuity that such places allowed, was integral to gay community formation. For him, promiscuity "knit together the social fabric of the gay male community."[16]

> Gay and lesbians who are content to live and love within the couple have to wake up to the fact that it is their promiscuous brothers (and, increasingly, sisters) who make the gay movement possible. Without that movement, there would be no safety for gays at all, not even for gay or lesbian couples tucked away quietly in the suburbs. (Popert "Public Sexuality" 30)

Popert argued that, while the bars, baths, and parks found in urban centres provided the physical context within which gay men were able to politically organize, it was the promiscuous behaviour that these spaces fostered that made a gay "collective consciousness" possible. In the piece, Popert contends that arguments against promiscuity, those that encouraged monogamy, that sought to define all forms of sex as "private," or advocated for the closing of bathhouses and backrooms, were tantamount to attacking the capacity of gay men to create politically viable, outward-looking gay communities that could effect any large-scale social change.

Into this already fraught mix of radical sex and oppositional politics, the HIV/AIDS epidemic made its unexpected and unwelcome appearance. In its first years AIDS provoked major political and social problems for gay communities. It challenged some of the basic tenets of gay liberation politics, associating gay sex, even among gay men, with disease and death. It stirred very real fears about the re-pathologization of gay men by medical authorities. Especially in the absence of a known cause, AIDS forced gay men to re-think sexual practices, inventing "safe sex" as a strategy to continue having sex, and being sex positive, while also taking care of themselves and each another. The crisis necessitated new organizations to fight AIDS, to educate people about the syndrome and safe sex, and to care for the sick and dying. And when HIV was eventually determined to be the cause of AIDS by the scientific and medical establishments, and a test for HIV antibodies was developed, the crisis prompted gay men to act proactively against legal and medical authorities, not to mention the Christian Right, who they feared would demonize and stigmatize gay men, and, frighteningly, quarantine HIV positive people as a matter of "public health."

AIDS quite famously came to the public's attention with a *New York Times* article published July 3rd, 1981.[17] The *Times'* story, "Rare Cancer Seen in 41 Homosexuals," describes clusters of Kaposi's Sarcoma cases among gay

men in New York and San Francisco. The article links this
cancer to gay promiscuity, reporting that these men "had
multiple and frequent sexual encounters with different
partners, as many as 10 sexual encounters each night up
to four times a week" (Altman).[18] From our vantage point
in history it may seem strange that Popert, writing about
politics of gay promiscuity in the July/August 1982 edition of *The Body Politic*, does not mention AIDS. The
*Times* article would surely have been known to him as
he was member of *The Body Politic*'s editorial collective,
which published critiques of the article in its September
and October editions, taking particular umbrage with
how the article linked the new cancer to gay promiscuity.[19] And yet, it is also *not* surprising given the immediate
political context of the gay community in Toronto, which
was actively protecting itself against State harassment,
censorship, and oppression. Additionally, the AIDS
epidemic in Toronto was at least two years behind that
of New York and San Francisco. Gay activists in Canada's
largest city were quite understandably sceptical of a "new
cancer" that *only* affected gay men, which was first called
"gay-related immune deficiency" (GRID). Even as late
as July 1983, when the AIDS Committee of Toronto
(ACT) was established, and there were twenty-seven
reported cases in Canada (only nine of which were in
its most populous province, Ontario), many of the city's
most experienced activists were conspicuous in their absence (Silversides 44).[20] Concentrating on the promotion
and growth of gay community, as they had since the early
1970s, these activists felt AIDS organizing in Toronto to
be "unnecessary and counterproductive to the growth
of the gay community," according to Robert Wallace
(qtd. in Silversides 44). Wallace was ACT's first media

coordinator, but even he recalls being "ambivalent" about the epidemic until a visit to San Francisco early in 1983 brought him face to face with the potential scale and fallout of the health crisis.

No comprehensive history of AIDS in Toronto (or Canada) has yet been written, which means, once again, the journalism/activism published in *The Body Politic*, and the many letters to the editors that contested the various views expressed therein, is the best source for gauging political reactions among gay men to the epidemic in the city.[21] Though it was a journal with an international catchment, because its most important journalists were also leaders in Toronto's gay community, its coverage provides the best barometer of the crisis as it developed in Toronto. The magazine's responses to HIV/AIDS were passionate and complex, and very much based in its gay liberation politics. As Mark L. Robertson suggests:

> The challenge [of HIV/AIDS] as *The Body Politic* saw it, was to respond effectively to the epidemic while preserving the community-based and sex-positive values of the gay community. After years of struggle, *The Body Politic* refused to surrender the hard-won freedoms of sexual expression and self-determination to professionals, pundits, and politicians. *The Body Politic* journalism shows how this new challenge to gay culture and identity was negotiated.[22] (Robertson "Aids Coverage in the Body Politic, 1981–1987: An Annotated Bibliography" 416)

Despite trepidation among Toronto's gay radicals, ACT and AIDS Action Now! (AAN) (1987) would be populated by many of the gay liberation activists involved with *The Body Politic*, notably Ed Jackson, Tim McCaskell, Bill Lewis, and, not surprisingly given

his radical politics and place in the community, Michael
Lynch. ACT's and AAN's early years were informed by
the sex-positive politics of autonomy and community
promoted by gay liberation and these activists; however,
these organizations also needed to create new political
models, mandates, and infrastructures that facilitated
working relationships with, and advocacy on the behalf
of, non-gay people affected by HIV/AIDS, as well as
government agencies and non-governmental health
organizations.

In the years before the discovery of the HIV virus,
journalists, doctors, and scientists in the straight and gay
press fervently debated what caused AIDS. Hypotheses
about its causes before 1984 ranged from divine retri-
bution to international conspiracy: from a gay plague
brought about by an angry God, to a Soviet plot that
aimed at destroying capitalism (Treichler 33). The two
primary scientific theories emerged out of the fields that
were associated with the new syndrome, virology and
immunology.[23] Virology proposed the "single agent"
hypothesis. Now the medically accepted theory, virology
holds that there is a human immunodeficiency virus
(HIV) that is contracted through a transfer of bodily flu-
ids (blood, semen, vaginal fluid, pre-ejaculate, or breast
milk). HIV causes the breakdown of the immune system
by attacking the body's white blood cells, leaving the body
susceptible to an array of diseases associated with AIDS.
Immunology proffered the "overload" or "promiscuity"
theory, which held that the causes of AIDS were multiple
and environmental. This hypothesis contended there was
no single agent but that the breakdown of the immune
system was caused by a combination of factors present in
the "lifestyles" of certain gay men. It hypothesized that

acquiring and reacquiring multiple sexually transmitted diseases combined with recreational drug use (amyl nitrate or "poppers" being an early suspect) and, quite literally, too much gay sex, caused the weakening of the immune system and the onset AIDS (Patton 61).[24] The immunology hypothesis reasoned that gay men had "overloaded" their immune systems by "polluting" their bodies to the point that they were as "dirty" as the "third-world" slums whose unsanitary conditions fostered other immunological diseases. The overload theory also "explained" why AIDS had appeared among Haitians, who suffered some of the world's lowest living standards, and who were labelled a "high risk group" along with haemophiliacs and gay men. While proponents of the immunological theory may not have been morally or politically motivated, the promiscuity theory could not help but be associated with, and taken up by, those who wished to re-criminalize and re-pathologize homosexuality and gay liberation. Once again medical discourses were yoking gay sex and gay promiscuity to sickness and to death.

As noted above, *The Body Politic* began to publish critiques, opinion, and commentary on AIDS following the publication of the *New York Times* article. Its first major coverage, however, came in the November 1982 edition. As there were no publicly confirmed cases of AIDS in Toronto, the two articles and the fallout they precipitated mark the public inauguration of the crisis in Toronto's gay community. "Living with Kaposi's" and "The Real Gay Pandemic: Panic and Paranoia," written by Michael Lynch and Bill Lewis respectively, advocate gay-liberation inspired, pro-sexual views on the first year-and-a-half of the crisis, challenging media and medical authorities inside and outside gay communities that connected AIDS to "the gay lifestyle." The articles got the magazine's top billing, with its front cover dedicated to them, reading: "A Special Ten-Page Feature. The New Diseases Among Us. The Case Against Panic: Getting the Information We Need to Make Choices about Sex, Risks, and Being Ill" (Cover).

Lynch, as I have indicated, was a long-time gay activist who in the intervening years became an important AIDS activist. Steeped in gay liberationist politics, he understood "the whole barely charted field of what is now being referred to as AIDS" as both a medical and political concern: a site of discursive contest that would impact how gay men lived their lives. Lynch's article was, in part, inspired by the fear he saw firsthand in New York, where he spent a considerable amount of both his social and professional time, including the previous summer on Fire Island, where the *New York Times* article was a topic of concern and interest. His article makes an impassioned plea for gay men and the gay community to remain autonomous, to hold on to the sexual freedoms they had fought for, and to not allow themselves to become subjects of medical authorities.[25] He writes:

> Another crisis coexists with the medical one. It has gone on largely unexamined, even by the gay press. Like helpless mice we have peremptorily, almost inexplicably, relinquished the one power we so long fought for in constructing our modern gay community: the power to determine our own identity. And to whom have we relinquished it? The very authority we wrested it from in a struggle that occupied us for more than a hundred years: the medical profession. (Lynch "Living with Kaposi's" 31)

The article is written in three parts. The first looks at Lynch's friend who, with his supportive partner and family, had been "living with Kaposi's" for over a year. Its narrative covers moments of fear and difficulty, strength and community, with an especial emphasis on "living," as its title suggests. The second provides an historical overview of homosexuality as a discursive formation since the end of the nineteenth-century. It takes medical authorities (some of them gay) and the gay press to task for what Lynch viewed as the politically regressive ways that AIDS was linked to "the gay lifestyle" and the re-pathologization of gay men. In the third section Lynch issues a call to arms to the gay community:

> We must launch an all-out campaign, of the scale undertook during the Bryant attacks, to fight the equations that gay equals pathology. We can only protest the inaccuracy and inhumanity of the anti-sexual straight press, but we can demand that the gay press give fuller human pictures of support groups and first-person experience. We must challenge the medical profession whenever it attempts to regain its power to define us, or to cloak a moral programme in medical terms. (Lynch "Living" 37).

In the article, Lynch does not minimize the seriousness of AIDS as a medical concern, which he deals with in intimately personal detail through the story of his friend. But Lynch is, however, as concerned about gay men ceding their autonomy, and diluting the sex-positive political philosophies and cultures, as he is with the medical threat. Guided by his gay liberationist politics, he preaches the virtues of gay community and insists that gay men confront this new threat with solidarity, and as a culture.

> We [have to] take our lives and our self-definitions
> back into our own hands. We have to make illness
> gay, and dying gay, and death gay, just as we have
> made sex and baseball and drinking and eating
> and dressing gay. [...] This is the challenge to us in
> 1982—just as the doctors are trying to do it for us.
> (Lynch "Living" 37)

Bill Lewis' article is similarly gay-liberationist in its
orientation, articulating an approach to AIDS that is
about knowledge, autonomy, and risk reduction. A former member of *The Body Politic* collective and professor
of surgery and microbiology at the University of Toronto,
Lewis focuses on sifting through the barrage of medical
"information and misinformation" unleashed since the
*New York Times* article was published a year and a half earlier (Lewis "The Real Gay Epidemic: Panic and Paranoia"
38). It begins with an overview of the current scientific
knowledge about AIDS, including who was expressing
the two primary AIDS-related diseases, Kaposi's Sarcoma
and Pneumocystis Carinii Pneumonia (PCP), and the
cities where these people were located. Like Lynch, Lewis
takes issue with media representations that characterized
AIDS as a "gay plague," which suggested it was "spreading like wildfire," and which argued it was "probably
only a matter of time" before it passed from gay men
to heterosexuals (Lewis "Real" 39). Lewis concedes that
the risk of contracting AIDS or any sexually transmitted
disease increases with greater numbers of sexual partners,
but he also contests the promiscuity theory by citing the
fact that some of the men who seroconverted had had
relatively few sexual partners, as low as four. Lewis also
reports that many of these men were not used drug users,
which was posited as one of the causes of immunological

collapse (Lewis "Real" 40). Coming out on the side of the single-agent theory, Lewis told his readers, "as with any sexually transmitted disease, having only a moderate number of sexual partners is no guarantee that AIDS will be avoided." Echoing Lynch, gay liberation politics, and anticipating the tenets of "safe sex," Lewis argues for an informed and autonomous approach to sex, noting: "If, as is mostly likely the case, AIDS is caused by a communicable agent such as a virus, we can still attempt to evaluate risk in order to arrive at decisions about our own sexual conduct" (Lewis "Real" 39).

In New York, where the epidemic was much more acute, advocates of both the single agent and the immunological hypothesis voiced their theories most prominently on the pages of the city's most important and widely-read gay publication, the *New York Native*. As if it were planned, the *Native* published an article advocating the immunological theory on the same day that *The Body Politic* containing Lynch and Lewis' critiques hit the newsstand. Michael Callen and Richard Berkowitz's "We Know Who We Are: Two Gay Men Declare War on Promiscuity," is a scathing, some might say guilt-ridden attack on gay promiscuity by two gay men. The article begins with the following statement:

> Those of us who have lived a life of excessive promiscuity on the urban gay circuit of bathhouses, backrooms, balconies, sex clubs, meat racks and tearooms know who we are. We could continue to deny overwhelming evidence that the present health crisis is a direct result of the unprecedented promiscuity that has occurred since Stonewall, but such denial is killing us. (Callen, Berkowitz and Dworkin 23)

Callen and Berkowitz promote the immunological/ environmental theory in their article by answering a series of questions about what they think causes AIDS, and by mounting arguments to counter the single agent/ virology hypothesis. They write:

> We, the authors, have concluded that there is no mutant virus and there will be no vaccine. We veterans of the circuit must accept that we have overloaded our immune system with common viruses and other sexually transmitted infections. Our lifestyle has created the present epidemic of AIDS among gay men. But in the end, whichever theory you choose to believe, the obvious and immediate solution to the present crisis is the end of urban gay male promiscuity as we know it today. (Callen, Berkowitz and Dworkin 23)

As this statement makes abundantly clear, Callen and Berkowitz cautioned that the *cause* of AIDS *was* a "gay promiscuous lifestyle," and the drugs and partying that were thought to go with it. The promiscuity theory that they promulgated pronounced the consequences of gay liberation, of not following the moral imperatives of heterosexual monogamy, to be disease and death. Callen, Berkowitz and other believers in the promiscuity theory, gay or straight, in effect blamed the "gay lifestyle" for the epidemic, which revealed deep-seeded sexual guilt among gay men, according to Lynch, and played directly into the hands of the Christian Right, according to Lewis. In the absence of an accepted scientific theory, however—and even long after one was developed—debates about the role of promiscuity in HIV/AIDS concerned gay communities all over North America.

Responding directly to a letter-to-the-editor written by Callen and published in *The Body Politic*, under the title "AIDS: Killing Ourselves," Lewis wrote "AIDS: Discounting the Promiscuity Theory." The article begins with the statement: "Promiscuity. That's the key word in the current debate about AIDS—the acquired immune deficiency syndrome in which the body's natural ability to resist infection collapses" (Lewis "Aids: Discounting"). It explains the "promiscuity theory," elucidates a number of arguments against it, and cites the dangers the theory posed to gay men's health, and to gay community.[26] Lewis maintains that, "although it remains to be proven, all scientific data currently available overwhelmingly supports the theory that AIDS is caused by a communicable agent such as a virus" (Lewis "Aids: Discounting"). Lewis concedes that he is medically more concerned about AIDS than he had been six months prior, but also emphasizes his alarm at the ways AIDS was being characterized as moral punishment for promiscuity by gay men such as Callen, voicing his worry that these arguments would be used against gay communities. To back up this fear up, he recounts the shock he felt when one-third of participants at a gay-organized AIDS conference in Dallas responded affirmatively when asked about closing backrooms and bathhouses as a means to fight AIDS by deterring the "promoti[ion of] multiple sex partners" (Lewis "Real"). With the bathhouse raids still so fresh in the minds of gay activists in Toronto, finding ways to continue to remain true to the politics of gay liberation and community, while also confronting the epidemic sensibly and pro-actively, was of paramount importance. Arguing against those who said "adopting a new sexual ethic we could end the epidemic," Lewis calls for gay men "to seek ways of making sex as healthy and risk-free as possible" and to "defend" community by "defend[ing] the existence of our sexual meeting places" (Lewis "Aids: Discounting").

As Lewis's call to action suggests, "safe sex" practices were developing in the grass-roots activities of gay communities at this time. Not unironically, the concept of safe sex is commonly attributed to Michael Callen and Richard Berkowitz who, with physician and scientist Joseph Sonnobend, published a pamphlet called "How to Have Sex in an Epidemic: One Approach," in May 1983. According to Berkowitz, he and Callen realized that gay men were going to continue to have sex and what needed to be developed were methods of engaging in sexual pleasure that did not spread diseases (Wein). As its title suggests, the pamphlet details ways to have sex in the age of AIDS, and crucially, it was not anti-promiscuity. It advises:

> The Key to this approach is modifying what you do—not how often you do it nor with how many different partners ... As you read on, we hope we make at least one point clear: Sex doesn't make you sick—diseases do ... Once you understand how diseases are transmitted, you can begin to explore medically safe sex. Our challenge is to figure our how we can have gay, life-affirming sex, satisfy our emotional needs, and stay alive! (qtd. in Patton 45)

Very soon thereafter, condom use became the central focus of safe sex education.[27] But condoms had never been part of gay male sexual cultures and, in the early 1980s, they needed to be introduced, explained and, most importantly, used. AIDS organizations such as ACT, public health departments, and gay magazines, as well as the dances, cabaret and theatre performances that were organized as fundraisers, were essential to disseminating information about safe sex and how to do it.[28]

In April 1984, when Federal officials in the U.S. announced that the HTL-III virus, later renamed HIV was the probable cause of AIDS, gay communities in the U.S. and Canada received this news with ambivalence. Many gay men were happy that progress was being made but they also worried the test could facilitate discrimination against "antibody positive" people in the name of public health. In March 1985, in advance of the release of the enzyme-linked immuno-sorbent assay test (ELISA), which tested for the presence of HIV antibodies, the National Gay Task Force along with multiple AIDS service organizations in the U.S. issued a statement encouraging gay men not to take the test. In Canada, at the first national AIDS conference, held in Montreal in May 1985, Vancouver AIDS activists Gordon Price asserted that concern about AIDS among gay men would soon shift from "How can I avoid AIDS?" to "Should I take the test?" (Popert "Taking Aim with an Empty Gun? The Red Cross Says Its Test Will Weed out Bad Blood" 14).

In an editorial written on behalf of *The Body Politic* collective, Ed Jackson and Andrew Lesk examined the difficult predicament into which gay men were placed by the development of the test. Because those in "high-risk" groups (prostitutes, drug users and homosexuals) have few rights under Canadian law, Jackson and Lesk recommended that these people should not take the test:

> The message to individuals in high-risk groups is the
> same regardless of the test results: practice safe sex.
> [...] As long as [medical] advice to antibody-positive

and antibody-negative individuals remains the same
and until more is known about the meaning of the
results, don't take the test. (Jackson and Lesk 8).

It is no coincidence that Jackson and Lesk's advice
is couched in legal and medical terms. Given the immediacy of the backlash against the gay community—the
raids on *The Body Politic* and on the bathhouses, the part
the "threat" of "gay power" played in the 1980 municipal election, not to mention the ongoing attacks of the
Christian Right—their editorial cautions against testing
because of the many potentially negative ramifications a
positive result might prompt. HIV positive people could
easily be denied services, housing, and employment, and
in the absence of antidiscrimination legislation there
were no laws to protect them from such maltreatment.
Agents of the state had acted against the gay community in Toronto for decades, but since the backlash in the
late-1970s it had done so in a much more aggressive and
malevolent manner. In the simplest of terms, politicians,
and the legal and medical establishments could not to
be trusted with the welfare of gay men. The authors' remarks also reflect the gay community's grass-roots efforts
to fight AIDS. Without any viable treatments, safe sex
was the only defence against acquiring or spreading HIV.
It remained the best and most autonomous way to take
care of oneself and others.

As we shall see in the next section, Gilbert was indelibly shaped by these events. His early life and career are
characterized by a slow movement away from the middle
class existence into which he was born and toward that
of a radical, gay theatre artist whose theatrical work was
his political activism. He began this transformation by

dropping out of graduate school, founding Buddies in Bad Times, and coming out as a gay man. He continued it by increasingly identifying the company with the city's progressively larger and more visible gay community, on the one hand, and the *avant-garde* aesthetics of the second wave of the Alternative theatre, on the other. This trajectory continued until 1984, when his work takes a significant dramaturgical and political turn with *The Dressing Gown*, his first major "cross-over" hit. With this play, and for the first time, he employed a traditional structure and presented a critical view of gay men and the "gay lifestyle"—negative depictions that I will argue must be understood within the contemporaneous debates about gay promiscuity and the "healthiness" of gay sex in the wake of the AIDS crisis, which I have just elucidated. Despite its conservative politics (or perhaps because of them) Gilbert's career was indelibly determined by *The Dressing Gown*. Dissatisfied with the considerable success he garnered by being critical of gay life and sexuality, he rejected the play and its politics with his next significant work, *Drag Queens on Trial*. As will be demonstrated in this essay's last section, the pro-sex, pro-promiscuity, and "sex radical" politics and aesthetics for which Gilbert has become both famous and infamous are first articulated in *Drag Queens on Trial*, and were a reaction to the success of *The Dressing Gown*. *Drag Queens* was a response to the backlash of the 1970s and early 1980s, and to the anti-promiscuity arguments that emerged in the wake of both the bathhouse raids and AIDS. It is the play that laid the foundation for all his subsequent work, and for the rest of his tenure at the most important queer theatre company in the country, Buddies in Bad Times.

## Becoming Radical: Sky Gilbert and the Early Years of Buddies in Bad Times

Schyler Lee Gilbert was born in Norwich, Connecticut in 1953. At the age of six he moved with his family to Buffalo, New York, where is father, a manager at the Travelers Insurance Company, had been transferred. With his mother and younger sister, he lived an idyllic, "*Leave it to Beaver* existence" (Gilbert *Ejaculations* 5). However, at the age of twelve, this life suddenly changed when his parents divorced. He and his sister had been involved with figure skating in Buffalo, and his parents had been avid curlers. Following the divorce, his mother decided to move him and his sister to Don Mills in Toronto, which she thought, with its good ice rinks and good schools, "would be an ideal place for us to start our new life" (*Ejaculations* 5-6). According to Gilbert's mother, Don Mills "rivalled New Rochelle, New York (where Dick Van Dyke and Mary Tyler Moore lived in the famous sitcom), as a clean, upwardly mobile middle class suburb" (*Ejaculations* 6). In Don Mills, he and his sister worked hard on their figure skating with their "pro" skating teacher Mr. Menzies. And although Gilbert designates his family "middle class," they were also members of the Granite Club, the prestigious, long-standing, invitation-only (not to mention expensive) private athletic club, where Mrs. Gilbert no doubt curled, and whose membership belies income or aspirations beyond those of the average middle class family.

For most of his childhood, Gilbert was bookish and eager to please his parents and teachers. In high school he became interested in Ayn Rand and classical music, and was "a passionate loner," spending much of his time

writing poetry, listening to Rachmaninoff (Rand's favourite composer), and searching for "inspired feelings"
(*Ejaculations* 7). Gilbert played cello in his high school
orchestra, and during a production of *Annie Get Your
Gun* he discovered he could experience these inspired
feelings in the theatre. "It seemed that being a part of
this production was so enthralling that it took me away
from my adolescence anxieties and propelled me into a
moment of ecstasy. I thought, *this is the way I want to
feel all the time*" (*Ejaculations* 7 emphasis original). With
this discovery, Gilbert made his first step away from the
middle class existence that was both expected and laid
out for him by dedicating himself to high school theatre
arts. He wrote a play about the Vietnam War, *The Mark*,
which won a Simpson Drama Festival Award for "dis-
tinctive merit." With this success he felt he had "found a
home" in the theatre (*Ejaculations* 8).

After high school Gilbert was accepted to York
University's acting program, but switched into playwriting and theatre criticism at the end of his first year
(*Ejaculations* 8). There he produced musicals and cabaret
evenings with the York Cabaret Theatre. Under the
auspices of an un-incorporated amateur group called
the Cabaret Company, he and friend Matt Walsh staged
some of these productions at libraries downtown, and
at the 519 Community Centre.[29] It was from one of
these performances that the name Buddies in Bad Times
was taken.[30] At this time Gilbert was obsessed with the
French Surrealists and their poetry, specifically the work
of Jacques Prévert. He and Walsh produced a musical
called "Buddies in Bad Times," based on the poems of
Prévert and Joseph Kosma which, according to Gilbert,
enjoyed success when it was staged at the University

of Toronto and then at the Harbourfront Theatre (*Ejaculations* 10-13).

Gilbert had battled his homosexual feelings since childhood (*Ejaculations* 4), had gay fantasies in high school, and was quite ashamed of them: "Ayn Rand didn't approve of homosexuals, and I knew that my family wouldn't either" (*Ejaculations* 7). Having finished his undergrad degree, he took a Master's at the Graduate Centre for Study of Drama at the University of Toronto. Upon completing his Master's, he briefly enrolled in the Centre's doctoral program, following a path that would most likely have led to a career as a theatre professor.[31] But he longed to come out and to be an artist: "I think I left the Drama Centre because I was yearning to come out. I just couldn't do it there [...] For some reason, being heterosexual was linked with university life; leaving there would mean I would *have* to be myself" (*Ejaculations* 10).

Having said goodbye to the straight world of academia, Gilbert incorporated Buddies in Bad Times Theatre with his friends Matt Walsh and Jerry Ciccoritti in 1978. The theatre's original mandate was "to explore the relationship of the printed word to theatrical image in the belief that with the poet-playwright lies the future of Canadian theatre" (Wallace "Theorizing" 143). Buddies' first performance, *Angels in Underwear*, was written by Gilbert and produced in September 1978 at the Dream Factory.[32] Following the company's mandate, and Gilbert's own poetic predilections, the play explored the poetry of the Beats, Jack Kerouac and Allen Ginsberg. The company produced its first Rhubarb! Festival of new works in January 1979, also at the Dream Factory. But Buddies did not hold everyone's interests equally: Walsh, primarily an actor, left after the company's first

Rhubarb!; Ciccoritti, who was more interested in film, and has gone on to have a significant career as a director, left in 1980 (Boni 22-23).[33] Following the departure of Walsh and Ciccoritti, Gilbert became the sole force behind the theatre, and he began to explore his sexuality more overtly in his life and in his theatrical works. He was twenty-eight, had just come out as a gay man, and was establishing himself as a professional artist.

In 1980, Gilbert's Buddies joined forces with Nightwood Theatre, A.K.A. Performance Interface, Theatre Autumn Leaf, and Necessary Angel to create the Theatre Centre. An artist-run space, the Theatre Centre provided rental facilities to its member companies, as well as other independent companies. According to Robert Wallace, the establishment of the Theatre Centre marks the beginning of the "second wave" of Alternative theatres in Toronto, and became "the main locus of the city's new and experimental groups, particularly after its move in 1984 to the centrally located Poor Alex Theatre" (*Wallace Producing Marginality: Theatre and Criticism in Canada* 102).[34] Its artists defined themselves against the first wave of Alternative theatres, "espous[ing] formal innova-tion and multidisciplinarity as [their] central priorities" (Wallace *Theatre and Transformation in Contemporary Canada* 45). Theatre Centre artists eschewed the first wave's conception of regionalism as *the* basis of Canadian nationalism and political theatre, which were basically synonymous. These artists began to explore new theatrical forms and to espouse new politics. Of the Theatre Centre companies, Buddies and Nightwood would, in Alan Filewod's words, exploit "the principle of regional differ-ence but freed [...] of geographic determinism." They would explore the "'region' of experience," or identity politics, examining gay, lesbian, and women's identities as the basis of their work (Filewod xv). By 1981, Buddies had begun to nominate itself a gay theatre, organizing itself and its theatrical productions around a politics of gay identity and community.[35] Importantly, as part of the Theatre Centre and the second save of Alternative theatre in the city, it was also defined by its *avant-garde* aesthetics. This context and these artistic and political commitments have been fundamental in determining Buddies' place in the city's theatre culture, and its particular melding of experimental aesthetics and gay and lesbian politics.[36]

Buddies' "coming out" and success as Toronto's gay-identified theatre was possible because of the gay community's increasing size, visibility, and its yearning to see itself represented on the city's stages. Economically speaking, by the late-1970s, Toronto's gay community constituted a market for gay work, which is evidenced by the large number of gay shows that toured to the city and by the not insignificant local productions of international gay hits. For example, Charles Ludlam and his Theatre of the Ridiculous Company brought their drag adaptation of *Camille* to the Factory Theatre in 1976; David Rabe's *Streamers* toured to the St. Lawrence Centre in 1977; *Hosanna* was revived by Richard Monette at Toronto Workshop Productions in 1977; Quentin Crisp's *An Evening with Quentin Crisp: The Naked Civil Servant,* was staged at Toronto Workshop Productions in 1978; and Lindsay Kemp's *Flowers* and *Salomé* toured to Toronto Workshop Productions 1978 and 1979, respectively. Productions of international gay hits were also numerous: *Boys in the Band* and *The Killing of Sister George* were both staged by Toronto Truck theatre in 1977; Doric Wilson's

*A Perfect Relationship* was mounted by Equity Showcase in 1979; Terrence McNally's *Next* was produced by Solar Stage in 1979; Tremblay's *La Duchesse De Langeais* was staged at the Tarragon in 1980; and Martin Sherman's *Bent* was staged at the Bathurst Street Theatre in 1981.

Despite the market for gay work, Gilbert was one among a small number of artists in the city who was "out," and the *only* one who was positioning his work as "gay" in the early 1980s.[37] His early work explores gay life through the recuperation of historical gay icons, employing what he calls the "'poet and his boys' model." Following his interest in poetry on stage, and slow to take on the full mantle of playwright, Gilbert typically selected a gay poet and used his verse and biography, exploring the bard's sexual relationships and his life experience as a gay man. Gilbert arranged the poetry and added his own writing where necessary to create the theatrical whole.[38] In terms of form, Gilbert's early works express his commitment to *avant-garde* theatre in their non-linearity, their experimental dramaturgical forms (i.e. poetic pastiche), and their image-based aesthetics (i.e. the stage image was considered as important as the words). He was inspired by similar work being done in New York by the Wooster Group, Richard Foreman's Ontological Hysterical Theatre, and also by his peers at the Theatre Centre, especially Cynthia Grant (Nightwood) and Richard Shoichet (AKA Performance Arts), who Gilbert credits with educating him about the importance of the stage image (*Ejaculations* 28-9). In terms of content, his early works adhere to the tenets of gay liberation: they celebrate gay love, sexuality, and promiscuity; they concern issues of oppression, and homophobia; they reclaim historical figures; and they used the theatre as a site to create contemporary expressions of gay community.

*Lana Turner Has Collapsed!: A Theatrical Extravaganza of Gay Life and the Movies* is an example of this genre. As the title suggests, the play investigates the life of a gay artist, Frank O'Hara, in a pre-Stonewall context. Performed at the Theatre Centre in September 1980, Gilbert regards *Lana* to be his first truly *gay* play because it published the word "gay" in its title and on its poster, an inclusion that he thought to be "very bold" at the time (*Ejaculations* 31). *Lana*'s structure is episodic and thematic. Its non-linear scenes primarily revolve around gay love, Hollywood movies, female celebrity and gay men's attraction to them. Its twenty-one characters, which include O'Hara and Turner, and the friends that peopled O'Hara's life and poetry, Larry Rivers, Willem de Kooning, Jane Freilicher, and Kenneth Koch, were performed by a cast of four men and one woman. It cleverly staged a number of O'Hara's gay love and sex poems, whose structure and conversational tone lend themselves to both theatrical performance and the creation of poetic images on stage. For example, O'Hara's well-known poem "Having a coke with you" is said as a monologue by a character called "Man," with the rest of the cast animating the poem's imagery, which are mostly art-historical references (O'Hara worked as a curator at the Museum of Modern Art in New York), such as *The Polish Rider*, an example of Futurism, and drawings by Leonardo da Vinci and Michelangelo.

*Lana*'s performance exemplified the sexual and political doctrines of 1970s gay liberation by staging poems and scenes that had political significance for its Toronto audience. Its staging of one poem in particular, "Ave Maria," illustrates this point. The scene in question has a character called "Lecturer" enter from off-stage and announce:

> Would everyone sit down please. I am going to do a
> lecture on child molestation, how to do it where to
> do it, etcetera, please sit down, don't push. (pause)
> Only kidding! What I have to say is a serious and
> discursive and concerns the movies and its especially
> directed to you Mothers! (Gilbert *Lana Turner* 23)

The Lecturer then recites O'Hara's "Ave Maria," a poem that encourages mothers to allow their children go to the movies where they might have their first sexual experience. The poem advocates for a view of family and motherhood that are quite contrary to conventional definitions of both, and aligns perfectly with the more radical views of gay liberation:

> they may even be grateful to you / for their first
> sexual experience / which only cost you a quarter
> / and didn't upset the peaceful home / they will
> know where candy bars come from / and gratuitous
> bags of popcorn / as gratuitous as leaving the movie
> before it's over / with a pleasant stranger whose
> apartment is in the Heaven on Earth Bldg / near
> the Williamsburg Bridge / oh mothers you will have
> made the little tykes / so happy because if nobody
> does pick them up in the movies / they won't know
> the difference/ and if somebody does it'll be sheer
> gravy / and they'll have been truly entertained either
> way / instead of hanging around the yard / or up in
> their room / hating you. (Gilbert *Lana Turner* 23)

While the poem's approach to sexual awakening and family is ironic and funny, it also echoes gay liberation's focus on the sexual liberation of everyone, including children, and its view of the nuclear family as an oppressive institution, especially for (gay) children.[39] In Toronto in 1981, with an audience of gay men cognizant of the trials of *The Body Politic* for publishing Gerald Hannon's *Men Loving Boys Loving Men*, and of the bath-house raids, the poem/scene would have humorously linked O'Hara's recollection of childhood to continued sexual oppression and the need of gay/sexual liberation in the present.

With *Lana*'s staging, Gilbert became Toronto's most visible gay artist, and Buddies its primary gay theatre. It garnered him his first mainstream-press review in the *Globe and Mail*, and, more importantly, his first profile in *The Body Politic*.[40] Written by David Roche, the byline reads: "Seems you can't go anywhere in Toronto without running into this fresh young upstart, heady with success" (Roche 27). Gilbert's success was *Lana,* which Roche attributed to both its quality and an advertisement placed in *The Body Politic*. But Roche also notes that the play suffered because of mainstream/corporate homophobia: the *Toronto Star* refused to review it "on the grounds that [it] is 'a family newspaper'" (Roche 27). The *Star*'s refusal to review the piece because it contravened notions of "family" conveys the extent to which being gay was still radical in this period, still clearly outside dominant ideas of "family," and still held some of the counter-cultural energy of 1970s gay liberation. Indeed, in this profile Gilbert equates his gayness with marginality and his marginality with being an artist:

> My purpose as an artist is not to make points about gay life or make political points. My purpose is to create art that comes out of my life, to express and communicate something of what's happening to me. What's happening to me has a lot to do with my relationships with gay men. Isherwood said, one of the reasons we were all gay in Berlin was because

we didn't want to fit into what society had set out
for us, and we rebelled. I don't fit in, and being gay
means I don't have to. I can find my own way and
chart my own course. (Roche 28)

For Gilbert, making plays that represented gay
men, their lovers, and a gay past for a gay community
in Toronto were radical gestures, though he was not yet
ready to position them as overtly political. Nevertheless,
because he was dealing pretty much exclusively with
gay issues, his work had very different political and
ideological implications than a touring gay company, or
a local "straight" theatre producing a "gay play." Staged
under the aegis of a gay-identified theatre, Gilbert's plays
expressed local struggles and the character of gay life and
community in Toronto. Gilbert recalls the practical significance of these identifications, and how they created
a markedly different environment in the theatre, in his
memoir. He writes that Peter Caldwell, an acquaintance
of his, told him that attending *Lana* was "the first time
I've ever gone to see a play and felt comfortable about
holding my boyfriend's hand" (*Ejaculations* 33). In a
manner unlike any other artist or company in Toronto in
the early 1980s, Gilbert and Buddies created a space that
fostered local gay community in the theatre.

Gilbert continued to use the "poet and his boys"
genre to investigate themes of gay life and love for the
next few years, gaining a small but significant following,
especially among gay men and experimental theatre fans.
Continuing to produce his plays at the Theatre Centre,
he would stage *Cavafy or the Veils of Desire*, based on the
poetry of Constantine Cavafy (1981); *Marilyn Monroe
is Alive and Well and Living in Joe's Head*, based on the

poetry of Joe Brainard (1982); *Murder/Lover* (1982) based on the poetry of Patti Smith, which concerns her relationship with playwright Sam Shepard; *Pasolini/Pelosi* (1983) based on the life and poetry of Pier Paolo Pasolini; and *Life without Muscles* (1983), based on the painting of David Hockney and the poetry of Thom Gunn. Gilbert abandoned this model, which he felt was becoming a creative rut, with *The Dressing Gown* (1984), and for the first time wrote and produced a play that was critical of gay men and gay promiscuity.[41]

Also staged at the Theatre Centre, *The Dressing Gown* was unlike Gilbert's previous work as it neither concerned an historical gay artist, nor did it incorporate extent texts. According to Gilbert, the play "was a direct result of my talks with Christopher [Newton]," the artistic director of the Shaw Festival (1979-2002), who sat on Buddies' board, and was one of Gilbert's influences at this time (*Ejaculations* 77). Following Newton's advice, Gilbert looked to theatre history for a structure that would allow him to be "challenging in content but accessible in structure," abandoning both the experimental dramaturgies he had developed in his earlier plays, and, as we shall see, his gay liberation politics (*Ejaculations* 77). *The Dressing Gown*'s structure is based on Arthur Schnitzler's *La Ronde* (1892), the famous *fin de siècle* play comprised of ten two-handed scenes that see each couple having sex, and one partner from each scene moving on to the next, constituting one part of the following sexual partnership until it has come full circle (thus, "la ronde"). *La Ronde* has been interpreted as an exploration of how venereal diseases are spread through all levels of society, an interpretation and history that is noteworthy as Gilbert's anti-promiscuity adaptation of the play was staged in the first years of the AIDS crisis, when, as detailed in the previous section, gay promiscuity was posited by some as the cause of AIDS. *The Dressing Gown* is organized in a manner similar to *La Ronde*: a series of seven two-handed scenes with one person from each scene moving in relay to the next until it comes full-circle, though not all of the couples in *The Dressing Gown* have sex. Schnitzler's play is quite clearly predicated upon characters that were culturally-recognizable types in turn-of-the-century Viennese society—the Count, the Young Wife, the Husband, etc. These characters' actions are posited as an expression of their particular psychologies, which are associated with gender, class and social position or social role (soldier, maid, etc.). In comparison, *The Dressing Gown* adds a metaphysical layer through the incorporation of "the dressing gown," which is passed from person to person and holds a kind of mystical, supernatural power. To put it another way, *La Ronde* suggests that our sexual actions are *comprehensible* expressions of our heredity and socialization, our psychologies.[42] The play presents this thesis in its study of sex among socially positioned types, rather than fully developed, individuated psychological characters. In *La Ronde* sexual impulses, common to all people, are negotiated even determined by our social positioning, specifically as gendered and classed subjects. *The Dressing Gown*, on the other hand, implies that our sexual desires and actions are impacted by unknowable and almost magical forces, which it conveys in the form of a mystical garment that exerts sexual power over those who wear it or see it.

*The Dressing Gown* was Gilbert's first major hit and, unlike the poet plays, it takes a critical look at gay men and their sexual relationships. In Gilbert's memoir he writes: "*The Dressing Gown* is about the superficiality and destructiveness of [gay] promiscuity. In some ways it's a very moralizing piece, and that's why I have mixed feelings about it now" (*Ejaculations* 78). The play is also a meditation on masculinity and sex, suggesting that men are inherently sadistic and abusive. It associates this sentiment with the dressing gown in the first and final scenes, which both see an older man giving the garment to a younger boy/man (it's the same young person: in the first scene he is a young boy and, as time has past, in the last he is a young man), giving the following advice: "The world is a cruel place [...] And men are sometimes the worst things in it. Men in our society are often very hard and cold, and they don't seem to know how to love. Sometimes it seems they'd rather kill each other than love each other" (Gilbert *The Dressing Gown* 80).

These rather essentialist ideas about gender, gay men and their sexual relationships are most explicitly expressed in the last scene of Act One. The scene depicts Larry, an S/M top and a banker in his thirties, and Jim, a submissive bottom in his early twenties. The two are engaged in an ongoing, purely-sexual sadomasochistic relationship. (Larry has an open relationship with his boyfriend, Barry, who we see in another scene being equally abusive to another young gay man). The scene shows how Larry and Jim's relationship is quite literally fuelled by Larry's sadism and Jim's self-destructive maso-chism. In the scene, Jim asks the older man to inject him with the drug MDA (methylenedioxamphetamine). He says: "Please sir please sir I beg you sir. Some MDA please [...] Don't worry about cleaning the syringe sir. (*pause*) I mean if it's too much trouble" (Gilbert *The Dressing Gown* 54-55). While humiliating Jim, calling

him a number of degrading names, Larry injects the
MDA into Jim's arm and the young man quickly and
violently overdoses, which is blamed on the "dirty
needle." Neither the scene nor the play mentions AIDS,
nor do they elaborate exactly what a "dirty needle" is, but
the point is nevertheless clear: this form of sexual play
is dangerous, pathological, and typical among gay men
who "don't seem to know how to love." Larry and Jim
are not sexually liberated adults engaging in healthy and
consensual sex; rather, the scene and the play suggests
that they are engaging in abnormal sexual activities that
are unhealthy and, potentially, deadly.

*The Dressing Gown*'s only female character, Martha,
continues this simple and essentialist approach to gender,
sex, and sexuality. In a manner that echoes the most
patriarchal conceptions of women, Martha is gentle,
loving, naïve, and submissive to a fault. A friend of Jim's,
she does not understand why gay men are so cruel to one
another. Worried for his safety, she visits him in hospital
to confront him about his self-destructive behaviour.

> MARTHA: (a little angry for the first time) No it's
> not stupid "I love you" stuff it's just me asking you
> as one person to another—why is sex so important
> to you?
>
> JIM: Oh God, I don't know … my dick gets hard,
> that's all—
>
> MARTHA: Yes but it's like I know you don't like
> me saying this but I love you and it looks to me like
> you are going from one man to another trying to get
> bigger and bigger cocks and highs and it all seems so
> self-destructive and ultimately a … waste. (pause)
>
> JIM: Are you finished?

MARTHA: Yes. (pause) I think so. But—

JIM: Shut up alright. (pause) I don't want anymore lectures. If you wan to come and visit me you just watch the fucking TV and shut up alright?

MARTHA: Yes. (pause) Sorry. (Gilbert *The Dressing Gown* 64)

Like the play, this scene suggests that sex outside of the "stupid I love you stuff" is at best a pointless waste of time, and, at worst, hazardous to one's health. It posits Jim's promiscuous sex as self-destructive and psychologically suspect: he is complicit in his own undoing. Moreover, Martha's goodness is located in her chaste (and heterosexual) love, which is confirmed when she reveals that, though she has tried to wear the dressing gown, she has been unable to do so. "I know you think I'm being mystical and stupid but I really … it wouldn't let me put it on. Isn't it weird?" (Gilbert *The Dressing Gown* 74). Weird indeed.

*The Dressing Gown*'s most problematic element is its central conceit: that the dressing gown has magical, aphrodisiac qualities that negatively affect the gay men. The play makes gay male sexual desire (not love, but sex) material in the form of the dressing gown, depicting it as a malevolent force beyond their control. The gay men who wear or are allured by the garment become victims of their uncontrollable sexual urges—to which women such as Martha are immune because they know what love is. The play suggests that gay men are under the spell of their sexual urges and cannot, therefore, love or respect one another, and will inevitably kill themselves and their sexual partners.

*The Dressing Gown* ran to sold out houses, was held over, and was Gilbert's and the Theatre Centre's biggest hit to date. Its success leads one to believe that its essentialist, sex-negative sentiments and quite nearly homophobic representations of gay were in the *zeitgeist* when it was produced in 1984. It received excellent reviews in the straight press, and its anti-promiscuity politics were not even condemned by *The Body Politic* reviewer, whose criticism takes issue only with the rather anti-feminist depiction of Martha. The closest thing to criticism that the play received came a few months later when Robert Wallace quite even-handedly wrote: "The honestly and relevance of Gilbert's perceptions in the play transcend their political and psychological naiveté to make it an artistically rewarding experience" (Wallace "Playing with Ourselves" 33). Given the play's immediate political contexts were the legal regulation of gay sex in the form of the bathhouse raids, the re-pathologization of gay men and the linking of gay sex with death in the wake of AIDS crisis, its negative representations of gay promiscuity and gay male desire are not exactly shocking, though they were politically dangerous.

Despite any misgivings about *The Dressing Gown*'s sexual politics, the play holds a seminal place in Gilbert's *oeuvre* because it prompted him to seriously examine the politics and aesthetics of his own success. In the introduction to the play, which was published in 1989, five years after its premiere at the Theatre Centre, Gilbert writes:

> The plays I wrote before *The Dressing Gown* were romantic celebrations of gay promiscuity (*Cavafy*, *Pasolini Pelosi* etc.) Suddenly, in *The Dressing Gown* it seemed to people that I was looking at my own kind with a critical, cynical, one might say even jaundiced eye. And I cannot help feeling that the fact that this play was seen as being critical of the 'gay lifestyle' has

in fact had very much to do with its success with the straight press. (Gilbert *The Dressing Gown* 9)[43]

With the play, Gilbert intervened into the promiscuity debates of Popert, Lynch, Lewis, Callen, and Berkowitz.[44] But within the politically divisive circumstances of the early 1980s, *The Dressing Gown*'s unprecedented success caused Gilbert to quickly realize that, unlike his previous plays, its stance against gay promiscuity and gay sex supported the status quo of heterosexual culture, and did not address the ways in which gay men and gay-male sexualities were under attack.[45] Indeed, it seems that the success of *The Dressing Gown* was at least partially predicated upon elements in gay and straight culture that, in 1984, wanted to blame the ills of gay life on how some of gay men understood and pursued pleasure, sex, and freedom.

With *Drag Queens on Trial,* Gilbert revolted against almost everything he had championed in *The Dressing Gown*. He created a play that humorously railed against essentialist conceptions of gender, and male and female sexuality. He indicted the mainstreams of both straight and gay culture for their hypocrisy, and for the ways they marginalize, criminalize and pathologize the sexually promiscuous, and the "gender deviant," which even gay liberation and lesbian feminism had failed to address adequately. In Gilbert's own words:

> I had just read *Queer Theatre* by Stefan Brecht [...]. It's a history of drag performers and filmmakers in the USA. It's also a cogent analysis of the rebellion that fired John Waters, Jack Smith (*Flaming Creatures*), and Charles Ludlam. [...] My knowledge of drag performance was pretty much secondhand [...] but [Brecht's] book gave me a theoretical approach. I

> could understand that Genet's queens were, in fact,
> rebelling against a whole society that supported
> the status quo, that drag undermines patriarchal
> power structures. At the time, I remember thinking
> that Toronto "The Good" needed a kick in the
> ass—that it should have its own drag queen theatre.
> (*Ejaculations* 85)

*Drag Queens on Trial*'s importance to the history of
gay theatre in Toronto moves in a number of directions
at once. First, its critique of society's liberal institutions,
especially the law, is clearly a reaction to the backlash that
the Toronto gay community suffered. As Gary Kinsman
argues, many gay men and lesbians felt that the police raids
on the baths were an "attempt to regulate the gay-male
community, and our sexualities, by applying criminal
categories—in this case, the bawdy-house legislation—to
cover gay men's sex" (Kinsman 341). Its setting in a court
of law, where the queens are on trial for *being* drag queens,
clearly resonates with this event, these sentiments, and the
generally poor relationship between the city's burgeoning
gay community and its legal establishment. Second, its
defiantly pro-sex and pro-promiscuity stance bolsters
a resolutely gay liberationist politic at a moment when
these politics were themselves on trial, having been made
that much more complex and controversial by the AIDS
crisis. Its defiant affirmation of autonomy and regretless
sexual liberty in the face of AIDS are clearly a reaction to
the debates about the place of sex and promiscuity that
the health crisis prompted. Its aggressively coalitional
politics, which encourages solidarity among those at the
margins of society, especially the sexual margins, and an-
ticipates the more overt AIDS activism that would soon
follow, as well as the emergence of queer politics and

theory at the end of the decade. Finally, dramaturgically, *Drag Queens* inaugurates Gilbert's deployment of drag, camp, and parody as seminal vehicles through which he would self-consciously combine *avant-garde* aesthetics and marginal, sex-radical queer politics, which he would develop and propagate for the remainder of his tenure as artistic director at Buddies in 1997, and over the course of his prolific career.[46]

## *Parodic Politics:* Drag Queens on Trial

*Drag Queens on Trial: A Courtroom Melodrama* is the story of Marlene Delorme, Judy Goose, and Lana Lust, three drag queens and occasional prostitutes who spectacularly resist the grinding oppression of their quotidian lives through a pointedly comedic, parodic, and metatheatrical staging of a courtroom melodrama, which sees them charged with the crime of *being* drag queens.[47] It begins with a dynamic and humorous opening sequence that appeals to performance conventions typical to theatrical/cinematic melodrama and gay male drag. This opening sequence is comprised of a series of tableaux, a dumb show that depicts the three rising from their beds and facing themselves without makeup in their bathroom mirrors, and a catchy popular song sung by the queens. It is followed by an ongoing backstage scene that shows the three queens preparing to stage the courtroom melodrama. In these backstage vignettes the three address the audience directly, quote lines from classic Hollywood melodramas, and sing and lip-sync a couple of songs. They complain about the ways masculine-acting gay men, and the gay community more generally, reject and degrade them for *being* drag queens. And, importantly, they speak frankly about sex, safe sex, and the current issues they face regarding AIDS.

The backstage drama is perforated by the staging of three courtroom scenes, which are announced by a "very deep, male [...] authoritative" and pre-recorded "Voice." In comparison to the backstage scenes, which are relatively verisimilar, "just three girls [...] shooting the shit," with the queens acknowledging their preparations and the presence of the audience, the three courtroom scenes are histrionic, employ voiceover, and follow the generic conventions of melodrama. These three scenes critique the legal, educational, and medical establishments, highlighting the hypocrisy of these institutions and demonstrating how they oppress the queens. Each scene self-consciously deploys the exact same structure: Marlene, Judy, and Lana state their pleas—Marlene and Judy pleading not guilty to being drag queens, and Lana pleading guilty—and are cross-examined by the prosecuting attorney. In each case, this testimony is spectacularly interrupted by the arrival of a surprise witness, a woman from each character's past that contradicts their statements before the court. Following the damning evidence of the surprise witness, Marlene, Judy, and Lana deliver a highly melodramatic monologue in which they defend themselves and then the scene ends. After the three trial scenes, the performance of the melodrama concludes with the queens collectively taking the roles of the prosecuting and defending attorneys, casting the audience as jury. In these roles, and speaking chorally, each attorney states his case and the audience is left to determine the queens' guilt or innocence. Following the audience's decision, the performance ends with a final metatheatrical backstage scene in which the three sing Judy Garland's *Get Happy*, because, as Lana contends, "a drag queen always leaves you tits up, humming a tune" (84).

*Drag Queens* is a metatheatrical parody of a Hollywood melodrama. It juxtaposes metatheatrical backstage scenes with parodic courtrooms scenes, highlighting the various discourses that foreclose upon the possibility that Marlene, Judy, and Lana's drag identities could be "real," "normal," or "true." In both performance modes, *Drag Queens* achieves its critique by parodically casting the characters' drag identities in the same essentialist terms used to privilege, reify, and coercively maintain heteronormative gender and sexuality, as well as mainstream gay culture's misogyny and racism. The parodic courtroom scenes thus dramatically elaborate the personal abuses the queens discuss in the ongoing backstage scenes, focusing more on societal institutions and less on the everyday realities of life within Toronto's gay male subculture. Taken together, the collective message of the two performance modes is clear: while the legal, educational, and medical establishments use their power to morally regulate the queens' lives, gay men's maintenance of normative (masculine) gender roles, their racism, and their exclusionary identity politics are also cited as factors in the queens' oppression. Finally, in the hysteria caused by the appearance of a HIV/AIDS, *Drag Queens* positioned medical, social, and legal/state authorities as malevolent. It espoused a politics of personal autonomy and solidarity by promoting a continued commitment to sexual freedom through safe sex, and coalition building among those at the sexual margins.

Parody and metatheatricality are the primary modes of performance that *Drag Queens* deployed to stage its particular political intervention. Parody is a practice in use across various genre and media, and, according to Linda Hutcheon, who has written extensively on the subject, it is "one of the major modes of formal and thematic construction of texts [in the twentieth century]" (Hutcheon 2). Hutcheon understands parody as a mode through which a whole range of modern artists have "com[e] to terms" with texts and forms from the past. For modern artists parody "signal[s] less an acknowledgment of the 'inadequacy of the definable forms' of their predecessors than their own desire to 'refunction' those forms to their own needs" (Hutcheon 4). According to Hutcheon, all parody employs some kind of "ironic inversion." Parodic texts exploit the conventions of other works of art and/or particular genres in a bifurcated manner that simultaneously cites and critiques discourses associated with the "original." For Hutcheon, modern parody is defined by its "ironic playing with multiple conventions." It is an "extended repetition with critical difference" that also "has a hermeneutic function with both cultural and ideological implications" (Hutcheon 7 and 2). In modern parody, these inversions, repetitions, and critical differences are not always enacted at the expense of the parodied text, they can, as *Drag Queens* does in its parody of 1950s Hollywood melodrama, celebrate, even revel in aspects of it (Hutcheon 6).

Metatheatricality most often refers to the dramaturgical practice of staging a play within a play, employing performance conventions that reveal or highlight their own construction, or plays whose dramaturgical structure, content, or action implicitly or explicitly put forward the idea that all the world is a stage, *theatrum mundi*. All of these practices are at work in Gilbert's play. Its most important metatheatrical convention, however, is its staging of a play within a play. This convention provides yet another layer of self-consciousness, dramaturgically and philosophically privileging *theatrum mundi*. The play's various metatheatrical practices, including drag, of course, enable a self-conscious form of identification and connection between the performing subjects on stage and the people in the audience, placing them in the same theatrical, social, and political world. In actual drag shows, musical numbers and skits alternate with direct interaction between the performer and the audience, which is also the case in *Drag Queens*. The performance of the staged melodrama is continually interrupted with performer-audience interactions that comment upon and contextualize it for and with its audience.

Melodrama's generic conventions and thematic concerns provide the basis for *Drag Queens'* parodic critique of heteronormative conceptions of sexuality and gender, and society's liberal institutions. Melodrama commonly focuses on female protagonists, the domestic sphere, and issues of gender and morality, which has made it of particular interest to feminists scholars.[48] A broadly democratic genre, its villains are usually those who enjoy societal privilege and power, while its heroines most often hail from the disadvantaged strata of society, and are oppressed by virtue of their status as women under patriarchy. Its plots are characterized by coincidence, chance, strange twists of fate, and typically "turn less on the triumph of virtue than on making the world morally legible, spelling out its ethical forces and imperatives in large bold characters" (Brooks 49). Its ethical messages depend on a simple construction of morality, with its characters being either innocent and absolutely good, or guilty and absolutely bad. The three queens love

Hollywood melodrama. They quote scenes from *Mildred Pierce* and other classic examples of the genre to much comedic effect. And like all drag queens, they are themselves spectacular, histrionic, and generally over-the-top, in their costuming, speech, and comportment. It is not, however, their genre of choice simply because they love it; rather, they choose it because its generic conventions allows them to unequivocally establish their innocence, on the one hand, and to clearly articulate the guilt of the cultures—gay and straight—that have so abused them, on the other.

The play's championing of the drag queen also conforms to 1950s Hollywood melodrama's tradition of confronting and critiquing the strained constructions of dominant morality. As Catherine Gledhill details in her study of the genre:

> Melodramatic desire crosses moral boundaries, producing villains who, even as the drama sides with the 'good,' articulate opposing principles, with equal, if not greater, power. In doing so it accesses the underside of official rationales for reigning moral orders—that which social convention, psychic repression, political dogma cannot articulate. Thus whether melodrama takes its categories from Victorian morality or modern psychology, its enactments of the continuing struggle of good and evil forces running through social, political and psychic life draws into a public arena desires, fears, values and identities which lie beneath the surface of the publicly acknowledged world. (Gledhill 32–33)

The play builds upon the melodramatic practice of revealing the oppressive effects of the dominant morality by making the queens' personal struggles with injustice the plot of a courtroom melodrama. Its most obvious parodic inversion is the substitution of melodrama's innocent but misunderstood feminine heroines for equally innocent but terribly vulgar and theatrical drag queens. Through its drag queens, the play demonstrates how gender variation is routinely disqualified from "reality," and how sexual promiscuity is similarly stigmatized by liberal institutions' not-so-subtle support of particular moral codes. The performance self-consciously plays with numerous melodramatic conventions within its play-within-a-play structure. This alienates its audience in the Brechtian sense, exposing the marginalized realities of the queens' lives, and privileging theatricality or *theatrum mundi* over the common sense conceptions of reality that uphold an oppressive status quo. The play repeatedly parodies essentialist understandings of identity by discussing the queens' drag identities in the same terms used to described sex, sexual orientation, and race. And, by placing its critiques squarely within the AIDS discourses current in 1985, the play indicted societal institutions for the parts they played in a dominant morality that hypocritically justified the marginalization of a sexualized underclass: the whores, drag queens, and "promiscuous" gay men whose poverty, illness, and deaths are made to seem inevitable at best and invisible or absolutely inconsequential at worst.

Hutcheon also contends that parody cites aspects of a text or genre's original historical circumstance, ironically invoking the characteristics associated with that time toward political ends in the present. *Drag Queens'* parody cites 1950s Hollywood melodrama and the post-war American culture from which these films emerged. Some remember the post-war period nostalgically, as a time

of great prosperity, simplicity, and moral purity: a time
when middle class nuclear families, with working dads
and stay-at-home moms, moved into new, safe suburban
communities, and enjoyed high standards of living—
much like the childhood the Gilbert describes. But for
many others it is remembered as a deeply repressive time.
A time when sexual and gender norms were aggressively
reinstituted and social "abnormalities" were intensely
scrutinized, surveilled, pathologized, and criminalized.
In this period, State agencies were brought to bear on
the sexual and "moral" lives of American and Canadian
citizens in the most pervasive and intrusive ways.[49] The
most famous example of such State repression in the U.S.
is the House Committee on Un-American Activities,
which was convened in 1945 by Senator Joseph
McCarthy. According to the Senator, Hollywood was full
of Communists and homosexuals had infiltrated all areas
and levels of government and the armed forces. Equally
damning for homosexuals was the passing of "Sexual
Psychopath" laws in a number of American states, with
similar laws being adopted in Canada. In 1937, J. Edgar
Hoover, director of the Federal Bureau of Investigation
called for a "War on the Sex Criminal." He suggested
that "the sex fiend, most loathsome of all the vast army
of crime, has become a sinister threat to the safety of
American childhood and womanhood." Hoover's "war"
was, ironically, mitigated by the Second World War;
however, during the "postwar decade the sex crime panic
gathered renewed momentum, peaking in the mid-
1950s" (Freedman 208). Many legislatures in the U.S.
revised earlier sexual psychopath laws while "twenty-one
additional states and the District of Columbia enacted
new psychopath laws," returning arrest rates of "perverts"

to their pre-war levels (Freedman 209). It is important
to stress that these were "sexual psychopaths," not just
"criminals." These people were considered clinically ill
and uncontrollably dangerous. In this period, legal and
medical authorities made objects of sexual "deviants," and
brought both the criminal and medical establishments to
bear on the lives of many gay men.

It is thus significant that *Drag Queens on Trial* is specifically a parody of a courtroom Hollywood melodrama,
and that its primary targets are the legal and medical
establishments and the educational system. In 1985, in
the wake of both the bathhouse raids and the advent
of HIV/AIDS, *Drag Queens'* parody of melodramatic
conventions invoked 1950s conservative morality, its
political witch-hunts, its imbrications of medicine and
criminality, and its generally paranoid and intense anxieties about issues of sex and gender. It depended upon
the audience's awareness of this history and this genre
as well as their knowledge, perhaps experience, of the
backlash and pathologization of homosexuality, which,
of course, had only been delisted from the American
Psychiatric Associations' *Diagnostics Statistics Manual* ten
years prior.

*Drag Queens'* use of drag and parody also follows in a
performance tradition that is specifically gay, with ante-
cedents in artists such as Charles Ludlam, John Waters,
and Jack Smith. Like these artists, who similarly employed
a mixture of drag and parody to enact simultaneously
comedic and political performances, the play enacted a
particularly gay form of parody, or "camp." Camp, according to Moe Meyer, a scholar whose has published
multiple books on the subject, is part of a distinctively
gay performance tradition and political praxis. Building

upon Hutcheon's definition of parody, Meyer argues that what distinguishes camp from other forms of parody is the ways it has been used by gay men to make their social and political existence visible. He quite expansively defines camp as "the total body of performative practices used to enact gay identity, with enactment defined as the production of social visibility" (Meyer 52). Camp, according to Meyer, has been deployed by gay men within gay communities to challenge the traditions of silence and marginalization that have historically undergirded heteronormative and patriarchal ideologies. Its particular form of parody has "piggy-back[ed] upon the dominant order's monopoly on the authority of signification," resignifying the texts of the dominant culture to express various alternative forms of gender, sex, and sexuality and the cultures organized around these identifications and desires (Meyer 43).

In its production at the Toronto Cinema, *Drag Queens'* parodic practices began with the set and venue of its performance. Its set was an identifiable court of law with all its basic accoutrements: a judge's bench, attorneys' desks, and witness box, but twice their normal size. Towering over the actors, the set's looming largeness represented the law as an intimidating and malevolent force in the lives of the innocent queens. By being staged in a pornographic theatre, a location with which many "respectable" theatregoers might not like to be associated, the play critiqued middle class morality of straight and gay culture. Its location brought theatrical performance into a place of overt and arguably illicit sexuality. Although the queens talk about their sex lives in frank and explicit terms, they do not perform sexual acts before the audience; nevertheless, the play's performance in a place where patrons viewed pornography and, presumably, engaged in illegal sexual acts (I mean, what was on those seats!?), announced its radical sexual politics.

In its formal conventions, the play's drag, camp, and its metatheatrical role-play privilege theatricality, and performed a critique of the essentialist thinking that delegitimized non-heteronormative identities in this period. Following the opening sequence of tableaus and blackouts, it shows the queens preparing to enact their drag identities: Marlene, Judy, and Lana putting on their make-up after they have awoken. It should be stressed that the queens are not transsexuals; they do not live fulltime as women, nor do they wish to become women—Marlene, for example, irreverently jokes that not being admitted into Chaps, a local Toronto gay bar, was "the most important thing to happen to [her] since [she] decided not to have a sex change" (31). Rather, they are *drag* queens who, we are told, live masculine identities as well. The play's metatheatrical form places greater weight on the queens' drag identities. Its metatheatricality posits the simultaneously real *and* performed status of these identities and, by extension, their other identities as well.

The play privileges theatricality throughout its backstage scenes, in which the three, apparently indiscriminately, prepare for and critique all of the parts they play in the courtroom melodrama—the judge, the attorneys, the surprise witnesses. This self-conscious role-play calls attention to the irony and injustice that, although all identities are performative, some are situated as authentic, while others, like those of Marlene, Lana, and Judy, are discounted as "lies." In the courtroom episodes especially, *Drag Queens*' metatheatrical role-play contributes to its critique of the law by effectively exposing and undoing the bond between the court, its officials, and the truth, justice, and morality with which they are supposed to be identical. In a manner that foreshadows Judith Butler's theory of gender performativity, and her invocation of drag as a political strategy, *Drag Queens'* central conceit, that the queens are on trial for being drag queens, parodies the straightforward relationship between sex, gender, and sexuality, and how those who challenge this naturalized trinity are regularly punished by multiple agents of social and political power.[50]

*Drag Queens'* metatheatrical role-play is an example of a classic camp strategy: the performance capitalizes on camp's ability to posit all the world as a stage, and thus highlight that all its men and women are, in fact, *merely* players. In this move is *Drag Queens'* political critique: along side its metatheaticality and parody of melodrama, the performance deploys camp to demonstrate the social privilege and stigma that attend different social roles. As David Halperin suggests, invoking one of Susan Sontag's famous "Notes" on the subject:

> It's camp's alienated queer perspective on socially authorized values that reveals Being to be a performance of being ('Being-as-Playing-a-Role') and that enables us to see identity as compelling acts of social theatre, indeed of as essences. That alienated vision performs a vital, indeed a necessary function for stigmatized groups. (Halperin How to Be Gay 195)

No group is more stigmatized that our three drag queens. Deploying camp conventions, *Drag Queens* embraces a performative conception of identity and enacts queer critique of essentialized identity that would become increasingly important as the decade wore on.

*Drag Queens'* first courtroom episode, the trial of
Marlene Delorme, critiques the legal establishment's corruption, and highlights the ways in which it criminalizes
particular social identities rather than crimes, demonstrating how the law maintains heteronormative middle
class morality by oppressing the queens. The scene begins
with Marlene pleading not guilty to being a drag queen,
which, of course, is funny because she so obviously *is* a
drag queen. Her plea, however, is an attempt to evade
punishment by a legal system that is corrupt: it has
already criminalized her with its bogus charges, which
equate drag with lying about one's true identity. When
asked to give an account of her childhood, she tells the
court exactly what she thinks it wants to hear, describ-
ing an "idyllic" life in Winnipeg, "much like that of any
blond-headed little boy" (37). But Marlene's prosecuting
attorney, played by Lana, is incredulous of her story.
Obviously, she conjectures, Marlene has "made some
fatal, ultimately tragic decisions," otherwise how did she
end up moving to Toronto and becoming "the rudest
most obnoxious drag queen in Eastern Canada?" (38).
Caught in this logic, Marlene parodies heteronormative
discourses of gender and identity by using its terms to
defend herself, declaring: "I base my not-guilty plea on
what I consider to be my God-given traits—my colour
sense, and of course, my passion for accessorizing which
I inherited from my grandmother [...] I am a drag
queen, and proud of my inherited traits" (40). Marlene's
humourous appeal to heredity as constitutive of her drag
identity parodies essentialized conceptions of gay identity
and the trite stereotypes upon which such arguments are
often predicated. Through this parody, Marlene's scene
also tacitly questions the value of pursuing civil rights,

the kinds of liberal legal approbation that mainstream
gay men and lesbians increasingly sought in this period,
and which were charged with doing little to nothing for
those at the margins of gay and lesbian communities,
such as drag queens and sex workers.

The court's corruption is confirmed by the appearance of Anita Hrupki, Marlene's surprise witness. Here,
parodying the conventions of the surprise witness and
melodramatic stock characters, Anita is just plain bad.
She is in cahoots with a corrupt legal system that is hell-
bent on conviction rather than justice. Following the
conventions of chance and dramatic revelation, she arrives just in time to confirm the prosecutor's conjecture:
Marlene is a drag queen who has perjured herself by lying
about her past. Anita tells the court:

> JUDY [ANITA]: Well, you see, this silly Bobby
> Fitch is making up these lies about his background
> just so that he can get off scot free. But he is guilty
> of being a drag queen. [...] The reason I say this is
> because, this so-called Marlene Delorme was never
> the blond-headed little boy she, sorry—he, claims
> to be. In fact, he once had brown hair, and I was the
> first one to dye it.
>
> [ ....]
>
> LANA [PROSECUTOR]: And you have not been
> coached or paid any money to make this unexpected
> surprise confession.
>
> JUDY [ANITA]: (*very memorized*) No your
> prosecutor. I have not been coached. (*she looks as
> judge, smiles*) Not to my knowledge.
>
> *She steps down and then stops to talk to the prosecutor.
> [The Prosecutor] slips her some money. She smiles at the
> judge and moves on.* (Gilbert <u>Drag Queens</u> 42)

Exploiting melodrama's obvious constructions of good and evil, as well as the often-corrupt nature of those who hold authority, in this case prosecutors who pay their witnesses, Anita is a participant in a legal system that is not objective but determined to criminalize the poor and innocent Marlene Delorme. The ridiculousness of the kangaroo court is also emphasized by the trite nature of the truth that Marlene is accused of contravening: hair colour and the biographical details of her childhood. In this fashion, *Drag Queens* parodies the conventions of melodrama to invoke the real-world attacks of Toronto's legal establishment on its gay community, especially its attempts to control gay men by legally regulating gay sex.

In light of Anita's damning testimony, Marlene defends herself by reversing the seemingly straightforward differences between truth and lies and, in so doing, privileges theatricality, promoting the performative conceptions of identity that run through the play. On her way to the stand, aping the filmic conventions of voiceover and melodrama, Marlene's thoughts are broadcast in the theatre:

> MARLENE: (*voiceover*) As I approached the stand, every nerve in my body quivering, I reviewed the accusations. They said I had lied, and I began to think about the lies, the years of lies, of living like a non person in Winnipeg, of gazing up at the clear blue sky and feeling small, ever so small. Yes, my life had been lies, nothing but lies, but wasn't that the essence of being a drag queen? And wasn't the drag queen somehow the lie that tells the truth? […] I had to make a stand and tell the truth, the truth in all its bitterness, its violence, its sordid detail. I had entered that courtroom Marlene Delorme, and whatever the outcome, I refused to leave it a cringing Bobby Fitch. (43)

Marlene's monologue posits her gender identity—
indeed any identity—as not inherent but socially constructed, suggesting that there is no right or wrong way
to "do" one's gender. Marlene's description of the "truth"
as bitter, violent, and sordid conveys the coercive ways
that masculine and feminine genders are naturalized as
"reality." It conceives of gender as a means to control a
subject's actions and behaviours in service of reifying the
power and morality of a heteronormative social order.
Once again the postwar period's highly restricted gender
roles are an important intertext in this regard, as her
monologue posits heteronormative gender and sexuality
not as essence but process: an array of social discourses
through which a subject's gender performances are either
recognized and affirmed or disqualified and outlawed.
Her assertion that her drag identity is simultaneously
truthful and fictive reveals the shift toward a social con-
structivist conception of gender and identity occurring
in queer communities in this period; indeed, through its
performance *Drag Queens* participated in this discursive
change.[51]

The play extends its critique of normative gender performance to the gay male community as well, once again
parodically invoking essentialist language to highlight
the hypocrisy of marginalizing those who do not perform
their genders appropriately.[52] This critique occurs most
emphatically in the backstage scenes, when the queens
talk about their everyday lives and the abuses they suffer
at the hands of other gay men. In the second backstage
scene, for example, Judy tells Lana and Marlene the story
of an altercation she had with a man who she picked up
while dressed in her masculine role. When she informed
the man that she is a drag queen, he demeans her and

invokes an essentialist view of gender identity: "Drag queens [a]re the lowest of the lows," he says. "[I']d never go out with a drag queen and [are you] a man or what?" (50). As his interrogation of Judy suggests, exhibiting a properly performed masculine gender, one which is continuous, (i.e. it is never *not* performed), self-identical (i.e. is an expression of one's "true" self), and clearly masculine, is also necessary if one is "to be a man" within the mainstream of gay culture. If a gay man performs both feminine and masculine personas, as drag queens do, or if his masculinity is insufficiently performed, he potentially forfeits his ontological status as a "real man." Ironically, Lana supports Judy and critiques essentialist conceptions of gender by appealing to essentialist language herself: "[You] should have told him off," she says, "He maligned our *race*" (emphasis mine 50). Lana's response to Judy's story parodies essentialist conceptions of ontology by invoking the problematic language of race. In doing so, Lana characterizes drag identities as the ontological equivalent of racialized identities, ironically privileging "theatrical" drag over the supposedly constant and "indelible" markers of racial identity. In performance this idea was doubly ironic because Leonard Chow, the actor who played Judy, was Asian, while Kent Stains, who played Lana, was white, and, therefore, would not be considered to be the same "race." While comical, the scene's focus on sex and dating also indicts the ways gender, racialization, and sexuality intersect.[53] It humorously details and how particular stereotypes and normative behaviours are punitively enforced within gay male sexual cultures through sex and stigma.

During the ongoing backstage scenes, the play also participates in educating audiences about condom use,

which was an urgent issue for gay men and others in
1985. In these interchanges, it rearticulates the kind
of safe-sex advice that sought to affirm gay sex and
(potentially) promiscuous behaviour, while also maintaining personal sexual health. In the second backstage
scene, for example, the realities of AIDS and condom use
are frankly discussed:

> MARLENE: [...] (*pause*, to JUDY) Did he fuck
> you?
>
> JUDY: I wouldn't let him. You know. AIDS
>
> MARLENE: I know. I always make them wait until
> the second date before I let them fuck me. And then
> they have to use a condom—ribbed.
>
> JUDY: Ohhhhhh. Condoms I hate them.
>
> MARLENE: But it is the only thing that saves you
> from AIDS, besides not fucking, and you can forget
> that.
>
> LANA: Yes darling. It's one thing to being fashionably
> self-destructive, but actually killing yourself and
> other people, well I draw the line there—
>
> JUDY: But don't you have trouble getting them on?
>
> MARLENE: No, and you can accessorize, see?
> (*pulling our a pack of fiesta condoms*) They come
> in lovely different vibrant colours to go with your
> bracelets and lingerie. I am particularly fond of a
> black bra with black condoms. I think the accents
> go quite nicely with my new dark lashes—(48)

By 1985, condom use was in the process of becoming the primary strategy for HIV/AIDS prevention

Hermione's testimony demonstrates how even childhood fantasies must be constrained by a heterosexual
moral imperative that does not include effeminate boys
or masculine girls. Her testimony shows how educators
pathologize children who do not exhibit "normal" gender
performances. The scene illustrates how these "signs of
pathology" were posited as means to control gay men and
other queers by placing their identities outside dominant
models of mental "health." This contention calls upon
the post-war history of gay pathologization, which was
especially current in the early days of the AIDS crisis,
as Michael Lynch's article "Living with Kaposi's" clearly
articulates. Indeed, it was not uncommon among men
of Gilbert's generation to have undergone psychotherapy,
aversion therapy, and even shock therapy to "cure" them
of their homosexuality.[54] In Hermione's final piece of
testimony, when she cites taking drugs, having "excessive"
sex, and listening to punk rock music as other examples
of "madness," *Drag Queens* accuses the educational system of hypocrisy, suggesting that its primary task is not
the educating and caring for the welfare of children,
but to maintain middle class morality by punishing and
weeding out any manifestation of sexual or gender non-
conformity in children.

In the final court scene, Lana's truthful and complex
expression of her gender identity and sexual practices
parody the "justice" of the legal system. Unlike Marlene
and Judy, she pleads guilty and is completely transparent about the complexities of her gender identity, and
the nature of her sexual practice. On the stand she says,
"being a drag queen is my life [...] I love to dress as a
woman. I always have. It makes life thrilling for me,
somehow. Who knows why? But for me, male clothing

is boring, restrictive, impractical, it's a contradiction, isn't it?" (71). By contending that she is following a desire that she has always had, Lana asserts that her gender identification is internal and abiding, and thus employs the language of essentialism. Ironically invoking this rhetoric she demonstrates how the law privileges some identities but disqualifies others, showing how the legal system serves a middle class, heteronormative morality by excluding drag queens or other transgender people. In the same manner, Lana's frank truthfulness about her sexual practices contravenes a legal system that privileges heterosexual monogamy. When asked if she has "sleazy sex with men in back alleys, toilets, steam baths and other dark and disgusting and dangerous places," she campily responds "as often as humanly possible" (71). Lana's honesty and integrity affirms her innocence and throws into relief the injustice of a legal system that does not punish people for doing harm to others or to property, but for their non-heteronormative sexual practices and gender identity. Parodically playing the role of melo-dramatic heroine, wrongly accused by an unjust society, her testimony indicts the law for deploying its resources to morally regulate queer identities and sex, with the Toronto bathhouse raids serving as the most egregious real-life example.

Lana's liberated honesty echoes the difficulties faced, and the tactics of resistance employed by Toronto's gay community in the wake of the bathhouse raids. Based on Lana's candid statements and admission that she is a drag queen, the prosecuting attorney concludes that the court has no choice but to find her guilty. Following the conventions of melodrama, however, Lana interrupts the attorney and states that she has something to say in her own defence. At this moment the audience hears her inner monologue while she histrionically enacts her own thoughts: "Well it suddenly occurred to me something about belonging, and well, I always think of Joan Crawford's words at the end of 'A Woman's Face' […] I want to belong to the human race" (73). In a conventional melodramatic plot, Lana would now deliver her climactic, emotional monologue. She would confirm her innocence while demonstrating the corrupt nature of the legal system and society that has so maligned her. This narrative arc would be especially rousing because it follows the same trajectory as those criminalized by the bathhouse raids: Lana's proud identification of herself as a promiscuous drag queen who has sex in public places is tantamount to the legal tactics and the "crimes" of the many "found ins" arrested during Toronto's bathhouse raids, with more than 90% of the accused having been acquitted by the time the play was staged (Spalding). Like them, Lana is now set to defend herself against the legal system that must, in typical melodramatic fashion, recognize her innocence. Her own proud invocations of humanity will prove that the law is duplicitous, unjust, and the real fraud in this scenario. But in a way that once again echoes the lives of gay men in Toronto, Lana's narrative is cut short by the arrival of her surprise witness, Dr. Dimchick. In the same manner that the gay community was placed into a state of disbelief, defensiveness, and paralytic shock with the arrival of emergence of HIV/AIDS, forced to confront serious questions about promiscuity and sexual liberation, Lana is suddenly and unceremoniously confronted by Dr. Dimchick, who has arrived to self-righteously condemn her for her sexual history by delivering the most damming testimony possible in this period: Lana has AIDS.

Dr. Dimchick's entrance into the courtroom is yet another parody of Hollywood cinema, one that has been quite famously adapted by gay male culture, and which positions her as evil incarnate. The stage directions read: *"MARLENE enters as Dr. Dimchick. She resembles Margaret Hamilton, the Wicked Witch of the West in* The Wizard of Oz" (73). Dr. Dimchick's arrival so disturbs Lana that she melodramatically takes out a gun and threatens to shoot. But Dr. Dimchick is unmoved and unafraid. "Don't worry," she says as she calmly approaches Lana: "No weapon is dangerous enough to protect you from the brutal truth. Sit down right now, you depressing, self-defeating, unfortunately-dressed, promiscuous slut" (74). Dr. Dimchick tells the court that she has been Lana's doctor since he was a "tiny effeminate child" named Davey Dollop (74). She informs the court: "Miss Lust has been avoiding me, refusing to answer my calls. Well I have finally caught up with her" (75). She proclaims to the court that Lana's "years of loose living, of flaunting authority" have all caught up with her (75).

> Dr. Dimchick: [...] Miss Lust has always favoured promiscuous sex, in which she has been the passive partner. She has swallowed busloads of male sperm, as well as drugging herself into a semi-conscious state every evening in order to loosen up her so-called inhibitions [...]. There is, in fact, no need to convict Miss Lust, for this human dogshit is going to perish anyway, and for all intents and purpose, by her own hand. Like many modern homosexuals, Miss Lust has committed a form of suicide due to her promiscuous habits, and now she must pay the price. (75)

Dr. Dimchick confronts Lana's seroconversion with the same moralizing arguments that circulated in this period, even among gay men. She blames Lana for her illness and, much like Callen, Berkowitz, and other advocates of the immunological theory, she cites promiscuity, too much sperm, and taking drugs as the *causes* of AIDS.

Dr. Dimchick's public declaration of Lana's diagnosis also resonates with the immediate political situation confronting the gay community in Toronto when the play was produced in November-December 1985: the politics of the newly available HIV test. As stated previously, the implications of the test had been a subject of debate and worry among gay men from the time that the virus was identified a year earlier. At the end of 1985 when *Drag Queens* was staged the HIV test was becoming widely available in Canada, and whether or not gay men should take it was becoming an increasingly pressing issue due to the potential repercussions of seroconversion in the absence of legal protections. Positing Dr. Dimchik as a malevolent medical authority that, like the court itself, is hell-bent on persecuting the queens, the play expresses the gay community's suspicion of these authorities in this period. The doctor's public disclosure of Lana's status in a court of law spectacularly announces the fears that attended the development of the test, which included many forms of social and legal discrimination, and the possibility that HIV-positive people could be tattooed or quarantined.

Like anyone receiving such grave news, and like the gay community in Toronto, Lana is stunned by the knowledge that she has seroconverted. Fragile, she wonders, as some gay men did, if what the doctor said could be true. Was she the architect of her own demise? Could this be a punishment that she deserves for her moral violations? Faced with what she initially sees as the "facts," though they are wrapped in the most insidious form of judgment, Lana once again approaches the stand.

> LANA (*voiceover*) [...] Surely every drag queen nay every homosexual dreams this nightmare. The sadistic doctor with the facts, the brutal facts, the balance sheet where it says in cold, hard computer printout—I was a passive partner in sex, as if all my passivity, all my femininity, all my womanliness which I always treasured was the essence of my disease, my heartbreak, my tragedy (75).

Identifying her illness with her femininity, Lana's testimony parodically invokes the cultural narratives that have traditionally connected the spread of sexually transmitted diseases to women, and which were redeployed in new ways in the context of AIDS. In his study of the representation of disease, Sander Gilman makes this connection between gender and sexually transmitted diseases, arguing that the context for the early depictions of AIDS was the "almost five-hundred-year-old iconography of the syphilitic" (248). Drawing on historical examples of visual sources, Gilman details how, by the time of the Enlightenment, the exemplary "image of the syphilitic shifted from male to female, but then only with the female as image of the source of infection" (Gilman 253-4). In the nineteenth century, Gilman argues, the gendered character and the moral overtones of these images, which depicted women as source, rather than sufferer of contagion, intensified. In representations from this period, "the female is seen as the source of pollution, but also as the outsider, the prostitute, the socially deviant individual" (Gilman 256). Gilman argues that this gendered and moral history of syphilis as sexually transmitted disease underlies early representations and thus understandings of people with AIDS, but with a significant alteration: "The male is not only the sufferer but also the source of his own pollution. [With AIDS] we have the conflation of the male and the female images traditionally associated with sexually transmitted diseases such as syphilis" (Gilman 258).

As a gay man in drag, Lana's thoughts about her doctor's diagnosis turn on the history of the representation of sexually transmitted disease that Gilman elucidates. While ironic and parodic, her thoughts cite common conceptions of contagion, which follow from this gendered, sexualized, and moralizing epistemological history. By specifically invoking tragedy, and because the performance was both a parody of melodrama and highly metatheatrical, Lana's reactions also link these conceptions of contagion, gender, and disease to the history of the tragic and melodramatic narratives that have rehearsed them. Lana's reaction ironically exposes what Raymond Williams calls a "structure of feeling," the often unconscious ideologies and values that underlie and effect specific affects and narrative constructions within a particular epoch. The "structures" that Lana's reaction makes evident are those of sexism, misogyny and homophobia, and the ways in which they have historically been deeply imbricated within discourses of morality and medicine. Her thoughts parodically posit how older epistemological paradigms, such as theatrical tragedy, melodrama, and representations of disease, are taken up and recoded through various modes of representation in the present. In the context of Toronto's gay community in the early 1980s, Lana's reaction demonstrates how these older paradigms insinuated themselves into the lives of people living with HIV/AIDS, while Dr. Dimchick's line of argumentation shows how these epistemological forms were used to justify the punishment of those who transgressed dominant narratives of masculinity, femininity, and monogamous heterosexuality.

As Lana re-approaches the stand, she notices "an attractive young man in the audience" that "a spotlight picks out," enabling the entire audience to witness their improvised interchange (76). Looking at this boy, she has the feeling that he is struggling with his sexual identity. With her thoughts once again broadcast in the theatre, the audience knows that she senses that "[he's at a] turning point in his life when he has to choose between becoming a normal productive member of society, or being a drag queen" (77). Though she is sick, weak, and fragile, attributes typical to a melodramatic heroine, her empathy for this young man gives her strength to go on. For his sake—and in this moment of metatheatrical direct address, for the sake of every gay man gathered in the theatre—Lana decides that she will not succumb to despair, defeat, or silence.

> LANA: Yes, it's strange, isn't it? I suppose I should be repentant, but I'm not. That is what we are like, those who don't live as others do—the different ones, those who do not surrender their mind and souls, their originality and spirituality to the multitude.

> JUDY: Don't you think this is a trifle pretentious? Perhaps you forget that you have admitted that you are a common prostitute.

> LANA: And who are you, who is anyone to judge? Yes, I am a drag queen and yes I am dying of AIDS. Perhaps I have made choices many would not agree

with but I followed my heart [...] I have not been
afraid to look inside myself, to live on the edge of
morality, society, of the world itself and if I must
die for it, so be it. And to all the little boys out there
who don't want to wear their blue booties but pick
out pink ones, to all the little girls who would rather
wear army boots than spike heals, to anyone who
has ever challenged authority because they lived by
their own lights I say don't turn back. Don't give up.
It was worth it. (78–79)

Lana's sentiments are iconoclastic, humorous, and
rousing. Despite being a person who is sick and down-
trodden, she bravely encourages others to live their lives,
to rail against conformity, to assert the inviolate importance of personal choice, and to have no regrets for doing
so. In her call to gay men, lesbians, and anyone who has
challenged authority, she promotes solidarity amongst
those at society's maltreated margins, its "sexual outlaws."

In Toronto in 1985, *Drag Queens'* AIDS politics
were audacious and pioneering, following a tradition
of gay liberationist activism and heralding the way for
increased AIDS activism in the city. *Drag Queens* was
the first play staged in Toronto to address AIDS and the
sexual politics associated with the syndrome, and Gilbert
himself has stated that the play is primarily about "AIDS
prejudice," though no one seemed to notice it at the
time (*Ejaculations* 93).[55] Its treatment of AIDS echoed
the pro-promiscuity and sexual liberated politics of
gay liberationists, like Lynch, Lewis and others at *The
Body Politic*. By citing people living with AIDS, gender
variant men and women, and by calling upon "anyone
who has ever challenged authority," *Drag Queens* cham-
pions the oppositional and coalitional politics emerging

within AIDS activism, and which would later be taken up by "queer" activists. In the same manner that *Drag Queens* advocates, AIDS Action Now! (1987) and Queer Nation Toronto (1991) would embrace a more fluid, self-conscious, and performative approach to gender, and promote a broader, anti-(hetero)normative approach to sexual practice as part of their political activism.

Gilbert's use of theatrical performance to intervene into AIDS politics is not unusual, though his radical sexual politics are. As Linda and Michael Hutcheon note in *Opera: Desire, Disease, Death*, there is an historical precedent for employing performance to redefine disease. Writing about AIDS plays in particular, they argue that this practice has been redeployed in significantly new ways.

> With AIDS and its gay activist politics, the tone and tactics have changed [...] This taking of control of the mechanisms of making meaning is often done openly, didactically, even outrageously—with irony and humour. It is also frequently eroticized, perhaps in an attempt to restore something of the hard-won liberation of pre-AIDS sexual life. (Hutcheon and Hutcheon 200)

The Hutcheons' analysis is convincing, though it is important to emphasize that the subjects of their investigation, *Angels in America*, *Falsettos*, *The Normal Heart*, and *As Is*, were, in comparison to *Drag Queens on Trial*, mainstream plays, produced by more established theatres in larger and more conventional venues.[56] Among other affirmations of liberal ideology and cultural values, each of these plays tacitly prescribes monogamy as a defence against AIDS through their affirmative representations of gay monogamous coupledom, and their negative representations of casual or promiscuous sex. Unlike *Drag Queens*, their critiques depend upon affirmations of liberal ideology, monogamy, and faith in progress. All American plays, each launches a critique of U.S. society for its inability to recognize the validity of gay love, for its heartless inaction around AIDS, and its failure to extend equal rights and protections to gay and lesbian citizens.

In comparison, *Drag Queens* rejects monogamy as the cornerstone of heterosexual morality, and the inclusion of gays within liberal legal frameworks, the ultimate aim of gay civil rights activism. Its parody undoes liberal society's conceptions of truth and justice by highlighting the ways these institutions construct their power, while its metatheatricality adds yet another layer self-consciousness and critical distance. It *shows* how the educational, legal, and medical establishments are predicated upon structures that need a scapegoat by literally *making a show* of the process through which these institutions define norms, rights, and their own authority by oppressing and criminalizing marginalized subjects. *Drag Queens'* form sidesteps the trap of re-affirming liberal ideology (a charge feminists following Brecht lodged against realism in this period) by deploying the double-pronged practices of parody, camp, and self-conscious metatheatricality.[57] These performance practices, indeed the parodic and self-conscious staging of a courtroom melodrama, allow the queens to demonstrate their lack of faith in these institutions and the realist modes of representation, whose narrative conventions and dramaturgical structures have been charged with tacitly maintaining them and the political status quo by theatre theorists since Brecht. The queens do not want acceptance or inclusion within the cultures or institutions that have always victimized and excluded them; rather, in self-consciously staging their own Hollywood melodrama, they want their innocence and maltreatment confirmed, and their talents and efforts affirmed, by adulation, praise, and applause only.

Despite the radical politics that I have elucidated here, the straight press received and promoted *Drag Queens* as a critical success at the time. The straight press saw liberal humanist conceptions of universality in its investigation of the queens' oppression and its advocacy of coalitional politics. It failed to comment on the political complexities of its parodic and metatheatrical staging, its invocation of AIDS, or the ways in which it critiqued the legal establishment. Although the press recognized the play as an example of radical performance, it only did so in terms of "taste" and "decency."[58] Henry Mietkiewicz, critic at the *Toronto Star*, for example, prefaced his review by writing:

> First, a word of caution. Although it does not actively promote homosexuality and chooses instead to advocate tolerance toward society's fringe elements *Drag Queens on Trial* is not for the faint-hearted. [...] Rarely does a minute go by without a four-letter word or some off-colour reference to genitalia or sexual deviation. ("Drag Queens on Trial Is Not for the Faint-Hearted")

Mietkiewicz ends his review by returning to the liberal values he views as the common denominator of his readership. He posits the queens as beyond the pale of middle class life, typically calling on universalizing rhetoric to justify the performance's value. He writes, "many of us will leave the theatre still convinced the drag queens are freaks. But that's hardly the issue. Gilbert has spoken eloquently about society's persecution and misunderstanding of non-conformity—and that's a theme that goes beyond the specifics of homosexuality" (Mietkiewicz "Drag Queens on Trial Is Not for the Faint-Hearted").

Critical reception in the popular press generally lauded the play, and recognized it as a watershed in Gilbert's career. It failed, however, to see the ways it actually solidified his desire to remain marginal and iconoclastic. This tendency is evidenced in a subsequent article written by Mietkiewicz:

> There are certain occasion in artists lives which, when viewed in hindsight, are recognized as obvious turning points. Rarer and more exciting, however, are events whose importance is revealed not after many years, but at the moment they occur. Such a milestone, against all odds, is *Drag Queens On Trial*, which should finally earn writer/director Sky Gilbert the broader acceptance he deserves after scrabbling for years on the fringes of Toronto's experimental theatre scene. (Mietkiewicz "Sky Is the Limit for Gilbert's Drag Queens")

Despite the positive cross-over rhetoric that Mietkiewicz espouses here, such a reception is not engendered by the play, nor is it what Gilbert intended. We get a sense of this when, at the end of the article, Gilbert acknowledges the "similarities" between queers and straights, but also states "there are many fundamental differences." He continues by elucidating his more anti-assimilationist politics: "The key is not to lie and say he's just like you, but to recognize the difference and understand it doesn't automatically mean there's something wrong with him" (Mietkiewicz "Sky Is the Limit"). Although Mietkiewicz is, in fact, attempting to honour the play by including the queens in the value system of the dominant culture, his commentary erases both the play's and its author's politics. Clearly Gilbert did not intend to write a universal story. He staged a self-conscious parody that critiqued the hypocrisy of straight culture's liberal institutions, which represented gay male misogyny and racism, and intervened into debates about promiscuity, sickness, and blaming the victim in the context of AIDS.

*Drag Queens'* tremendous success confirmed Gilbert's and Buddies' place in Toronto's theatre ecology, and put him and his theatre firmly on course to become the most important queer voices in the city and the country. Buddies had produced work by other theatre artists since its inception, primarily through the Rhubarb! festival, which it co-produced with Nightwood theatre from 1980 to 1985. In the wake of *Drag Queens'* success, the theatre began a new, more independent and politically radical chapter in its history. In 1986 Buddies parted ways with Nightwood theatre and began to produce Rhubarb! independently. The reason for their split is significant as it reveals Buddies' commitment to boundary-pushing sexual politics. According to Gilbert:

> [the] problem was I felt that [Nightwood's] politics weren't as sexual as Buddies. I know they objected to some of the images used in a Rhubarb! show. And that was problematic. Because Buddies had started the festival, I felt strongly about reclaiming it. [...] if they had their own sexual politics, they should have created their own festival. And they did. They started Groundswell. I did not think there was any room for the censoring of a piece in terms of sexual content at Rhubarb! or at Buddies. They agreed, and they decided they didn't want to be part of Rhubarb!

> any longer. [...] At the same time Nightwood
> left Rhubarb, I began to see the importance of
> supporting lesbian work. It was hard trying to get
> lesbians interested in what was at the time, a very
> male-identified company. Although, the company
> did have some lesbians involved. (Boni 18)

Following *Drag Queens'* extended run, Buddies also produced its inaugural "Four-Play" festival, its first programming officially mandated to producing lesbian and gay plays by artists other than Gilbert.[59] In the years that followed *Drag Queens*, Buddies would chart its own way and begin to engage a diverse array of gay, lesbian, and *avant-garde* artists.[60]

Since *Drag Queens'* staging, drag, parody, and self-conscious theatricality have the become mainstays of Gilbert's work and the primary vehicles of his iconoclastic critique. *Drag Queens in Outer Space: A Dream Play* followed as a sequel to *Drag Queens on Trial* in 1986. Focusing its critique on the mainstream of gay community, it concerns Marlene Delorme's decision to succumb to the pressures of "macho" gay culture by abandoning her feminine persona, acting "butch," and becoming "a Church St. monogamist" (Taylor). Gilbert used drag to critique various aspects of both gay and straight culture in *Suzie Goo: Private Secretary*, *Lola Star Builds Her Dream Home*, and *Jim Dandy*. Gilbert also became a drag queen himself. Not long after his first foray in drag at *Drag Queens'* premiere, Gilbert's alter ego "Jane" emerged and has become a celebrity in her own right. Jane hosts parties, readings, cabarets, and stages performances in theatres and in public places. For example, she has taken groups of people with her to the Eaton Centre to go

shopping "for a frock." She has also conducted walking
tours of Toronto that take her patrons to the places where
she has had outdoor sex, regaling them with all the ter-
rifically tawdry details.[61]

In 1990 Jane played the central role in a simultaneously theatrical and very real performance that saw Jane
charged and have her day in court, confirming in the
most realistic of terms the political realities parodied in
*Drag Queens on Trial.* In January of that year Jane was *en
route* to a theatre benefit in a taxi in the west end of the
city (R. Smith). As the cab was travelling through the
Queen and Ossington area, which, in 1990, was not a
good part of town, the police stopped it, apparently for a
burnt-out headlight (Glick). Gilbert recounts what then
occurred in his memoirs:

> [The police officers] were very rude to me and
> searched my purse and my 'person.' I was in a
> notorious area of town and I think they thought
> I was a transsexual, drug-addicted hooker. A chick
> with a dick. When they couldn't find any drugs on
> me, they finally gave me a ticket for not wearing my
> seatbelt. (*Ejaculations* 167)

As fate would have it, when Gilbert related the details
of the story to Tim Jones, Buddies' General Manager,
Jones realized that the court date coincided with the
theatre's 1990 Queer Culture Festival, the annual festival
of queer art that it had been producing since 1989. Jane's
court date would become theatre: Gilbert would go to
the trial as Jane, and her appearance on the stand in the
very real world of an Ontario Court would be included
in the Queer Culture festival's brochure as one of its
many performances (*Ejaculations* 168). It would be an
opportunity for Gilbert to make the kind of critique of

the legal system that he had made in *Drag Queens*, but in a performance that quite literally blurred the lines between theatre and reality.

On the day of the trial, Jane was chauffeured to the courthouse in a rented limousine. On her way, she and her small entourage sipped champagne and watched pornography on the limo's television. When she arrived at Old City Hall, she was greeted by a group of fans who made their way with her into the courtroom. As one reporter described the scene:

> It was now traffic court as a performance art installation. Jane sauntered over to the stand in that fluffy shag white coat, that peroxide wig, that make-up that made Tammy Faye look like a nun. [...] Jane opened by stating to the judge that she was dressed in drag to make a statement, to show how she was dressed the night she was busted ... to demonstrate how anyone who dresses or looks unusual is a target for the TO [sic] police. (Glick)

In the end, Jane got off on a technicality: it is not illegal for a patron to ride in a taxi without wearing a seatbelt. The judge, Brian Hudson, said that Jane/Gilbert "is a reasonable individual and was a passenger in a strange cab. The charges are dismissed" (R. Smith).

In relation to Gilbert's biography, and its historical context, *Drag Queens* represents an artist and a community at a crossroads. Following the unprecedented success of *The Dressing Gown*, Gilbert took stock of the moral conservatism, and the anti-sexual and homophobic currents that ran through straight and gay culture alike, which had risen to a fever pitch in the wake of the backlash, the bathhouse raids, and the emergence of HIV/AIDS. Since *Drag Queens,* he has consistently advocated

and celebrated promiscuity, has challenged assimilationist tendencies in gay culture, and has radically questioned
the medical establishment's understanding of HIV/
AIDS.[62] For the gay community in Toronto, the play
expresses the incredible success of a revolutionary politic
that created and consolidated a politically effective and
visible minoritized community, complete with its own
gay-identified theatre. In 1985, its staging intervened into
the debates current in the first years of the AIDS crisis,
about promiscuity, and the decline of gay liberation. It
reacted to the nascent mainstreaming of gay politics in
Toronto, the increasing and contested importance of gay
civil rights, and it portended both radical AIDS politics
and the queer critiques of identity and community,
which would take centre stage at Buddies and in the gay
community in the decade that followed.

## Endnotes

1. It was anthologized in the fourth edition of Jerry
   Wasserman's Modern Canadian Plays. See Jerry
   Wasserman, ed., *Modern Canadian Plays: Volume I*
   4th ed. (Vancouver: Talonbooks, 2000).
2. The Metropolitan Police Force was renamed
   Metropolitan Toronto Police Service in 1995, and
   the Toronto Police Service in 1998, when the city
   and its boroughs were amalgamated.
3. Institutionally complete is a term used by sociolo-
   gists to describe ethnic or religious communities that
   have developed to a point that the average member
   can fulfill most of his or her daily needs within the
   institutions of the community.

4. This kind of identity politic, the idea that gay men and lesbians constituted a political minority, was a nation wide phenomena in Canada. For analysis of this turn in Toronto see Catherine Jean Nash, "Toronto's Gay Ghetto: Politics and the Disciplining of Identity and Space 1969–1982," diss., Queen's U, 2003. In Canada see Tom Warner, *Never Going Back: A History of Queer Activism in Canada* (Toronto: U of Toronto P, 2002), Gary Kinsman, *The Regulation of Desire: Homo and Hetero Sexualities,* 2nd ed. (Montréal: Black Rose Books, 1996), Peter Knegt, *About Canada: Queer Rights* (Halifax: Fernwood P, 2011).

5. Bryant was only unsuccessful in Orange Country, California, where Proposition 6 was defeated in 1977.

6. Similar anti-Bryant groups were formed against across Canada. For more on the rise of the Christian Right and social conservatism in Canada, see Tom Warner, *Losing Control: Canada's Social Conservatives in the Age of Rights* (Toronto: Between the Lines, 2010).

7. In November 1986, after much lobbying by the Coalition for Gay Right is Ontario (CGLRO), Bill7, which included an amendment to the Ontario Human Rights Code to prohibit discrimination based on sexual orientation, was passed by Queen's Park. See Warner, *Never Going Back: A History of Queer Activism in Canada* 197–99.

8. Political activities around the age of consent and the extension of sexual liberation to children created real division between gay men and lesbians in this era. For an article on lesbian feminist reaction to this

incident in particular, see Becki Ross, "Like Apples and Oranges: Lesbian Feminist Responses to the Politics of the Body Politic," *Queerly Canadian: An Introductory Reader in Sexuality Studies*, eds. Scott Rayter and Maureen FitzGerald (Toronto: Canadian Scholars' P 2012).

9. This is the basic thesis that Nash elucidates in her dissertation.

10. The owners and those who were working for the baths were charged as "keepers" of a "common bawdy house," while the patrons were charged as "found ins."

11. In *Track Two*, Burt also speaks about how his experience of the raids—being forced into the street naked, being called degrading names, and feeling completely at the mercy of a malevolent state authority—made him understand "for the first time" the kind of experiences his parents must have faced during the second World War as Jewish survivors of the Holocaust. See Harry Sutherland, *Track Two,* Film, Canada, 1983.

12. Gay Pride was not a parade with municipally licensed street closures until 1985. See Mariana Valverde and Miomir Cirak, "Governing Bodies, Creating Gay Spaces: Policing and Security in 'Gay' Downtown Toronto," *British Journal of Criminology* 43 (2003).

13. Beginning in 1984, Canada Customs began to seize international materials destined for Glad Day, as well as Vancouver's Little Sister's bookstore, the censorship trials for which continued into the 1990s. The Canadian Committee against Customs Censorship was established in 1986 to protest the actions of Canada Customs. See Brenda Cossman, *Bad Attitude/S on Trial: Pornography, Feminism, and the*

*Butler Decision* (Toronto: University of Toronto Press, 1997), Aerlyn Weissman, Cari Green, Homeboys Productions. and Moving Images Distribution., *Little Sister's Vs. Big Brother*, videorecording, Moving Images Distribution, Vancouver, B.C., 2002.

14. The RTPC was dissolved in July 1992, but the "Court Watch" column continued. See Bob Krawczyk, *Remembering the Rtpc*, 1991, Canadian Lesbian and Gay Archives, Available: http://www.clga.ca/Material/Records/docs/remrtpc.htm, August 20 2011.

15. Also see Scott Tucker, "Our Right to the World," *The Body Politic* Jul–Aug. 1982.

16. As Popert's use of the term underlines here, promiscuity was not pejorative among gay liberationists.

17. I say famously because the article is cited in popular representations of AIDS such as Larry Kramer's play *The Normal Heart*, and the early AIDS film *Longtime Companion*, the latter of which begins with a montage of different people in various New York locations reading and responding to the article.

18. It is now known that there was a rash of uninvestigated AIDS deaths in the 1970s among intravenous drug users, which, at the time, was called "junkies' pneumonia." Cindy Patton notes that AIDS was not recognized in this population because junkies were already considered sick and unhealthy, making their untimely deaths unremarkable. See Cindy Patton, *Inventing Aids* (New York: Routledge, 1990).

19. See Bill Lewis and Randy Coates, "Moral Lessons; Fatal Cancer," *The Body Politic*.77 (1981).

20. By comparison, four months earlier, in March 1983, when Larry Kramer wrote his famous article "1,112

and Counting," there were more the five hundred AIDS diagnoses in New York City, of which 195 had died. See Larry Kramer, "1,112 and Counting," *The New York Native* 14–24 Mar. 1983.

21. The notable exception is Ann Silversides' excellent biography of Michael Lynch, which focuses on his work as an AIDS activist. See Ann Silversides, *Aids Activist: Michael Lynch and the Politics of Community* (Toronto: Between the Lines, 2003).

22. This quotation is taken from the introduction of Robertson's annotated bibliography of AIDS coverage in the *Body Politic*. Also see his annotated chronology of the history of AIDS in Toronto: Mark L. Robertson, "An Annotated Chronology of the History of Aids in Toronto: The First Five Years, 1981–1985," *Canadian Bulletin of Medical History* 22.1 (2005).

23. Immunology and virology were the primary medical fields of research because AIDS illnesses were those usually associated found in people with impaired immune systems, on the one hand, but its spread seemed similar to that of a virus, such as syphilis and hepatitis, on the other.

24. One hypothesis suggested that immune system breakdown among men may have be triggered by exposure to too much semen (though this was not a danger to women). See Patton, *Inventing Aids* 61.

25. Lynch was an American by birth, having immigrated to Toronto to take a post at University of Toronto. He spent a lot of his time with friends on Fire Island, and in New York City, where he also conducted some of his academic research.

26. The promiscuity theory was dangerous to gay men's health because it held that AIDS could not be contracted through a single sexual encounter with an infected person, and that if gay men changed their lifestyles, the epidemic would end.

27. For an account of both the development of safe sex practices, and how safe sex has been negotiated among gay men, see David M. Halperin, *What Do Gay Men Want?: An Essay on Sex, Risk, and the Subjectivity* (Ann Arbor: U of Michigan P, 2007).

28. The first campaign undertaken by Toronto Public Health began in August/September 1983; the first ACT educational pamphlet was published in December 1983 and the first AIDS Awareness Week was launched in June 1984; *The Body Politic* had, of course, been publishing information about AIDS since 1981, but the first full-scale "Safe Sex" article appears in the December 1983 issue, see Rick Bébout, "Is There Safe Sex?," *The Body Politic* Dec. 1983.

29. Since resigning from Buddies in 1997, Gilbert has continued to write and produce work in Toronto under the auspices of the Cabaret Company. He also founded a theatre company in Hamilton, where he resides, called Hammer Theatre.

30. The musical's title came from a Prévert poem called "Le concert n'a pas reussi," which Eric Bentley translated as "Buddies in Bad Times," and which served as the closing finale for the musical.

31. Ironically, when Gilbert resigned as artistic director of Buddies in Bad Times in 1997 he once again enrolled in the doctoral program at the University of

Toronto and eventually became a professor of theatre
at the University of Guelph.

32. The Dream Factory was run by Vincent Kambrek
and Ari Giverts, housed in an old brewery on the
north side of Queen Street East at Sumach Street.
See interviews with Gilbert, Matt Walsh, and Jerry
Ciccoritti in Franco Boni, *Rhubarb-O-Rama!: Plays
and Playwrights from the Rhubarb! Festival* (Winnipeg:
Blizzard, 1998).

33. The first festival was called Rhubarb! Rhubarb! Boni,
*Rhubarb-O-Rama!: Plays and Playwrights from the
Rhubarb! Festival 11.*

34. Richard Nieoczym of the Actor's Lab was also part
of the founding group, but that he left within a year.
See Boni, *Rhubarb-O-Rama!: Plays and Playwrights
from the Rhubarb! Festival* 11.

35. For a history of Nightwood, see Shelley Scott,
*Nightwood Theatre: A Woman's Work Is Always Done*
(Edmonton: Alberta U P, 2010).

36. In Gilbert's memoirs he posits his disinterest in making work for middle class gay audiences as one of the
reasons he resigned as artistic director of Buddies in
1997. See Sky Gilbert, *Ejaculations from the Charm
Factory: A Memoir* (Toronto: ECW P, 2000) 264. For
an examination of how Buddies move into its current
home at 12 Alexander Street required the company
to become more "mainstream" in its politics and its
aesthetics, see J. Paul Halferty, "Queer and Now: The
Queer Signifier at Buddies in Bad Times Theatre"
*Queer Theatre in Canada*, ed. Rosalind Kerr, vol. 7
(Toronto: Playwright Canada Press, 2007).

37. The notable exceptions from the 1970s are Larry
Fineberg, John Palmer, and Paul Bettis, though, none

of these playwrights overtly positioned their work as "gay" in a political sense in this period. Palmer would begin to identify his work as gay in the 1980s; for his view on being a gay theatre artist in Toronto in the 1970s, see the interview between him and Robert Wallace in the anthology of his plays, *The End/A Day at the Beach*. The other notable gay artist doing gay work in the first few years of the 1980s is David Roche. He, however, would quickly become part of the Buddies scene. Additionally, Brad Fraser would hit the theatre scene in Toronto with his play *Wolf Boy* in 1985, produced at Theatre Passe Muraille.

38. In his memoirs, Gilbert suggests that he used this form, and was reluctant to take on the mantel of playwright, because of his anxieties about having his writing judged by others.

39. On the difficulties of dealing rationally with childhood sexuality, see Jane Rule's Jane Rule, "Teaching Sexuality," The Body Politic Jun. 1979. She wrote this in response to the "Men Loving Boys Loving Men" controversy.

40. For Gilbert's first review, see Ray Conlogue, "Lana Turner Intrigues, but Fails," *Globe and Mail* 4 Oct. 1980.

41. In his memoirs, Gilbert suggests that the first play for which he was billed as playwright was *Radiquet*, and that he wrote *The Dressing Gown* in the wake of its failure with critics and audiences (72–75). This, however, is not the case. In reviews of Gilbert's early plays he is often listed as writer, and *The Dressing Gown* was staged in October 1984, while *Radiquet* was staged in March 1985. *Radiquet* is a play that is inspired by a poet but does not incorporate his

poetry. Its failure in March 1985 was, perhaps, another element that fired his desire to rebel against the gay community with *Drag Queens on Trial.*

42. As if to validate the validity of *La Ronde*'s psychological observations, Sigmund Freud quite famously wrote to Schnitzler, on the occasion of the playwrights sixtieth birthday, telling him that what he realized through intuition with his plays had taken Freud years of careful work and research.

43. When it was published in 1989, Gilbert actually re-wrote one of the scenes, changing "'Eliot's' little lecture about the gay lifestyle [in which] there was a lot of talk about penises being 'evil'; of the ways in which men's psychological makeups [sic] cause them to be cruel" Sky Gilbert, *The Dressing Gown,* 1st ed. (Toronto: Playwrights Canada P, 1989) 8.

44. In his memoirs, Gilbert says the play emerged out of his own personal hurt after a failed relationship, and his disappointment with the gay community for not always supporting his work. He also writes that it can "be seen as *prescient* in terms of AIDS hysteria" (*Ejaculations* 78). While this may be the case, debates about the place of sex and promiscuity in gay life had been current since the bathhouse raids, if not earlier, and they had only become more heated with the advent of AIDS.

45. For Gilbert's thought on these issues see Gilbert, *Ejaculations from the Charm Factory: A Memoir.* 77–85.

46. "Pro-sexual" is a term that Buddies would incorporate into its mandate when it moved into its current home at 12 Alexander Street. See Robert Wallace, "Theorizing a Queer Theatre: Buddies in Bad

Times," *Contemporary Issues in Canadian Drama*, ed. Per K. Brask (Winnipeg: Blizzard, 1995).

47. Marlene Delorme was played by Doug Millar, Judy Goose by Leonard Chow, and Lana Lust by Kent Stains.

48. See Christine Gledhill, *Home Is Where the Heart Is: Studies in Melodrama and the Woman's Film*, Reset ed. (London: British Film Institute, 2002).

49. See Gary Kinsman and Patrizia Gentile, *Canada's War on Queers: National Security as Sexual Regulation* (Vancouver: U British Columbia P, 2010).

50. See Judith Butler, *Gender Trouble: Feminism and the Subversion of Identity*, 10th anniversary ed. (New York: Routledge, 1999), Judith Butler, "Performative Acts and Gender Constitution: An Essay in Phenomenology and Feminist Theory," *Theatre Journal* 40.4 (1988).

51. Gilbert may have got this phrase from a book published in 1984 by Philip Core, called *Camp: The Lie that Tells the Truth*. If this was the case, his decision to switch the focus from camp to drag specifically reveals his and, presumably, the culture's renewed interest in gender.

52. While *Drag Queens* does not include lesbians within its critique, some lesbian feminists viewed gay male drag as misogynist. Marilyn Frye, for example, writing in early–1980s, argues "gay men's effeminacy and donning of feminine apparel displays no love of or identification with women or the womanly. For the most part, this femininity is affected and characterized by theatrical exaggeration. It is a casual and cynical mockery of women, for whom femininity is

the trappings of oppression, but it is also a kind of play, a toying with that which is taboo" See Marilyn Frye, *The Politics of Reality: Essays in Feminist Theory* (Trumansburg, N.Y.: Crossing P, 1983) 137.

53. This was also an issue that was being debated in the pages of *The Body Politic*. See Tim McCaskell, "You've Got a Nice Body … For an Oriental," *The Body Politic* Apr. 1984, Ken Popert, "Race, Moustaches and Sexual Prejudice," *The Body Politic* Jun. 1983.

54. For example, in "Blessed are the Deviates: A Post-therapy Check-up on my Ex-psychiatrist," an article in which Michael Riordan recounts his experience of "aversion therapy," "electric shocks, three times a week, an all-out assault for a year, to straighten me out, to kill the homosexual." See Michael Riordon, "Blessed Are the Deviates: A Post-Therapy Check-up on My Ex-Psychiatrist," *Flaunting It!: A Decade of Gay Journalism from* The Body Politic, eds. Ed Jackson and Stan Persky (Toronto: Pink Triangle P, 1982).

55. Its AIDS message was, however, noticed by John Glines, whose New York theatre company, "The Glines," had successfully produced William Hoffman's AIDS play *As Is* in March 1985. According to Gilbert, Glines expressed interest in producing *Drag Queens* but on the condition that he delete its references to AIDS. New York was at least two years ahead of Toronto in the crisis and, along with San Francisco, was at its epicentre in North America. In the absence of universal health care, and with a municipal and federal government that were belligerently negligent in their response, it was hit very hard by the epidemic. Gilbert was, of course, overjoyed by

the possibility of having a professional production of his *Drag Queens* in New York, but he refused to change the play: "I can't do that, it wouldn't be my play anymore if I did that." According it Gilbert, Glines refused to produce the play as too many people were dying in New York, and "people want to see positive stuff" (*Ejaculations* 94). The Glines subsequently produced *Drag Queens* in 1994 with its AIDS elements intact.

56. *As Is* enjoyed critically successful run at Toronto Free in Theatre in January 1986, shortly after *Drag Queens* was produced. It was a co-production between Toronto Free and Shaw, and was the play's Canadian premiere. The TFT/Shaw co-production toured to the National Arts Centre in February.

57. See Elin Diamond, "Brechtian Theory/ Feminist Theory: Toward a Gestic Feminist Criticism," *The Drama Review (TDR)* 32.1 (1988), Jill Dolan, "'Lesbian' Subjectivity in Realism: Dragging at the Margins of Structure and Ideology" *Performing Feminisms: Feminist Critical Theory and Theatre*, ed. Sue-Ellen Case (Baltimore: Johns Hopkins U P, 1990), Jill Dolan, "Practicing Cultural Disruptions: Gay and Lesbian Representation and Sexuality," *Critical Theory and Performance*, eds. Janelle G. Reinelt and Joseph R. Roach (Ann Arbor: U of Michigan P, 1992).

58. The only real exception is found in Jay Scott's review in the *Globe and Mail*, though he does not really investigate the play's politics. Scott, who was also gay, thought that the queens' protests against both straight and gay culture were genuine and

courageous. See Jay Scott, "Between Immortality and Irrelevance: Drag Queens Tackle Stereotypes," *The Globe and Mail* 21 Oct. 1985.

59. Gilbert had produced other gay plays through Rhubarb! but they were never marketed or positioned as such.

60. Fostering equality between gay men and lesbians in the theatre, and issues of sexual and racial diversity more generally, have been ongoing concerns for the company, and it has had both successes and failures on these fronts. For a discussion of the place of lesbian work in Buddies' history, see Moynan King, "The Foster Children of Buddies: Queer Women at 12 Alexander" *Theatre and Performance in Toronto*, ed. Laura Levin, vol. 21 (Toronto: Playwrights Canada Press, 2011).

61. Gilbert still regularly appears as Jane at theatre functions such as the annual Dora Mavor Moore awards. I, for one, took great pleasure in seeing Jane walk up to the stage this past spring (2011), having received the Dora for best new play in the independent theatre division for *The Situationists*.

62. Gilbert has been part of an organization called Health, Education, AIDS Liaison (HEAL), founded in New York by Michael Ellner. HEAL questions the science of HIV/AIDS. In Gilbert's words, they "question whether HIV has ever actually been isolated, and whether it is capable of the kind of cellular carnage that it discoverer, Robert C. Gallo, attributes to it." See Gilbert, *Ejaculations from the Charm Factory: A Memoir* 94–95, Sky Gilbert, "Positive," *Toronto Life* June 1999.

# Works Cited

Altman, Lawrence. "Rare Cancer Seen In 41 Homosexuals." *New York Times* July 3 1981.

Bébout, Rick. "Is There Safe Sex?" *The Body Politic* Dec. 1983: 33–37.

———. "Promiscuous Affectations". Toronto, 1999. May 10 2011. <Http://Www.Rbebout.Com/Bar/1977.Htm>.

Boni, Franco. *Rhubarb-O-Rama!: Plays And Playwrights From The Rhubarb! Festival*. Winnipeg: Blizzard, 1998.

Brooks, Peter. *The Melodramatic Imagination: Balzac, Henry James, Melodrama, And The Mode Of Excess*. New Haven: Yale U P, 1995.

Butler, Judith. *Gender Trouble: Feminism And The Subversion Of Identity*. 10th Anniversary Ed. New York: Routledge, 1999.

———. "Performative Acts And Gender Constitution: An Essay In Phenomenology And Feminist Theory." *Theatre Journal* 40.4 (1988): 519–31.

Callen, Michael. "Aids: Killing Ourselves." *The Body Politic* Apr. 1983: 5–6.

Callen, Michael, Richard Berkowitz, And Richard Dworkin. "We Know Who We Are: Two Gay Men Declare War On Promiscuity." *New York Native* 8–21 Nov. 1982: 23–29.

Conlogue, Ray. "Lana Turner Intrigues, But Fails." *Globe And Mail* 4 Oct. 1980, Sec. E: 10.

Cossman, Brenda. *Bad Attitude/S On Trial: Pornography, Feminism, And The Butler Decision*. Toronto: University Of Toronto Press, 1997.

Cover. *The Body Politic* Nov. 1988: Front Cover.

Diamond, Elin. "Brechtian Theory/ Feminist Theory: Toward A Gestic Feminist Criticism." *The Drama Review (TDR)* 32.1 (1988): 82–94.

Dolan, Jill. ""Lesbian" Subjectivity In Realism: Dragging At The Margins Of Structure And Ideology " *Performing Feminisms: Feminist Critical Theory And Theatre*. Ed. Sue-Ellen Case. Baltimore: Johns Hopkins U P, 1990. 40–53.

———. "Practicing Cultural Disruptions: Gay And Lesbian Representation And Sexuality." *Critical Theory And Performance*. Eds. Janelle G. Reinelt And Joseph R. Roach. Ann Arbor: U Of Michigan P, 1992. 263–75.

Filewod, Alan. "Introduction." *The Ctr Anthology: Fifteen Plays From The Canadian Theatre Review*. Ed. Alan Filewod. Toronto: U Of Toronto P, 1993. Xi–Xx.

Freedman, Estelle B. "'Uncontrolled Desires': The Response To The Sexual Psychopath, 1920–1960." *Passion And Power: Sexuality In History*. Eds. Robert A. Padgug, Kathy Lee Peiss And Christina Simmons. Philadelphia: Temple U P, 1989. 199–225.

Frye, Marilyn. *The Politics Of Reality: Essays In Feminist Theory*. Trumansburg, N.Y.: Crossing P, 1983.

Gilbert, Sky. "Drag Queens On Trial: A Courtroom Melodrama." *Painted, Tainted, Sainted: Four Plays*. Toronto: Playwrights Canada P, 1996.

———. *Ejaculations From The Charm Factory: A Memoir*. Toronto: ECW P, 2000.

———. *"Lana Turner Has Collapsed!: A Theatrical Extravaganza Of Gay Life And The Movies "*: Unpublished, University Of Guelph Archives, 1980.

———. "Positive." *Toronto Life* June 1999: 100–03.

———. *The Dressing Gown*. 1st Ed. Toronto: Playwrights Canada P, 1989.

Gilman, Sander L. *Disease And Representation: Images Of Illness From Madness To Aids*. Ithaca: Cornell U P, 1988.

Gledhill, Christine. *Home Is Where The Heart Is: Studies In Melodrama And The Woman's Film*. Reset Ed. London: British Film Institute, 2002.

Glick, Ira. "Court Appearance As Performance." *Xtra* April 27 1990.

Halferty, J. Paul. "Queer And Now: The Queer Signifer At Buddies In Bad Times Theatre" *Queer Theatre In Canada*. Ed. Rosalind Kerr. Vol. 7. Toronto: Playwright Canada Press, 2007. 239–55.

Halperin, David M. How To Be Gay. Cambridge, MA: Belknap P Of Harvard U P, 2012.

——. *What Do Gay Men Want?: An Essay On Sex, Risk, And The Subjectivity*. Ann Arbor: U Of Michigan P, 2007.

Hannon, Gerald. "Men Loving Boys Loving Men." *The Body Politic* Feb. 1977: 29–35.

——. "Sewell: Unleashing The Whirlwind." *The Body Politic* Feb. 1979: 8–10.

Hutcheon, Linda. *A Theory Of Parody: The Teachings Of Twentieth-Century Art Forms*. 1st Illinois Pbk. Ed. Urbana: U Of Illinois P, 2000.

Hutcheon, Linda, And Michael Hutcheon. *Opera: Desire, Disease, Death*. Texts And Contexts. Lincoln: U Of Nebraska P, 1996.

Jackson, Ed. "Media Raise Fear Of Undue Gay Power As Sewell Endorses Hislop Campaign." *The Body Politic* Oct. 1980: 9–10.

Jackson, Ed, And Andrew Lesk. "Little Knowledge, Dangerous Thing." *The Body Politic* Dec. 1985: 8.

King, Moynan. "The Foster Children Of Buddies: Queer Women At 12 Alexander " *Theatre And Performance*

*In Toronto*. Ed. Laura Levin. Vol. 21. Toronto: Playwrights Canada Press, 2011. 191–202.

Kinsman, Gary. *The Regulation Of Desire: Homo And Hetero Sexualities*. 2nd Ed. Montréal: Black Rose Books, 1996.

Kinsman, Gary, And Patrizia Gentile. *Canada's War On Queers: National Security As Sexual Regulation*. Vancouver: U British Columbia P, 2010.

Knegt, Peter. *About Canada: Queer Rights*. Halifax: Fernwood P, 2011.

Kramer, Larry. "1,112 And Counting." *The New York Native* 14–24 Mar. 1983: 1,18–22.

Krawczyk, Bob. "Remembering The Rtpc". Toronto, 1991. Canadian Lesbian And Gay Archives. August 20 2011. <Http://Www.Clga.Ca/Material/Records/Docs/Remrtpc.Htm>.

Lewis, Bill. "Aids: Discounting The Promiscuity Theory." *The Body Politic* Apr. 1983: 11.

———. "The Real Gay Epidemic: Panic And Paranoia." *The Body Politic* Nov. 1982: 38–40.

Lewis, Bill, And Randy Coates. "Moral Lessons; Fatal Cancer." *The Body Politic*.77 (1981): 43.

Lynch, Michael. "Living With Kaposi's." *The Body Politic*. 88 (1982): 31–37.

———. "Media Fosters Bigotry With Murder Coverage." *The Body Politic* Sep. 1977: 1–2.

Mccaskell, Tim. "You've Got A Nice Body ... For An Oriental." *The Body Politic* Apr. 1984: 33–37.

Meyer, Moe. "Reclaiming The Discourse Of Camp." *An Archaeology Of Posing: Essays On Camp, Drag, And Sexuality*. Madison, Wis.: Macater P, 2010. 32–52.

Mietkiewicz, Henry. "Drag Queens On Trial Is Not For The Faint-Hearted." *Toronto Star* 20 Oct. 1995, Sec. G: 4.

——. "Sky Is The Limit For Gilbert's Drag Queens." *Toronto Star* 25 Oct. 1985.

Nash, Catherine Jean. "Toronto's Gay Ghetto: Politics And The Disciplining Of Identity And Space 1969–1982." Diss., Queen's U, 2003.

Orr, Kevin. "Condoms: Gay Men Try Them On For Size." *The Body Politic.*109 (1984): 31.

Patton, Cindy. Inventing Aids. New York: Routledge, 1990.

"Pneumocystis Pneumonia—Los Angeles." *Morbidity And Mortality Weekly Report* 30.21 (1981).

Popert, Ken. "Dangers Of The Minority Game." *Flaunting It!: A Decade Of Gay Journalism From The Body Politic.* Eds. Ed Jackson And Stan Persky. Toronto: Pink Triangle P, 1982. 138–39.

——. "Public Sexuality And Social Space." *The Body Politic.* 85 (1982): 29–30.

——. "Race, Moustaches And Sexual Prejudice." *The Body Politic* Jun. 1983: 34.

——. "Taking Aim With An Empty Gun? The Red Cross Says Its Test Will Weed Out Bad Blood." *The Body Politic.* 116 (1985): 14–15.

Riordon, Michael. "Blessed Are The Deviates: A Post-Therapy Check-Up On My Ex-Psychiatrist." *Flaunting It!: A Decade Of Gay Journalism From The Body Politic.* Eds. Ed Jackson And Stan Persky. Toronto: Pink Triangle P, 1982. 14–20.

Robertson, Mark L. "Aids Coverage In The Body Politic, 1981–1987: An Annotated Bibliography." *American Review Of Canadian Studies* 32.3 (2002): 397–414.

——. "An Annotated Chronology Of The History Of Aids In Toronto: The First Five Years, 1981–198." *Canadian Bulletin Of Medical History* 22.1 (2005): 313–51.

Roche, David. "On The Party Circuit With Sky Gilbert." *The Body Politic* Feb. 1981: 27–28.

Ross, Becki. "Like Apples And Oranges: Lesbian Feminist Responses To The Politics Of The Body Politic." *Queerly Canadian: An Introductory Reader In Sexuality Studies*. Eds. Scott Rayter And Maureen Fitzgerald. Toronto: Canadian Scholars' P 2012. 139–50.

Rule, Jane. "Teaching Sexuality." *The Body Politic* Jun. 1979: 29.

Schnitzler, Arthur, Frank Marcus, And Jacqueline Marcus. *La Ronde*. London: Methuen, 1982.

Scott, Jay. "Between Immortality And Irrelevance: Drag Queens Tackle Stereotypes." *The Globe And Mail* 21 Oct. 1985, Sec. C: 12.

Scott, Shelley. *Nightwood Theatre: A Woman's Work Is Always Done*. Edmonton: Alberta U P, 2010.

Silversides, Ann. *Aids Activist: Michael Lynch And The Politics Of Community*. Toronto: Between The Lines, 2003.

Smith, Miriam Catherine. *Lesbian And Gay Rights In Canada: Social Movements And Equality-Seeking, 1971–1995*. Toronto: U Of Toronto P, 1999.

Smith, Ray. "Queen For A Day In Court." *The Toronto Sun* April 12 1990: 44.

Spalding, Roger. "The 87% Solution." *The Body Politic* Apr. 1983: 12–13.

Sutherland, Harry. *Track Two*. Film, Canada, 1983.

Taylor, Bill. "Drag Queens In Outer Space, All Good, Not-Too-Clean Fun." *The Toronto Star* 6 Nov. 1986, Sec. B: 3.

Treichler, Paula A. "Aids, Homophobia, And Biomedical Discourse: An Epidemic Of Signification." *Aids:*

*Cultural Analysis/Cultural Activism*. Ed. Douglas Crimp. Cambridge, Mass: MIT P, 1988. 31–70.

Tucker, Scott. "Our Right To The World." *The Body Politic* Jul–Aug. 1982: 29–33.

Valverde, Mariana, And Miomir Cirak. "Governing Bodies, Creating Gay Spaces: Policing And Security In 'Gay' Downtown Toronto." *British Journal Of Criminology* 43 (2003): 102–21.

Wallace, Robert. "Playing With Ourselves." *The Body Politic* Feb. 1985: 32–34.

——. *Producing Marginality: Theatre And Criticism In Canada*. Saskatoon: Fifth House, 1990.

——. *Theatre And Transformation In Contemporary Canada*. Toronto: Robarts Centre For Canadian Studies, 1999.

——. "Theorizing A Queer Theatre: Buddies In Bad Times." *Contemporary Issues In Canadian Drama*. Ed. Per K. Brask. Winnipeg: Blizzard, 1995. 136–59.

Warner, Tom. *Losing Control: Canada's Social Conservatives In The Age Of Rights*. Toronto: Between The Lines, 2010.

——. *Never Going Back: A History Of Queer Activism In Canada*. Toronto: U Of Toronto P, 2002.

Wasserman, Jerry, Ed. *Modern Canadian Plays: Volume I* 4th Ed. Vancouver: Talonbooks, 2000.

Wein, Daryl. *Sex Positive*. U.S.A, 2008.

Weissman, Aerlyn, Et Al. *Little Sister's Vs. Big Brother*. Videorecording. Moving Images Distribution,, Vancouver, B.C., 2002.

Essays on Selected Plays

# It Started with a Kiss & The Roman Spring of Mrs. Thompson

## Hope Thompson

*I*t *Started with a Kiss*
      As it often does.

I have been a fan of Sky Gilbert's (and later, desperately in love with him) since I saw my first play of his in 1979 at the Palmerston Library theatre in Toronto. The play starred Peter Noble, my sister's boyfriend at the time, which was perhaps why I saw the play. But I like to think there was another reason I ended up in that darkened theatre on a bright, sunny afternoon in 1979—that somehow, it was preordained; we were meant to be together, eventually, and that this was simply the beginning. I was in high school at the time and was accompanied by my then boyfriend, JT (whose initials have been changed to protect his identity).

As we walked from Bathurst Station along Bloor Street West, I remember that he had a skateboard with him. I tried to talk to him, to have a conversation, but he would shoot ahead on the skateboard, out of earshot. Having decided to bring a skateboard seemed childish to me. We were going to see a play, after all. I distinctly remember feeling irritated but then learned that boys mature later. Perhaps this was an example of that. However, in defense of JT who, like myself, would become gay, I have always been a bit "uptight." Instead of trying to confront and overcome this problem through costly therapy sessions, I decided, long ago, to simply work with it.

I no longer remember the plot details of that first Sky Gilbert theatre experience but I do remember being thrilled, astonished and riveted by the events on stage. My reaction was stimulated by the fact that the play featured an open-mouth and sustained kiss between the leading man and leading lady. To my young and inexperienced self, it was thrilling, and perhaps even avant-garde. As JT and I were both "peri-homosexual," the romantic side of our liaison was hotly unsatisfying (for me, anyway). Our interests were elsewhere, though we hadn't yet admitted it to ourselves. All I could think about was that onstage kiss—between a man and a woman. But it didn't make sense. Surely, I would be kissing a woman …

Only later, would I realize the true identity of that man and that woman.

Flash forward thirty years.

As a late bloomer, I had now written a play and Sky Gilbert was acting in it. By now, I had seen many of his plays, socialized with him, laughed with him but working on a show together was quite unlike anything else. As the rehearsals progressed toward opening night, so did the intensity of my feelings for Sky. I was falling in love and I knew it. If rehearsals are foreplay and the actual show is the climax, then I was certainly ready for a fag when it was all over. This was a serious infatuation. My heart felt like it would launch out of my ribcage, overflowing as it was with a heady mixture of desire, joy and confusion. In a situation like this, there is only one course of action.

Daydreaming has always been one of my strong points. As a child my parents noted that I stared out the window, silently, and for hours during long car trips while my siblings cried and fussed. Only after a clean psychiatric evaluation did they shrug it off as "a rich mental life."

To fully enjoy my infatuation with Sky, I decided on a Roman theme. I knew that Tennessee Williams had spent time in Rome with his boyfriend, Frank Merlo, and that they had caroused about with Italian actress, Anna Magnani. For clarity, I ditched the boyfriend and cast myself as Anna and Sky as Tennessee. Then, later, I found I had to switch those roles, to drive up the passion. Still later, I re-cast us again, as ourselves—but with some slight modifications. For example: I was someone he wanted to spend time with. In the daydream, I accepted completely that he had another life—with men, at bars. I loved him regardless and was content to moon around the apartment, waiting, wondering, stirring pots. fussing with pillows. When he would finally return, we would, well … the fantasy didn't really play out beyond the pillow fussing and anticipation of his arrival at the door of our Roman walk-up.

It seemed enough, inside my mind, that Sky Gilbert was coming home to me.

## The Roman Spring of Mrs. Thompson

MUSIC CUE #1: *Sky comes on stage moving to music in headphones. Music stops abruptly when he pulls out postcard from inside jacket.*

Dear Sky,

Remember how we used to say that in a perfect world, we'd have an apartment in Rome?

Well, guess what? It's a perfect world! I'm here. I'm in Rome! I've paid first and last on our apartment and I'm ready for you so just ... come on over!

It's a beautiful apartment. There's lots of closet space for your shirts and trousers and whatever other things a man brings on holiday. Shaving items? Don't ask don't tell, right?

You'll love the location. It's just off the Via Condotti by the Spanish Steps—you know the ones made famous by Vivien Leigh in the *Roman Spring of Mrs Stone* when she trotted up and down them looking for her young Italian lover only to find Warren Beatty. What a gigolo! And he's not even Italian. Much like how they cast Charlton Heston in *Touch of Evil*. Were there no Italian or Mexican actors in 1950s Hollywood? I mean, how ridiculous. We'll talk about things like this when you get here. Oh, I can't wait. Hey, perhaps we could act out scenes from some of are favourite Roman movies? I have a camera.

Or, you can act out scenes with other people. I mean, we don't need at be joined at the hip! (STRANGE GLANCE; SHE WISHES THEY WERE)

Obviously I just want you to be happy. I am!

Just sitting here by the window, writing this letter, anticipating your arrival at Leonardo Da Vinci Airport—airport code FMO for when you book your ticket, which hopefully will be soon. No pressure!

It's a two-bedroom apartment.

Obviously.

Me, I've got some books and maps and Italian-English dictionaries to keep me busy. You, on the other hand, are free to just be yourself and do whatever it is that you do! (That line is actually from Judy Garland's Carnegie Hall recording during the first intermission when she tells the audience to just go drink or smoke or do whatever it is that you do!) Isn't it tragic when lesbians try to be like gay men?

We will NOT talk about that when you get here.

On a typical evening, when you get back from being out at your clubs or darkened streets or wherever it is that you go, me, I'll be waiting with a steaming pot of spaghetti, should you be hungry after your adventures. Then again, you could even stay out all night! It's absolutely no problem. Don't worry about me. I'll have my face buried in a good book.

I'm totally content to just do my thing.

And wait. And wonder. Oh sure, maybe I'll be a little bit curious. I'll scratch my head, "where's he gotten to now?" But I won't be upset. Just looking forward to seeing you.

Like I am right now as I write this postcard. Please don't be long in getting here, but obviously take as long as you like. I know you're busy with stuff in Canada. *La Dolce Vita* awaits—when you're ready, of course.

Caio.

Esperanza

That's "Hope" in Italian. Hope Thompson. You do remember me? It doesn't matter if you don't—just please get here …

Anyway. Arrivederci!

(BEAT)

MUSIC CUE #2

## *Heliogabalus*: A Lover's Story

## Ian Jarvis

Of all Sky's plays this has to be one of my personal favourites—I mean how can it not be considering it's a play about me being the Emperor of Rome! Even if I am compared to an effeminate dictatorial tyrant, it's still extremely flattering to have a play written about you. I've been Sky's partner for more than a decade and have had the fortunate—or some might say the unfortunate—experience of being his muse. If anyone has gone out with a writer, they are well aware of the fact that nothing in their lives will ever again be sacred. They are running the risk of having themselves—and their loved ones—used and exploited as good material.

My friends and myself have appeared throughout Sky's work. Whether it is in his books, poems, or plays—sooner or later there always comes a passage with a reference to something from our lives, something more than a little close to home. When this occurs, thankfully, Sky is kind enough to mask the details or twist a few facts around, so they go publicly unnoticed and save the people involved too much embarrassment. It often tends to be a case of art imitating life. The truth always seems to be stranger and much funnier than fiction.

In this respect *Heliogabalus* is no different—except the audience is getting a one-sided look at the story. So gather round! It's time for the Emperor of the Sun to speak about the play in his own words. Let's take a look at some of the real truths and distortions of the writer's mind at work—from an up close and personal perspective.

*Heliogabalus* deals with an amazing range of issues and subjects and is packed with lots of ideas that were based on truths from the past. The play came about when I was on a trip in England, and stumbled across a book entitled *Caligula: Divine Carnage: Atrocities of the Roman Emperors* by Steven Baber and Jeremy Reed. Sky is right to depict me in the play as having a love for the grotesque, the morbid and the bizarre. The book was a real page-turner for me as it was filled with non-stop decadent sex and extreme violence. It shows a more brutally real account of Rome than we are used to seeing depicted in sanitized history books and Hollywood films. I'd definitely recommend this book to anyone wanting to learn more about the true extremes of Roman debauchery. But you have been warned—it's a graphic read, not for the faint of heart.

Inside the book there is an entire chapter set aside about Heliogabalus (also spelt Eliogabalus). It was this chapter that would become the Holy Grail for much of the historical information the play is based upon. I was amazed to come across the Emperor's story, as nowhere in any of my history courses or my gay reading material had I ever heard of this fascinating historical character. Even on the Internet there is little writing or information about Heliogabalus. The truth is Rome—and the entire Roman Empire—had once been ruled by a 14-year-old, cross-dressing, homo—who loved sex and putting on wild parties. He created the first women's senate, and sunk the entire Roman naval fleet, because he had such a strong hated for masculine men and their games of war. He filled the courts of Rome with mass orgies, and gave the highest positions of office to hairdressers and sex workers. Why don't they teach this stuff properly in the schools? Here's a solid gay 'party icon'—one that's way better to know about than Britney or Lady Gaga! It's sad though, because (as in the play) the military macho men of the empire couldn't take Heliogabalus anymore, and the beloved Emperor of the Sun was killed when he was only 18. It's said that during his four-year reign he did more damage to the Roman reputation than anyone before or after. However, during those four years, the world of Rome was a queer place—full of pure sex, pleasure and unyielding decadence—a place that makes the culture of the 60s and 70s look pale, and incredibly uptight, in comparison.

Well as soon as I was done reading the book I passed it along to Sky, who—unlike me—can't stand the hint of violence or blood. Sky will often close his eyes in a horror movie or just look away. However his passion for hearing the legend of a gay girly boy Emperor won out, and (thankfully) he was compelled to read it cover to cover. Shortly after, a regular pattern—one I've seen many times over the years with Sky—began. He hunkered down for hours in front of his laptop listening to shrill opera music blaring through headphones. He's almost manic. Nothing else exists or matters in the world, and he's in a true state of creative bliss. He'll never tell anyone what he's working on under any condition, at least not until it is firmly completed—and you wouldn't dare interrupt him to ask. All you know is he is doing something he has to do, and it's best to leave the master alone with his craft. Happily for us all, the life and times of Heliogabalus emerged from all this. It was just too important a story not to be shared with an audience. Unfortunately, in order to bring this great tale into the modern world, Sky required the use of our relationship, and me.

Okay. So I'm going to begin by admitting to some—but not all—of the horrible truths about me in the play. I am not a neat freak, and I am more than a little messy around the house. In fact I may even border on the verge of being a hoarder. Before Sky and I decided to live together, we went out for two years. I agreed to move in with him on one condition—that I would never ever have to wash a single dish. And still, to this day, more than 10 years later, I haven't.

Now. Before you all start to think "How horrible he is!" and "Life with the Emperor of the Sun must be exactly as it's depicted in the play!"—it's very important that you know a detail or two about my partner (whose real name is Schuyler Lee Gilbert Jr.—named after his Dad—then shortened to Sky). He loves cleaning up, taking out garbage and washing dishes! You see what isn't clear in the *Heliogabalus* play is that Sky / Hierocles actually takes the greatest of great pleasure from doing these things. In fact it just further glues us together as a couple. I love making the mess and he loves cleaning it up. It sounds a little sick, even as I write about it. But let the truth be told. If it was really so horrible living with me all these years he wouldn't still be here. Though not always understood from the outside in many ways, this arrangement makes—for us—the perfect symbiotic relationship.

Sky also got the part about me liking to try new and exotic foods dead on. However, anything is considered exotic when your diet consists of only meat and potatoes! For years Sky would only eat the blandest of foods, and not many of them are very healthy. It's always been a bit of a challenge—and a chore—for us to go out to dinner together. It's only recently that I've been able to get him inside of a Sushi restaurant. He still won't try anything more risqué then teriyaki chicken—and on a good day maybe a few pieces of a California roll. The idea of fish, let alone raw fish, is just too much for him. So yes, if you consider eating anything beyond this you are—to him—indeed, a mad man. I'm not sure where the "honey garlic" references come from in the play. But is honey garlic really such a weird flavour? Well maybe if you're Sky Gilbert it is.

Sky's mother died recently, and my own mother is blind—so I can thankfully say neither will be reading this book anytime soon. This means I can spill the beans without getting caught. Both of us have had a constant, and relentless, battle with our mothers. They have been far from being what you would call sweet, nice old ladies. Instead they have both been stubborn, opinionated—and about as right wing as you can get. They both also have taken great passion in inflicting relentless guilt onto their children. In the play, Heliogabalus struggles when dealing with his mother—both in the modern world and in the past. This little detail could have just as much been about Sky as it could have been about me.

Sky's real life mother was called Pat, and was referred to in the play as Bev. She was a proud Republican woman who was extremely overbearing and had no problem dominating a room. Yes, Sky is an American through and through. (On a side note—he still has to compulsively watch CNN every day and knows very little about

Canadian politics). You might be able to take the person out of America, but good luck taking the American out of the person! Believe me, I've tried. His mother moved them up here when Sky was 13, supposedly to avoid any chance of Sky being drafted into the Vietnam War. The real, and more likely reason, was to escape any dealings with Sky's father—and even more likely so Pat could enjoy her newfound single life in Toronto. I remember meeting her for the first time and just being stunned. She reminded me so much of Joan Rivers! She had a deep, gravelly voice from years of the drinking and smoking that would eventually send her to her grave. She was always dressed to the nines, with talon-like claws, and a hairdo that would have put the *Dynasty* women to shame. Sky's mother loved to shock, and was always brutally frank about her sexual activities. She'd take the greatest of pride in talking about the details of her sexual relationship with Sky's father. That being said you would never dare talk about your own sexual adventures. If you were in Pat's company you were there to listen. There just wasn't enough space in the room. It should come as little surprise that Sky has ended up basing so much of his loveable drag character "Jane" on her.

Like the two characters in the play, Sky and I have always had an open relationship. From day one we've always had it set up like this, and neither of us has had any desire to have it any differently. The idea of monogamy is repellent to both of us, and I personally just don't understand why anyone would ever want to be that way. To me the greatest thing about being gay is that you get to test drive all the cars you want in the world, and never have to get stuck with a lemon. I have so many straight friends who would kill to have this freedom in their lives, yet these days so few gay people actually take advantage of it. You can have your cake and eat it to—and needless to say this play and many other pieces of Sky's work have been peppered with this ideology. Again, I know it's very trendy right now for gays to get married and adopt children from overseas—Africa and the Far East. If you are one of those people, you probably aren't going to like a lot of Sky's work. I wish you the best of luck with it. Nothing kills the fun of a party like the sound of a baby. Love is something very different than sex, and I can honestly say I really don't believe we would have lasted as long as we have as a couple if our relationship had been any different.

With this all being said, having an open relationship doesn't mean it's a total "free for all." We have clearly defined rules and guidelines for how our relationship operates. For example, we aren't allowed to sleep with each other's friends, or inside our work circles. Sky once had a gay boss at University. You could imagine the difficulties if I had started to sleep with him. Our relationship has gone through a lot of negotiations, figuring out what rules work, and what best suits both of our needs.

Heliogabalus has a scene where they are working on figuring out one of these sacred and rather difficult rules. Heliogabalus is pushing the boundaries by wanting to be able to have a guy take him away for a weekend to Montreal, and Hierocles is adamant that this is a "no go." Yes, Sky and I did go through a period of trying to figure this issue out between us. In the end we got it sorted out, and we now have rules and conditions around it.

There are some details that were dropped from the play—like the fact I never did go to Montreal with another guy, as I knew it was something Sky / Hierocles didn't want, and I loved him much more then an all-ex-pense-paid weekend trip away. More importantly, what's often missed in the play is the fact that Heliogabalus is being extremely honest and open with his partner about having this need to go away and have fun. Lots of people lie to each other instead. It's often plain easier to just do it on the side than to own up. Heliogabalus could have just told Hierocles he's going away on a business trip or to handle some royal duties in Greece. Instead he chose to be truthful out of love. As difficult as it is for Hierocles to hear this, I think it would pain him much more if he had been lied to. Having any sort of relationship between two people is work, but in the end I really believe it's worth the effort to be honest about what you're feeling. I'm happy to say the real Heliogabalus now does get to go away on vacations with tricks—and in the end the real Heirocles is happy as can be with it. After all, he gets the whole house to himself—and a nice break from the Emperor of the Sun!

Sky is 17 years older than me. He's also twice my size. I only weigh in at a svelte 128 pounds. There are a lot of references to this in the play—both about size, and the perception of one's gender role. Sky's main body of work really deals with a few centralized issues. One of these core issues—next to sexuality—is gender.

At the time Sky wrote *Heliogabalus* we where try-ing to buy a house in Hamilton where we now live. As much as I love Sky, he can be a total idiot savant when it comes to doing or understanding anything technical or financially related. He has a great big blind spot. I still come home to find things broken. It's almost a game of—"What will Sky break next?" His secret answer to fixing things is gaffer tape. Often I've come home to see everything—from computers to TV sets—covered in it. Anyway, when it comes to running the house (as in the play), it's the boy Emperor that's wearing the pants. At the time of the play we where going into bank offices to talk about mortgages. By default the staff would always start by talking to him—mostly because he looks so big, burly and tough. Therefore he must be the one in charge. It couldn't possibly be the younger, softer, girly one. Well it wouldn't take me long to set them straight. And by the end of the conversation they knew that if they were going to get any sort of deal out of us—well, it was me they'd be doing business with. I'm definitely like Heliogabalus— what one would best describe as a "fem top." Sky, on other the hand, is more like a big pussycat. For both of us this can be a challenge, as the inside doesn't match too well with what people expect from us on the outside.

Unfortunately, as important a figure Heliogabalus was, and as important a message that the play *Heliogabalus* has to offer, it was never as well received as some of Sky's other works. *Heliogabalus* deals with everything from gender politics and hedonistic delights, to sex workers and AIDS. It's a challenging play. It pushes audiences, and requires their direct participation. Actors are placed inside the crowd, and forced onstage to masturbate, while others are poisoned from drinking blue mysterious liquids. Young muscle boys put on sex shows.

The real Heliogabalus had a dinner party where the guests were placed in a room and fed the most amazing feast. At the end of the meal they were subjected to a rain of blue orchid petals. The petals kept falling down from the sky, until the room was filled to the rafters— and everyone choked to death. Sky managed to capture this; the audience is subjected to a similar experience.

However, unlike in Rome, no one dies, thankfully, because Sky doesn't have the financial resources that the Emperor had! Even though many people who came to the play were challenged, the play still doesn't present half the reality of what life was like in the real Rome. *Heliogabalus* audiences—by Roman standards—really get off lucky. And it's plays like *Heliogabalus* that remind us just how tame and uptight our society is, compared to what came before.

The truth is I love Sky to death, and I'm probably not the best person to write about one of his plays. I mean, I'm really one of the biggest Sky Gilbert fans the world has ever seen, or will know. I remember being 17, and skipping out of high school with my boyfriend to see one of his plays—*Lola Starr Builds her Dream Home*. It changed my life, and I've been in awe of him ever since.

If you are thinking of dating a writer, my advice is: be extremely careful. Even if Sky writes about me as a despotic, dominating, boy-bitch form ancient Rome, warts and all—I will still always love him. However, if Brad Fraser tried to do it, I'd feed him straight to the lions!

# "I'm Not Sure Where You Get Your Information."[1]

## Keith Cole

Sky Gilbert and his many characters lead the same life. They live together, eat the same food, drink hard liquor together, listen to Opera at the same loud volume, read together in the same tiny home library, hit the bathhouses together, and are in constant transit with each other in one commute to the next. They also love to hate how much television they watch together, they connect with each other in every single movie theatre and they make lots and lots and lots of art together. Sex is a collaborative effort as well. Their families, however, have a different relationship—one is real and the other is explored with violence, hatred, dread, humour and often brutal honesty on the written page and the performative stage. This sameness or parallel life Sky has with his many creations are manifested differently in the words they say or how they process this kinship with Sky in their own individual work that they perform in one of his plays, poems or films. These differences are found in the location the characters find themselves in, the life experience that has been thrust upon them by their author and the political / sexual stance Sky positions them in. What is evident in the final outcome is that Sky and all his characters share a common sense of legacy: they will all be held personally responsible for taking down the foundations of civilization—whether they like it or not.

I know the man known as Sky Gilbert as an individual for many years. Friend, director, playwright, drinking chum, bathhouse buddy, audience member, mentor, employee, co-actor, arts grant signee and the list goes on but I have never been able to fully unravel the mystery of my epigraph—*where does the information come from?* The place where the commonalities, personalities and the occupations that Sky and his characters share—where does this world exist and what does it reveal to the viewer and the reader?

Sky and his characters have been passing on information and the theatrical baton of stage magic for several years now. Information and the value of it is a concern for Sky and his otherworld creations. All those relevant are located theatrically through their deeds, situations and words and this allows Sky and his merry gang to extend their points of view, passions and mad musing to the great outwards and beyond without losing their imperative message: written history must and will change and the future must also enjoy the same fate in the hands of Sky and his many beloved or much maligned characters.

Sky as woman. Sky as mother. Two absurd sentences. Sky is a biological off shoot of a woman, his mother. Sky has re-generated his woman-mother as the object and a highly characterized, desirable product who lives generously in a community of Sky's work. But when is Sky his mother? When is one of his characters playing the woman who is known as Sky's mother? Going back and forth from one gender and generation of a Gilbert—one can easily feel the confusion—which one is coming and which one is going? Who is playing whom? Sky and his characters do not let their fans and haters easily situate themselves or each other in an easy fluidity of ebb and flow.

The female spectre character looms large in Sky's work: either as oral and aural confrontational visions or as oral and aural haunting woman who is plaintive, incoherent and pleading who needs to be released from their mental fog and sexual recession and repression before they fade into the void known as the past.

Inside Sky's creative mind his characters demand a ritualistic exorcism as they announce their readiness and need to be released—often a duty that Sky must reluctantly meet. Sky's only function is as medium for his creation's redemption from within him. He becomes the object of a filial fulfilment in that, just as he created these characters and they were once his for caretaking, the roles are now reversed and Sky becomes the patient as his creations go into the world and they take care of him and his artistic and personal business and values.

The empty space inside Sky's mind is the birthplace of his characters and when ready they stride out as real or imagined people full of humour, confusion, contention, purpose, clear eyes or complete lunatic. Sky's work is not frozen. His plays and beyond are full of forward move-ment; nothing can impede their progression through time and place. There are, however, several moments for audience reflection and occurrences of thoughtful isolation.

What does Sky demand of his characters? Should he inspect them or are they inspecting him and us? These characters scrutinize the viewer / reader tossing back onto us our own fetishizing tendencies and ask us if we are the normal ones? Female and male bodies and voices assert themselves responding to and asking questions of us. There is repetition and the doubling and doubling back and the re-double of questions, problematized situations, generalized statements that are offered as truth, aggressions, permissions being granted or asked for and the refusal to speak or to be heard by character, audience and author. Sky draws back the theatre's curtain (real or imagined) and the sharing of secrets between himself and his characters begins. The audience may or may not be made privy to the information revealed—what is said but most importantly what is not being said. Whatever it is that is kept inside the audience can never have full participation with Sky's people. Perhaps these imaginings require us to repair and restore ourselves first as a society before they can establish an elaborate personal relationship with us.

When spending time with Sky's multiple characters, we are reminded that they are constructed out of tiny and discrete elements but, when they appear on the stage, the page or on film, their figures are monumental, often reflecting back onto the people who play them—more than the sum of all their parts.

## Endnote

1. A line spoken by the character of Mandy, played by Moynan King, in *The Birth of Casper G. Schmidt*

# Playing Straight in Sky Gilbert's Metatheatre

## Moynan King

In the spring of 1999 Sky Gilbert called me and asked if I would perform in his new play, *The Birth of Casper G. Schmidt*. The production was scheduled for July in the Toronto Fringe Festival. "I wrote this part for you," he said over the phone. "I hope you like it." Despite his cool, public persona, Gilbert is humble and casual in his request for artists to work with him. He's also a formidable force in Canadian theatre: founder of Toronto's legendary Buddies in Bad Times Theatre and the most prolific theatre maker I have ever met. He writes and directs all of his own work and currently produces two full productions each year. By the spring of 1999 Sky had left Buddies and formed a new alternative company, *The Cabaret Company*. Sky and I had worked together before, extensively—he had produced three of my plays at Buddies between 1992 and 1997, and in 1994 he asked me to join the company as his Assistant Artistic Director (a position I held until the summer of 1997)—but I had never acted in one of his shows.

When I got the script, I was deeply touched by the powerful and sympathetic character he had written *for me*. The character's name was Mandy.

In Gilbert's *The Birth of Casper G. Schmidt*, the characters, performers and audience are swept into multiple currents of meaning and interpretation that splash between form and content until finally they merge into a dreamlike pool where anything is possible; but in the end, only the most fantastic conclusion seems probable. The theatrical devices deployed by Gilbert do not break the illusion of the play. They constitute the illusion that *is* the play, and the contract between performers and audience comes with an almost infinite number of appendices so that art, in this case, reveals itself to be an inter-textual experience.

From 1999 through 2003, over the term of a sporadic but expansive tour[1], I became Mandy. *I became Mandy.* In the context of metatheatre[2], which is central to my theoretical inquiry, this statement requires some serious investigation. Did I become Mandy, and if I did, to whom did I become Mandy? Or, did Mandy become (*mise en abyme*[3] to) me, Moynan, the actress? What happens to my identity in the process of embodying a pregnant heterosexual woman? Or conversely, what impact does my body, playing a role that was written for me, have on a character in a fictional metatheatrical narrative?

Before attempting to answer these questions I would like to consider two pivotal concepts (embedded in the two quotes below) in relation to the form and content of Gilbert's play.

> *Tragedy cannot operate without the ultimate assumption of an order. For metatheatre, order is something continually improvised by men.* (Lionel Abel, *Metatheatre* 113)

> *There are, however, not one but two main classes of contagious illness in man: infectious diseases (spread by germs) and contagious forms of psychological disturbances (spread by suggestion).* (Casper G. Schmidt, *The Group Fantasy Origin of Aids*)

Each of these statements touches on a theoretical conviction that life, in short, is a dream; that the confines of our reality are limited only by our beliefs, and that nothing is incontrovertibly "true." Abel, in *Metatheatre: A New View of Dramatic Form,* (the text wherein the term metatheatre is coined), focuses his examination on a cross section of important plays, most notably Shakespeare's *Hamlet,* and Calderon's *Life is a Dream.* His definition, at times porous and intractable, finds relevance for my inquiry with its emphasis on metatheatre's stylistic intervention in tragedy. Abel's identification of metatheatre relies on a comparative analysis of the "values and disvalues of tragedy and metatheatre" (113). In *The Birth of Caspar G. Schmidt* a tragedy is predicted then thwarted through a complex layering of metatheatrical devices and inter-textual references.

In 1984 (the real) Casper G. Schmidt published a controversial article in *The Journal of Psychohistory* that, as the quotation above suggests, questioned the fundamental nature of the AIDS virus and the conditions of its rapid and devastating spread through the gay community in the 1980s. The section quoted above sums up the conviction behind Schmidt's analysis and finds indisputable contiguity with the premises of Abel's metatheatre; both perceive human identity as Protean and unstable. And both of these theories, in evidence in Gilbert's play, create the potential for the diversion of a tragic outcome.

The plot of *The Birth of Casper G. Schmidt* is simple. It involves three characters: Mandy, an open-minded young woman; John, Mandy's boyfriend; and Howard, their gay friend. We learn, in the course of the play, that Mandy is pregnant with John's baby; that John and Howard, at one point, had sex; and that Howard *may* have AIDS. Even though the child is unborn and the exact diagnosis of Howard's illness is uncertain, the probable outcome of this scenario is that Mandy and John's baby will be born with AIDS. This plot, from the viewpoint of tragedy, demonstrates our "vulnerability to fate" (Abel 113), but through the metatheatrical lens of Gilbert's production, the plot is complicated and questioned by the characters (and performers) and the story is transformed from one of despair to one of hope.

The play begins with Mandy standing downstage centre and directly addressing the audience:

> We had just returned from a late screening of *The Truman Show*. John and Howard and I were relaxing over a drink. (81)

This brief but loaded introduction serves to 1) identify Mandy as interlocutor, who is both a performer and a character, 2) align the work with a contemporaneous example of metadrama—*The Truman Show*, and 3) demand from the outset that the audience step out of their role as passive observer and take stock of more than one layer of reality. This introduction asks that the audience be aware that the scenario about to be played out is a re-visitation of events gone by—it is a theatricalization. Mandy uses the past tense in her introduction and then, as she moves into the main setting, transitions into a representational present that the audience is compelled to follow. Mandy's experience is now the audience's experience. And though Mandy has introduced the scene to come, once she steps into it she, like the audience, does not know where it will go. Within the primary narrative there are no "winks" to disrupt the naturalism of the scene, but the door to imaginative interpretation has been opened and the leakage of this interpretation saturates the scene's meaning.

Gilbert's repeated conflation of reality and theatricality through the use of metatheatre creates overlap between the narrative of the play itself, the idea of truth, and the performativity of lived experience that slip over onto the characters' journey—a metatheatrical journey that undermines authority and subverts the idea of fixed reality.

In the opening scene, which begins with Mandy's introduction quoted above, the tension rises and the characters' personalities are on the verge of conflict when the action freezes and, again, Mandy steps out of the scene to directly address the audience saying:

> Maybe it was seeing *The Truman Show* or something, but it just occurred to me that we were in a play. (84)

And, having identified the play they are extending as Noel Coward's *Design for Living* she suggests that:

> The scary part is that we might have sort of all picked up this idea of what a witty, brittle conversation can be and when we are together we feel compelled to be that way, to act that way, that we are not being ourselves. We are being some idea that we've

> formulated either directly or obliquely through
> Noel Coward, an idea of what the ultimate human
> interaction really is. (85)

Thus Gilbert has loaded yet another layer of interpretation onto the work as Mandy reveals that not only is
she in a play, but that the characters in the play are acting
out yet another play (potentially one by Noel Coward)
that they simply can't stop themselves from performing.
They are compelled to be that way, to *act* that way because life, like the world of the play, is an inter-textual
experience. Mandy's frequent communication with the
audience puts her in a good position to gain their trust.
She is aligned with them. She understands that the scene
they have just watched was a bit over the top—too witty,
too brittle, and too strangely intimate. She lays bare the
very artifice of their collective theatrical experience but
(for the time being) maintains her identity as Mandy,
the open minded young woman. Later in the play she
will interrupt a scene not as Mandy, the character, but
as Moynan, the actress. In essence, she (Moynan) enters
as dramaturge and says (using the other actors' real
names) that this part of the play really should have had
a workshop.

Howard, the character, had, at this point, stopped
the action (in the midst of his sexual pursuit of John—
literally chasing John around the stage), to remind the
audience that they were watching a play and, further, to
inform them that the actors in the play were all available
for sex after the show. Gilbert invokes, in the service
of sexual liberation, an ideology that defines actors in
general as dissembling and sexually promiscuous. This
statement brings the only female in the production, the
actress playing Mandy, on to the stage to debate Gilbert's

politically problematic representation of actresses with
the actor playing Howard. What ensues, surprisingly, is
not just a battle of moral conviction but indeed a battle
for the role of narrator (or perhaps, more accurately, the
role of playwright) between the actor playing Howard
(Clinton Walker) and the actress playing Mandy (me,
Moynan). This is a debate about the history of theatre,
the sexualization of actors, and the status of women on
the stage; this is not an argument for Mandy, the open-
minded young women, but for Moynan, the actress,
queer, activist and feminist. Their argument culminates
with Clinton saying:

> You're out there selling your personality and your
> looks all the time at auditions, it's just some stupid
> sexophobia that makes you unable to sell your body
> in the bargain. I mean, don't get on your high horse
> with me. Don't tell me you're not a slut. All actors
> are sluts. It's a tradition. (97)

The argument ends with Moynan, frustrated and
angry, storming off the stage arguing against Gilbert's
inappropriate sexual representation of women. That Sky
wrote this part for me becomes clear in his exploitation
of my voice to challenge his own appropriation of the
female character's voice and her problematic sexual
representation. Mandy's voice (and Moynan's) become
subsumed, throughout the course of the play, by one
authorial power after another (Noel Coward, Howard,
Sky Gilbert and Casper G. Schmidt) and the identities
of the two characters, Mandy and Moynan, merge. What
is revealed in this scene is a metatheatrical convention
that is strange yet still convincing, and Gilbert's intuitive
casting process creates an ephemeral, but very tangible,

link between believability and identification—between the integration of character and actor on stage. At the end of this scene, after the actress, Moynan, has lost the argument with the actor, Clinton, she will no longer speak directly to the audience. Mandy (and Moynan), for the rest of the play, revert to the purely representational role of a character in a tragic scenario where it is revealed to her that her baby might have AIDS.

The title of this paper, *Playing Straight in Sky Gilbert's Metatheatre,* refers to the multiple meanings of straight associated with playing Mandy. First of all, in the sense of me, the queer actress, playing a heterosexual role—and in direct opposition to the flamboyantly gay character Howard; second, in the sense of the comedic character convention—Mandy is Howard's *straight man*, often providing the set up for his best joke lines; and third, in reference to her somewhat rigid attitude toward accuracy and truth. Mandy's paradoxical rigidity in relation to the concept of truth is evidenced several times in the play. For example, in her word play with Howard in an early scene, she insists that he not use the word *Soignée* if he doesn't know what it means. In short, she repeatedly transgresses against her own endorsement of fluid narrative making. Mandy begins as interlocutor, introducing and deconstructing scenarios as she goes along, and aligning herself with the audience, but her need for clarity, truth and accuracy ultimately disqualify her for the role of narrator in a Sky Gilbert play. The conclusion of this play, this theatrical group fantasy, this meta-journey through tragedy, requires a more radical, queer and provocative voice—and that voice belongs to Howard, the play's hyper-theatrical, obsessive-compulsive, asthmatic, sex-addicted, gay character. The illusion that the performer, Clinton, exerts control over the playwright will ultimately translate to his ability to convincingly exert a metatheatrical prognosis onto a tragic diagnosis.

Gilbert not only uses all the devices available to him in the lexicon of metatheatrical convention in this play but he throws in one more surprising curve to further destabilize the concept of singular truth even within his own character conventions by ultimately replacing Mandy with Howard in the role of narrator. Once Mandy has left the stage and Clinton is alone with the audience he challenges them to change, and subsequently change the end of the story, saying:

> But I want you to think, when you see this next
> scene, of whichever stupid role models from movies
> or whatever, you're basing your life on and stop. I
> just want you to stop. And just be your own person,
> okay. Whatever that is. Which is kind of scary. (98)

Gilbert, in the voice of Clinton (the actor), propositions the audience with a shifting quintessence of truth—one that favours the messy complexity of humanity over the dogmatic restrictions of consistency.

The real-life Casper G. Schmidt, whose article is quoted above, claimed that AIDS was not a real disease but a product of "epidemic hysteria." Gilbert has deliberately conflated his idea of cathected epidemic and the group fantasy ritual of theatre itself. This conflation is implanted in the identity of the unborn child and is ultimately *mise en abyme* to the entire work. Schmidt, the real Schmidt, is reduplicated, or metaphysically mirrored, in the play, a fact that highlights an embedded process of deconstruction within the work, beginning with the very title of the play, by collapsing the real and the theatrical.

The play ends with a monologue delivered by Howard that posits an outcome for an HIV positive baby that is not tragic—in fact it is idyllic, joyful and entirely made of hope because, as Howard says, Casper G. Schmidt believes "that just as faith can kill, faith can create life. And to have faith in Casper G. Schmidt means to have hope ... All you must do is believe" (110).

"Tragedy," as Lionel Abel has asserted, "glorifies the structures of the world, which supposedly reflects its own form. Metatheatre glorifies the unwillingness of the imagination to regard any image of the world as ultimate." (113) This assertion resonates well with the structure of *The Birth of Casper G. Schmidt* wherein the playwright invites the audience to interpret the outcome for themselves. "I'm always interested in destabilizing points of view," says Gilbert. "That's one of the reasons I'm a playwright and always write my novels as monologues [and not] from a perspective of an omnipotent narrator. It has to do with my general anxiety about not getting it right" (personal interview). Gilbert's unwillingness to regard "any image of the world as ultimate" in this "utopian AIDS dream-world, allows us to attempt to conquer our greatest fears regarding an ever changing, every growing AIDS pandemic that can no longer be scapegoated as the gay plague" (Bateman 8).

The queer view of the world that suppurates through all of Gilbert's work is poignantly perpetrated in this, the most *meta* of his plays, where Gilbert not only exploits the devices of the metatheatre but also fully consummates the form. The theatrical construct of this work inhabits the space of a dream—a dream that the characters articulate and perform as a means of thwarting the confines, and inevitable tragedy, of the plot. Reality and mimesis are collapsed into an intoxicating theatrical prescription as the play layers textual reference upon reenactment, upon character embodiment, upon the actors' emergence from behind their characters, until truth is revealed as a moving target. And in the end, the tragic diagnosis of an unborn child gives way to the hopeful prognosis of a character's conviction—a conviction built upon the fault lines of reality exposed in the play itself.

"There is," Abel has insisted, "no philosophic alternative to the two concepts by which I have defined the metaplay: the world is a stage, life is a dream" (83).

The final image of the play is a staged manifestation of its utopian dream world reminiscent of iconic Christian renderings of Joseph, Mary and Jesus. John stands slightly upstage of Mandy with his hands on her arms, looking over her shoulder at the baby Casper cradled in Mandy's embrace. They are surrounded by warm light and Mandy slowly lifts the baby upward toward the source of the light. By metaphysically echoing the appearance of the saviour, the play's "strange and fantastic vision" (Gilbert 109) is complete. If life, in the world of *The Birth of Casper G. Schmidt,* is a dream, then who, we must ask, is doing the dreaming? What begins as the dream of (the real) Casper G. Schmidt becomes the dream of the playwright Sky Gilbert who places the dream inside a metatheatrical conflation of reality and mimesis where it spreads, like contagion, by suggestion to the cast, the characters and finally the audience. The dream that will save the unborn baby, that will unmake the AIDS epidemic, is now everyone's dream, and for a moment, at the conclusion of this meta-journey, the dream is made real.

Through the truth-destabilizing techniques of metatheatre, Moynan, the actress, did become Mandy for the audience, and the conflation of my identity and the character's was completed by them. Mandy's experience is the audience's experience and her embodiment of the *saviour* slips from the stage into life—into me, the actress who, with the fictional Casper in utero, signifies the collective dream. The audience is willing to claim Mandy's baby, "her prize and her punishment," (Gilbert 110) as their own, because they want to believe.

## Endnotes

1. *The Birth of Casper G Schmidt* was performed at the Toronto Fringe Festival, The High Performance Rodeo in Calgary, the Edmonton Comedy Festival, Off Off Broadway (one night only), the Factory Theatre Studio (one night only), and the Columbus Gay and Lesbian Theatre Festival where it was honoured with three awards: Best Director, Best Playwright and Best Ensemble Performance.

2. The term metatheatre is most commonly used to refer to the theatrical device of "the play within the play" but its meaning is more complex and can briefly be defined as any theatrical device that makes a character aware of his or her own theatricality.

3. The term *mise en abyme* (literally, *to put in the centre* in heraldry) was popularized as a critical term by André Gide and suggests a self-reflexive embedding in art or literature.

# Bibliography

Abel, Lionel. *Metatheatre: A New View of Dramatic Form.* New York: Hill and Wang, 1963. Print

Bateman, David. "Closets, Cornfields and Cashmere Sweaters" in *Avoidance Tactics: Three Plays.* Fredericton: Broken Jaw Press, 2001. Print

Gilbert, Sky. *Avoidance Tactics: Three Plays.* Fredericton: Broken Jaw Press, 2001. Print

Gilbert, Sky. Personal Interview with Moynan King. March 1, 2012

Schmidt, Casper G. "The Group Fantasy Origin of AIDS," in *The Journal of Psychohistory,* Summer 1984 online: http://www.virusmyth.com/aids/hiv/csfantasy.htm

# Designs on *Wit in Love*

## Hillar Liitoja

### *Tabula Rasa*

Just as every piece of writing begins with a blank page, so a state of neutrality—coupled with limitless freedom—forms the ideal *tabula rasa* for the creation of any installation. One wishes for a space that permits both additions and eliminations, preservations and alterations, as well as realignments and reconfigurations of existing elements. Go ahead, tear down that wall, make a rose-bush grow out of the floor, puncture holes in the ceiling so it may drip vodka. No wonder I have created my installations exclusively in my own home. Who is there to forbid me anything? And who else, but myself, will bear responsibility for any and all consequences?

Nevertheless, our *tabula* for *Wit In Love* was not perfectly *rasa* as a couple of restrictions were self-imposed before we even began serious contemplation. Seeing as my kitchen had formed part of a previous DNA installation, *The Observation* (2002), we would avoid all references, direct or oblique, to any of its elements. We also obliged ourselves to create a look completely different from its normal state, meaning as it is commonly known to friends and artistic associates. Finally, we determined to closely examine each detail of Sky Gilbert's kitchen-description and then either adhere to it, reject it or give it a twist.

## Sometimes a Kitchen is not just a Kitchen

Designing *Wit* also began with key principles we set out to accomplish, principles we wanted to put into play. The installation had to be infused with complexity, with richness. Resonances, reverberations were essential along with the engagement, the stimulation of all our senses. The underlying theme that emerged was constellations. And even though everything occurs in Wit's *brother's* home, we felt it important to inject some elements of Wit's *own* nature, personality, character.

The bulk of the action in the novella's chapter takes place in the kitchen. My living quarters have a spacious, high-ceilinged kitchen with most everything one expects to find—stove, sink, fridge, table, cupboards, etc. So the foundation of the installation was already present. All we needed to do was to build upon it, to transform the room into exactly what we wanted—something more dense than just a kitchen.

\*\*\*

Gilbert's text does not specify precisely when the events unfold but Wittgenstein, at the time, is a university professor. If we assume him to be in his mid-thirties, the action occurs shortly after 1930. One arrives at this date by adding thirty-odd years to his birthdate, not because the text conveys any indications of the era—no foxtrotting flappers, no Duke Ellington jazz tunes or mention of Depression's ravages to indicate the end of the "roaring" twenties. A sense of timelessness pervades.

In keeping with the elimination of a time frame, we also removed any sense of place other than accepting the obvious—the performance did, after all, occur in Toronto. In the text, Wit goes to visit his brother in Cornwall but it would have been ridiculous for us to Anglicize the setting. Lake Ontario is an effortless substitute for the North Sea. Specificity with regards time and place would have necessitated a senseless "suspension of disbelief." In fact, we made a point of having nothing in the kitchen that would have spelled "Toronto." (Never mind the loose Canadian bills and change—they could have been souvenirs from one of the brother's tours). This kitchen could easily have been located in any so-called first- or second-world country.

The kitchen's transformation was a gradual, leisurely process taking about two months to complete. We covered most of the floor with a large light-coloured rug and replaced my sensible utilitarian chairs with an armchair while adding other discreet chairs for the audience. A vase gushing tulips arrived on the table. Now we had the distinct feel of a living room.

We placed a little bookcase in my armchair-corner, topped it with a stereo system and placed the speakers on mini-shelves we screwed into the upper walls. That corner was soon flooded with unruly stacks of books—a wide variety of novels, cookbooks, composers' biographies, Susan Sontag's essay collections, Samuel Beckett's complete works, etc., totalling over a hundred. Music scores landed on the floor and table. The addition of a table-lamp, a sizeable sketch-pad, a mug sprouting multi-coloured pens completed the sense of being in a study.

*** 

Up until this point we had remained in the world of credibility—albeit a trifle strained—but it was not long before we started to edge into another realm. In one of those flashes of pure inspiration I had a vision of the air dotted with girls' underwear. It really did not seem to make any sense whatsoever, but I ventured this notion to my close artistic associate Magda who, to my surprise, immediately agreed it was an interesting idea. (One discards such flights of fancy, without examining them more closely, only at one's own peril).

I went to the mall and found exactly what I was look-ing for—boxes of inexpensive, simple, single- and multi-coloured, plain and patterned cotton panties appropriate for every-day use by your average teen girl. We sifted through dozens of these and selected a pleasing variety which we hung on three clotheslines that ran on differ-ent angles from the table-top eye-hooks up to different points where wall meets ceiling. A hint of laundry-room became superimposed on the existing kitchen / living room / study.

Interestingly enough, it was Magda who took the undies to a new level. Once they were in place, not interfering with sightlines or any other elements, I had thought the matter closed. After all, these were not objects of Wit's brother's mention or interaction. But Magda started wondering: *What if a few pairs had not yet completely dried?* And: *Suppose a pair was so soiled as to*

*remain forever stained?* So every few days she would take a
pinch of freshly-ground coffee—more on that later—and
smear it in the appropriate place. I should also note it was
a particularly lovely pair, hanging at eye level, which she
chose for this impudent little desecration.

Through trial and error, Magda finally managed to
perfectly moisten the bottom part of one pair—she did
not want them to drip. This pair was again hanging at eye
level where a number of audience members had to pass
them in order to reach their places or seats. I suppose the
idea was that some people would bump their forehead
against that wetness and possibly recoil in surprise or dis-
pleasure. I don't remember whether or not that actually
happened but I do know that I became its regular target.

Magda would do this "moisturizing" while I was in
the front room putting on my costume; I never saw her
perform this exercise. Later, while she was "processing"
the audience in that same front room, I was at the back,
going through the critical connector-lines that were most
likely to cause trouble. At the precise correct clock-tick
I would emerge into the performance space in order to
do the final pre-set—kill the fridge, turn on lights and
gas, etc. I would be so focused on my pre-performance
tasks I think I never even saw those panties hanging in
wait for me. Most likely my gaze was aimed down at the
fridge's electrical outlet. But invariably—and I mean
*invariably*—I would get a sloppy moist touch on my
forehead. And then I would go through the exact same
sequence: curse Magda, smile at the innocent cunning of
the trap, blame myself for falling into it, and then forget
all about it. Only to get panty-kissed again the next night.

\*\*\*

Let's consider the accuracy of my description of the space. If you were present at a performance you may well think: *I studied everything on the table very carefully and I am certain there was no money on it.* Another person may express different doubts: *Out of sheer boredom I spent a lot of time staring at the floor and I know there were no musical scores strewn about.* Well, you would both be right.

Installations, like so much else, evolve. All the chief elements of the space were in place on Opening Night but over the course of two runs we made a number of tiny adjustments. Right from Opening we were pleased with what we saw but that did not mean we were ever so satisfied as to be complacent.

These tinkerings came naturally. We never sat down and asked ourselves: *How can we make this installation better?* It was more a question of curiosity: *I wonder what it would look like if we were to …* At other times there would be a nagging feeling—for weeks in the case of the table—that something was missing. When confronted with a certain lack we don't just place *anything* on the table to fill that seeming emptiness—it was already pretty crowded—but we wait for the right thing to present itself, in this case some bills and loose change.

It took some time to clearly hear that little bowl crying out for an avocado. And once she got that avocado there were no more tears. In any case, there is no point in looking for rhyme or reason, purpose or intent. All that matters is that avocado *looked* right, it felt *at home*. Nothing more is needed, no explanation, no justification.

Did I just feminize that little bowl? Hear her cry out? Yes, I did. It's not as though we anthropomorphize each and every object. But sometimes it *does* help to give, say, a knife, a sense of humanity, to consider the potential of it possessing human emotions. Before you take these words to be a confirmation that I clearly belong on the loony fringe, consider the following: creating *She Alone* (2007) Magda and I would often speak to objects, admonish them, ask for favours—but I suppose this should be addressed when I take that DNA work under consideration. It is clear, though, that altering your viewpoint, giving an object human perspective, may assist in arriving at a lovely solution. And I am perfectly content to be consigned—in your mind—a place among the crazies, if my thought-processes result in wholly satisfying, if not ingenious, solutions to festering artistic problems.

\*\*\*

The north wall of my kitchen is particularly prosaic and easily divided into three sections—a sizeable fridge; an oversize deep sink over which hang two rows of small pots and pans; a chest of drawers (cutlery, tablecloths and napkins, big pots and casseroles) below a big cupboard (plates, bowls and glasses). However once we had finished transforming that area any sense of the commonplace had disappeared.

Normally I keep a variety of sundry items on top of the fridge—garbage bags, coffee filters, Kleenex boxes, potato chips bags, etc. In this case it was the tissue boxes that provided the inspiration and, given the fair amount of space between the top of the fridge and the ceiling, we decided to build a sculpture. Off we duly went to the nearest drug store to make a selection of colours and patterns we felt would most allow a harmonious combination. We preferred the pastel-coloured boxes with horizontal lines interrupted by various-sized circles; the ones with deep-green bamboo stems; and still others with arrays of oval-shaped pebbles amongst occasional bright flowers.

Fortuitously enough our chosen boxes were all on sale—but with the irritating proviso of six per customer. So a trip or two to the drug store was incorporated into our daily routine and after two weeks we had begun to amass the many dozens of boxes needed to fill a thousand cubic inches of space.

Building this structure was not stressful. Minor technical problems were surmounted with ease and box-selection was simplified as many were not visible. Boxes once amassed, within only a few hours we had our final product—an irregularly-shaped "staircase" with hints of pyramid, ziggurat, perhaps a slice of the Tower of Babel.

Then, somehow, we came across a pair of identical twins: two diminutive wooden ladders. After fastening one end to the other we ended up with an etiolated ten-foot climber that we placed near the foot of our "staircase" and extended over the sink to rest on top of the cupboard. A pathway to heaven? Well, not quite. The ceiling was in the way.

*** 

That extra-large sink of mine is divided in half—not only very practical but perfect for our desire to convey a sense of the contrasts between Wit and his brother. The great philosopher was famously fastidious in matters of sanitation and order. Cleanliness was not only next to godliness but a catalyst for clarity and "clean" thinking.

Naturally enough, his half of the sink was empty and spotless. His brother was … not quite so punctilious. His side was crammed with pots, pans, dishes, glasses, cutlery. On top of this mess, no doubt just to irritate Wit, he would occasionally butt out his cigarette on the divider between the two halves.

I must say this part of the installation was by far the easiest to create. When Magda and I would finish our soup-break or occasional dinner—always in the front room on a white tablecloth laid out on the carpet—we would simply deposit our dishes, higgledy-piggledy, into the sink, taking care only not to crush anything below. After a week the brother's portion of the sink was full and the result was pretty disgusting if not rebarbitant. And once the run was over you can imagine how revolting it was to soak and scour everything to its original pristine condition.

\*\*\*

The solution to the chest of drawers' surface was the last piece of the puzzle to slide into place. We simply lacked a vision. No doubt we would remove the items normally there—two dish racks—but what to replace them with?

I do not remember any undue suffering on this account. We were not pressed for time and if both our creative brains were to simply stop functioning I could always take solace in my readiness to delay Opening if necessary. To succumb to frustration or anxiety is never helpful. To force a solution is to court mediocrity and regret. One learns to be patient, to have faith in one's creative powers. Give it time. Do not suffocate the problem—allow it room to breathe. The right idea will present itself when it is ready.

In the end, the idea that did "present itself" was to design a constellation of glasses containing coffee and salt. We were certainly aware that both Wit and his brother were engaged in thinking about the nature of the world and how it is ordered, if ordered at all. Wit's brother's arrangement of glasses in one field of vision, his juxtaposition of coffee and salt, both containing a range of colour, flavour and texture—all this was a possible tool in his quest for comprehension and coherence, a manifestation of his thought processes.

Once that door was opened our discussions were fertile, our decisions rapid. We wanted every glass to be beautifully shaped as well as elegant; the glasses had to be of differing heights and capacities; no glass was allowed a protruding rim; identical glasses were welcome.

We again made the rounds of Value Villages—with great success—and arrived back at DNA with more glasses than we would ever need. Not only would we have replacements in case of breakage but a very important principle was reinforced—never paint yourself into a corner, always have more materials than you need. Excess is truly preferable to falling short and then having to arrest the creative process.

Magda and I never discussed how many glasses we needed. It was clear we required quite a few but what was the point of deciding upon a number when we needed luck to find *any* glasses that met with our qualifications? We would snap up all those that pleased us and innately intuit when we'd gathered a sufficient number to work with. It is only to one's advantage to have more materials at hand—it allows room to manoeuvre; more choices and possibilities are now available. Besides, a glass that might have seemed acceptable in the store may, under a different light, turn out to not quite meet the standard. Excitement, having fun, may skew discernment. The relationship between glasses obliges serious considera-tion. Any given glass may be stunning but end up being discordant within the array. One must learn to reject a shard of beauty when the harmony of the whole is jeopardized.

Magda enjoys coffee, she drinks it regularly, whereas my contact with the brew is an occasional sip from her cup. Thus it made sense for her to select the various types, making sure the beans' colours ranged from pale brown to deep black. She began by restricting one shade to each glass but ended up creating colour-layers reminiscent of superimpositions in the Earth's crust.

The sense of smell was a vital consideration in our choice of coffee. I have always found the communication of a fragrance to be particularly challenging. I suppose the difficulty lies in its inherent evanescence. I sometimes wonder—and surely there is a chemical explanation— why the smells most people consider intolerably mephitic are the ones that last longest. A starburst of freshly-cut carnations in a vase will exude its scent but for a short time, the nose-full dissipating rapidly. In order for that fragrance to persist one would need the audience in a closed room whose surfaces are covered with hundreds of blooms. Yet hammeringly malodorous effects are so much easier to achieve—simply place a champagne bucket of freshly-excreted shit alongside a pot of putrefying meat near a platter of week-old shellfish and, oh, don't forget to piss in all four corners a couple of days before you let the audience in.

We were aiming for something a touch more subtle. Almost directly before the house was opened, Magda would grind the beans and pour the pulverization into the selected glasses. The time-delay was, of course, unfortunate. Over half an hour would pass before the first audience member actually entered the kitchen. However most everyone was obliged to walk past the glasses in order to arrive at their placement and surely several people did get at least a whiff of the aromas. The most appreciative were those few blessed with a sharp sense of smell and seated right next to the coffee/salt display.

As for the question of salt, Magda and I are united— we both take lavish pleasure in it. We love the taste, the flavour-enhancement, but we also derive aesthetic delight in the colours, the shape and translucent brilliance of the crystals. Life is thrilling when part of one's job is to go salt-shopping!

To peer into our glasses was to enter a connoisseur's gallery: the finest-grained, stone-ground, sullen-grey *sel marin* from Brittany; glistening pink- and orange-flecked Himalayan rock salt (sounding distinctly more glamorous and exotic than the actual product from Punjab, Pakistan); pure-white Aegean Sea salt, each sharp-edged crystal like an opaque snowflake, all alike, none a duplicate; and, most spectacularly, another Himalayan salt, retaining the yellows, greens, lavenders and deep purples of seaweed-slivers.

In the centre of this coffee/salt display we placed an amphora of murky herbs-infused olive oil. Why? A purely subliminal, if not sublime, decision—that made me gasp when, weeks later, its implications became apparent.

Interestingly enough, this constellation was never fixed. We had spent part of an afternoon putting the glasses in place, working very fluidly, always taking turns. Yet every night, when all the freshly-ground coffee had been poured into the respective glasses, Magda would make small adjustments. That made sense—glass number three might receive a new-coloured coffee, the appearance of a differently-layered glass might necessitate a shift in position. I was never part of this process, getting into costume and focusing on my performance ahead. Nevertheless, as part of my last-minute preset ritual, I would study the latest configuration and usually make one or two meticulous adjustments, lining up this glass with that one, moving one "star" a tiny bit closer to another one.

Please believe me now, when I say that only while writing the last paragraph did I realize how appropriate all these daily miniscule re-alignments were. We had conceived these glasses to be a microcosmos with the amphora as its centre. All the heavenly bodies, in reality, are in relentless perpetual motion. No stars, no planets appear in identical positions one night after the other. In that case, why should our constellation not experience similar, nightly, almost imperceptible shifts in position?

I must confess experiencing a profound rush of pleasure, just moments ago, upon stumbling on this revelation. At its core is the huge question of volition. As well as Magda and I create together, we have profoundly differing views on a critical mystery—the role that fate or destiny plays, or does not play, in our lives. Our sharply opposing opinions became apparent as we worked on DNA's *Fate* ballet (2004).

I maintain that tonight, when I made myself a vodka and tonic at 7:32 pm, that was exclusively my decision. I could just as easily have made it one minute earlier or twenty minutes later. My call. The same applies to the squirt of lime I added as well as the little stir I gave the drink to integrate the lime with every mouthful to come.

Magda would say the only role I played was physical— I poured the vodka and the tonic, etc. I had no part in the decision-making process—none of the choices (the timing, glass-selection, drink-contents, measurements, stirring) were mine. They were all fated.

Magda would go even further and claim that everything that happens in our lives is utterly beyond our control, much as we may imagine otherwise. She avers that, for example, it was not at all her decision to create this installation with me but simply the machinations of fate. Moreover, the course of everyone's life, down to the tiniest detail, from the moment of our conception to our last breath, has all been annotated by God, fate, destiny, call it what you will.

Both of us believe what we believe and neither of us has any interest in converting the other. It is overwhelmingly likely we will both die not knowing who is right and to what degree. Ultimately it makes no difference in the way we lead our lives. Magda will still ponder a difficult question even though she knows the answer (and even the pondering's route) has been pre-ordained—just as I will mull over an issue in hopes of arriving at a new, more ideal solution.

What makes this moments-ago revelation of mine so interesting—and why it has led to an unintended digression—is the way it reinforces a core belief of mine. For some time now I have maintained that if you do your utmost to realize your artistic vision, if you are as thorough, as attentive, as sensitive as possible, the consequences will reach beyond your intent. It is as though some unknowable force intervenes in the work's favour, a force not only thoroughly in tune with your vision but even more intimate with it than you are yourself.

The fact remains that Magda and I made nightly adjustments to our coffee/salt constellation—the only one with movable parts—without ever discussing whether or not we would do this. This already is strange because, as I said, neither of us would make changes without talking it through with the other. Perhaps it has nothing to do with some "unknowable force." Perhaps by this time we were so deeply imbued by the installation we were acting subconsciously, out of pure instinct.

Ultimately—I need not know. All that matters is both of us were delighted by the final results—the rest is stimulating speculation. No doubt lingers in my mind that had I been conscious of the integral logic underlying those nightly colour-changes, mini-adjustments, I would have presented that case to Magda—and I am sure she would have agreed. In the end the results would have been the same—but they would have been the indisputable expressions of our will instead of …

***

The east wall may just as easily be divided into three sections: a waist-high counter-top between a chimney-cupboard and a stove/oven. The chief interest of this wall lies in the field of lighting, with one exception—the large white bowl, placed in the middle of the counter.

Late in the evening Wit's brother makes spirited offers of "really delicious" cocaine that Wit rejects with increasing irritation. These offers were punctuated by a series of sharp cork-throws aimed into the bowl. Even if they found their mark, as they often did, these corks would often bounce out of the bowl and ricochet wildly.

Early on I mentioned a striving for resonance—in this case the desire was purely literal. The sound of cork hitting clay bowl was satisfying but, alas, one-dimensional. The remedy was simple—we placed a much smaller Pyrex bowl inside the large one. Not only did we now have the contrast of a brighter-sounding *ping* but I also had the pleasure of hearing when the cork had hit the mark dead centre.

At this point I must salute the audience members who, almost without exception, never flinched and remained frozen during this mini-barrage of mini-missiles. Perhaps they instinctively—and correctly—realized their stillness would aid the accuracy of my aim. However, is it possible that awareness of my legendary marksmanship has spread much wider than I had ever imagined?

\*\*\*

Behind this wall was the bathroom, which served as a separate viewing area as well as the site of another constellation—the Exploded World.

As previously mentioned, the desire to understand the world's workings was a continual preoccupation of both brothers. One approach might be to divide Earth into a number of components, the better to singly examine each element. We decided to enact this most literally. We favoured the cobalt blues of the oceans as well as the brilliant whites of the polar caps and, two atlases later, the floor was covered with dozens of sharp-edged multi-sized world-fragments that later we glued, with haphazard frenzy, all over the wall behind the bathtub.

To balance this carnage we added two unviolated halves of the world yet could not resist cutting two other worlds in half and then gluing them back together a tiny bit off kilter. Roughly in the middle were our blue lights, the centre and seeming cause of this cataclysmic explosion.

Earlier we had isolated all references to the world in *Tractatus Logico-Philosophicus*, the only work Wittgenstein published in his lifetime—to some the irrefutable proof of his genius, to others (like ourselves) an impenetrable incomprehensible density. We made a selection of our favourites, sentences we thought we could actually understand—*The world is independent of my will … The world and life are one. I am my world.*—and then scattered these quotes amongst the Earth-shards.

In the end there was world-shatter amidst world-analysis, something to contemplate or be horrified by, yet impossible to view in its totality due to the confines of the bathroom.

***

People who are not creators often fall into the trap of ascribing inevitability to works of art they consider "perfect." In their minds there could have been but one possible way this beautiful poem could have been written. They think—*It could not have been otherwise.* Thus respect and adoration may spawn illusion and deception. No role is given to chance, luck, accident in the creation of a work of art. Just like the discovery of penicillin resulted from mould ruining bacteria cultures in a petri dish left unintentionally uncovered, so the creative process is rife with fortuitous discoveries, serendipitous omissions, unlikely coincidences. The Grand Design, the product of Wit's brother's desire to better understand the philosophy of Schopenhauer, is a perfect case in point.

Alex Malow, an old friend from my piano-playing days, erstwhile painter, acolyte of Sviatoslav Richter, worshipper of Rossini, was conducting a purge and offered me various items he no longer wished to keep. I gladly accepted a lovely dark painting of a candlestick beside a rug—which found its way into our installation—as well as a slender volume full of photos of magnificent ancient Greek architecture: temples to gods and goddesses, some facing the sea. What a hoard of beauty, most of it unknown to me!

Over the next weeks I would occasionally turn the pages and gaze at the wondrous images. Amongst the buildings was the photo of a large vase, covered with writing. After admiring it for awhile my mind made a huge leap of extrapolation—this indecipherable (to me) text contained a code, the foundation of Greek existential principles. All the temples were linked to this vase. Of course! They had to be!

I excitedly showed the book to Magda and she agreed that this link—however tenuous—could be made. We went through the book, selected our favourite photos, cut them out and put them aside for a couple of weeks. We occasionally revisited them and began our culling process, never discarding the rejects.

My kitchen's south wall is dominated by a large window. The idea was to get a board that would cover its entirety, then fasten it to the moulding and ledge in a way that would block out all the light. We would paint the board white, affix the photos, draw the connections and, at one point, I would open the curtains and—voilà—the Grand Design.

Gord Peck, our ingenious, problem-solving, hyper-efficient Production Manager, arrived, took measurements, and soon returned with the appropriately-sized sheet of plywood and put it into place. We looked at it with awe—how was it possible that an ordinary sheet of plywood could look so beautiful? The large number of multi-sized whorls in the wood were captivating, inspiring.

This reminds me of another guiding principle in making an installation—always examine every component carefully, try to look at it with "fresh" eyes. Never proceed blindly with a plan of action. Better to stop after each step and reconsider for a moment—a different, previously unconsidered direction may prove superior. Fine ideas may well be superseded by even better ones.

As Magda and I continued to be transfixed by this "ordinary" sheet of plywood—already, in truth, blessed with a constellation—it became inconceivable to cover any part of it with paint. Instead we began to wonder how best to enhance, bring to the fore, this gift of delightful wood-knots.

Enter Seth Turack, a young writer and actor who had helped "process" the audience in DNA's *The Large Glass* (2005). He had just returned from a stay in Vancouver and pure happenstance made him walk by my house just as I was outside on the porch. During a brief chat he offered his services and a couple of days later was on board. Little did I know how indispensible he would become, lugging home cases of Carmenère, seducing strangers to purchase those tissue-boxes, performing numerous time-consuming tasks.

One of Seth's most tedious chores was highlighting those whorls by outlining the perimeter of more than a dozen of them with transparent silicone—some needed only a coat or two but others were to be much thicker, extruding by as much as an inch. Since each layer had to dry before a new one could be applied it must have taken Seth two weeks before he was finally done.

Meanwhile we made our final selection of photos and began positioning them. This task was more exacting than might seem. The photos were not exactly fragile but we could not risk damage by repeatedly fastening them to the plywood and moving them around at will. We had to take the time to get it right because once glued to the surface, they could no longer be jockeyed about.

We measured the photos, took a piece of mat paper, spread out the Sharpies, and Magda began a lovely in-scale rendering of the images. Not for the first time during this collaboration did I have the sensation of being taken back in time to a grade-school art class, looking in wonder at the girl beside me, watching her make drawings so apparently more accomplished and beautiful than anything I myself would ever be capable of. When I mentioned this to Magda, she said she had the same feeling, being eight years old, sitting behind a desk, cares of the world blotted out, crayon in hand, concentrating exclusively on drawing a picture.

That writing-covered large vase was, naturally enough, in the middle as everything emanated from it, and we drew red and black arcs with arrows to indicate our fancied relationships. We were so pleased with her drawing that when it came time to do the gluing we religiously adhered to it, making only tiny adjustments to accommodate the whorls. When it came to the connecting lines, we would always alternate turns, always stating our intention and never beginning before receiving the other's approval. First time, only time. No allowance for erasures. At the very last minute though, we made one change for greater visual effect—the red lines remained solid whereas the black ones became dotted.

So in the end, thank you, Alex. With your kind and timely present we were able to fashion the Grand Design. Without it we will never know what contours would have shaped it.

***

To one side of the window is an unopenable door. We both liked the paint-smeared windows, the grease-spattered surfaces—and just let it be.

To the other side—and now we are back in the book-stacks corner—is a wall that is nigh-covered with an over-the-years accumulated mostly-yellowing miscellany: a postcard of Paris rooftops, a number of poems and quotes, *sake* labels and terminology, an obituary of John Leonard, the great literary critic, etc. Keeping in mind that Wit's brother's character *was*, after all, based on myself, we felt it best to leave it untouched.

However one item did provoke a short discussion—RM Vaughan's article, *For Canadian 'freaks', a patron saint*, that lauds the huge influence of none other than Sky Gilbert. Was it excessively self-reflexive to leave it up on the wall? When we considered how poorly that part of the room would be lit, we decided the question was moot. And so the article remained in place.

***

Finishing our clock-wise tour of the room, we arrive at the west wall. Between the audience-entrance door and the continuation of the "study's" library lie two identical cupboards. On top of the upper one we placed two candlesticks alongside a tilted unframed mirror; the other surface held a chopping board, a glass-dome cheese-tray containing a desiccating maple leaf, and that avocado-desirous little bowl.

Of some curiosity was the lower cupboard's door which led to the cheese I would need at a later point in the show. This door would emit a most distinct *click* whenever opened, a somewhat startling sound we were both fond of. The only problem was we had a couple of workmen doing minor repairs some weeks before we opened. These people have a tendency to automatically fix anything they find amiss so I remember pointing out this fault and begging them to ignore it. They did. Good. I imagine it would have been considerably more difficult to restore that sound than to eliminate it.

On the floor we placed the aforementioned painting by Alex, resting it on a slim blond-wood case, the better to accentuate its presence. And now I must turn to the saddest part of my reminiscences, the role that Ed Fielding ended up *not* playing in the creation of *Wit*.

First and foremost, Ed was an artist whose immensity of talent was exceeded only by the complete and utter lack of recognition accorded it. Excepting DNA. Ed fulfilled several commissions for us, starting with huge portraits of all the major characters of *Hamlet* (1989) through the disturbing painting of Persephone for *Sick* (1991) and the exquisite flower-sculptures for *The Observation*. What we had hoped for was a couple of miniature, not larger than 15 square inches, colour-intense abstract paintings that would hang, unframed, on a cupboard door or two.

At the time he agreed, he was already ill, but still painting on most days. After a while, when he had not produced anything for us, he explained he was presently

engrossed with architectural drawings. I asked to see
them, reflecting on their potential appropriateness considering Wittgenstein's interest (and occasional practice)
in that field. He came for a visit and I pointed out the
ones that most pleased me and encouraged him to try
his hand at a smaller format. He said he would accede
to my wishes—but too late. The cancer eating away at
his insides led to increasing frailty, relentless enervation
and debility. The pace of his physical disintegration
would only accelerate and in November 2009 he died.
We mourn the passing of a friend, a man whose multi-
faceted, fervent contribution to DNA is matched by a
mere few.

***

The beat-up antique wooden table was the room's
centrepiece and we wanted it to equally reflect aspects of
both brothers' natures. Equal being equal we divided the
table into two neat halves.

Wit's brother's area was a mess of clutter: sketchpad;
coffee-mug blossoming pens and scissors; perspiring
lemonade bottle; wooden matches and tranquilizer in
shot-glass; vase of petal-shedding tulips; bowl of corks;
Bombay Sapphire gin bottle; plate nestling two eggs
(were they raw?); fractured cognac-snifter or wine glass;
bills and change; novels and Beethoven. A snapshot of
scatter-shot turbulence.

Here I must tip my hat in gratitude to Henry
Sansom, talented filmmaker, DNA video archivist, warm,
intelligent, generous, a man of such equipoise he would
say—*Thank you*—in response to every policeman's shove
during the Toronto 2010 G7 demonstrations.

We had invited Henry for dinner—with the proviso he would endure and comment on a talk-through of my performance. This was early in the process, a time when I used wooden matches as a prop, occasionally threatening to light a cigarette but never actually doing so. Henry suggested we lay down a rug. (Why had we never thought of *that* ourselves?) Then he added an intriguing question: *Had we ever seen* Last Year at Marienbad?

Though I had not seen that film in decades, I knew exactly what he was getting at. In this glorious Alain Resnais masterpiece there is a game played between two people involving a number of wooden matches laid out in the shape of a triangle. The rules matter less than the fact that the skilled player will always win, whether he moves first or second. Magda had never seen the film so Henry arranged a proper viewing.

I am old enough to realize one's tastes evolve, how the accumulation of life's experiences alters perspective, making a once-gripping novel tawdry, elevating a formerly-dismissed symphony to the sublime. Yet watching this hauntingly enigmatic film I was as spellbound and mesmerized as in my mid-twenties.

Sometimes one must persist in a course of action before its error becomes apparent. *Last Year at Marienbad* made me not only discard that cigarette but gave shape to the matches' geometric patterns I began to assemble while musing about the irascible nature of my brother.

\*\*\*

Wit's table-half was in sharp contrast to his brother's—a model of cleanliness, order, austerity, conditions all necessary and conducive to his philosophical thinking.

Gilbert's text refers to three knives stuck in a wall and this developed into a perfect example of us creating a twist to his kitchen-depiction. We really had no choice. Gilbert's inspiration for those knives in the wall came, in fact, from *The Observation*—references to which we had disallowed—where there was an entire congeries of knives either plunged into a wall or captured in a mid-flight liberation-struggle from another wall's grip.

Yet the knives formed a significant part of the brothers' conversation so their presence was ineffaceable. We landed on the idea of creating another constellation, not of the brother's sensuous coffee/salt variety but something more cold and implacable.

As with the glasses, we devised criteria for the knives—Value Village needed to supply us with a wide selection: varying sizes, wooden handles, blades both serrated and true, duplicates welcome. Seth would stain any excessively light handles to their desired darkness after enduring the tedium of removing the blades' protective scotch-tape sheathing and restoring their brilliance with lighter-fluid.

We knew we were going to lay down a pure white tablecloth which would be impaled by these knives, all blades facing outwards in the same direction. We began to make sketches—again that invaluable mat paper was cut into scale-size pieces with each dot representing a knife, Magda claiming the black colour, myself the blue. However we soon realized our attempts were dissatisfying, lacking coherence. Rules were needed.

We decided the one who goes first must always place three knives in the shape of a triangle. The next one must not only form another triangle but have it intersect the previous one. And so on, my dots always in relation to

hers and vice versa. No maximum number was ever allotted to the knives. Right at the end of each sketch we took
a red pen and made final single additions, remembering
to take advantage of the entire surface and making sure
at least a few knives ended up in close proximity to each
other.

Once we had made around a dozen sketches, we laid
them out and chose our favourites. And then put them
away. It is important to remember we never completed
any of the installation's design components at one go.
Advancing bit by bit we allowed every step to gestate.
Distance cleanses and freshens the mind. Revisiting our
designs weeks later we would invariably arrive at new
favourites.

Strangely enough, considering all the effort we had
put into the prototypes, we never even bothered to
consult them once we got down to the business of hammering those knife-tips into the table. Yet, perhaps not
so strange after all. Our method was deeply ingrained,
well rehearsed. Most likely we both sensed, without any
discussion, the best approach was to just attack.

Just as with the Grand Design, we always described
each placement pre-hammering, thus allowing for
discussion—*Are you sure you want that tall one in the
corner?*—and suggestions—*What about placing that little
guy a little closer to the big guy?* Patiently, cautiously we
would proceed, holding our excitement in check. What
immense pleasure to finally see our imaginings begin to
take shape and become real!

Little did we know what recalcitrant creatures some
of those knives were, repeatedly swerving from their assigned direction. Addressing them in a reasonable tone
to no avail, we needed to devise techniques of trickery

and deception in order to make them toe the precise line. Despite the nature of some refractory characters I don't think it took us much longer than an hour to complete the constellation. We stood back and examined our handiwork—from all angles, high and low, up close and from a distance. Very important, this. If any aspect of your installation will be looked at from different vantage points it behooves you to take the time to consider all audience members' perspectives.

Magda and I were very pleased—the constellation bore up to our scrutiny, no changes were necessary and the knives remained in their original position for the entirety of the run. I seem to remember we were both proud enough to beam. We had—without ever directly intending it—realized our own interpretation of one of the Exploded World's lines: *Objects make up the substance of the world.*

\*\*\*

One day Magda came over all excited—*Guess what? I'm going to Norway. With Ola and Dorota.* Ola, a ballerina at the Polish National Ballet, and Dorota, a masseuse and beautician, have been Magda's two closest friends for over half her life. I remember once asking her: *So who do you consider to be your absolute best friend?* No hesitation: *That's an impossible question. All three of us are equally close to each other.* The three Musketeers come to mind—*all for one and one for all.*

I was, of course, very happy for Magda because I know how much she loves travelling, but, selfishly enough, even happier for myself. The chapter we were performing ends with a revelation on Wit's part—he must escape the confines of Cambridge and go, alone, to Norway, back to the isolation of his lake-side cabin, the solace and refuge from where his most productive thinking always emerged.

Norwegians in Toronto seem to be a self-effacing reclusive bunch. We most certainly wanted to have some reference to that legendarily troll-infested country, perhaps a keepsake or two Wit had brought back home to remind him of the tranquillity so lacking in England. So we tried to find a bookstore, a delicatessen, a ceramics shop. Nothing. Not even a Norwegian House, an edifice most European ethnicities in Toronto deem necessary to introduce and take pride in their culture. Yes, Magda in Norway could certainly be put to good use.

I asked: *So where do you plan do go?* Her clear voice: *We land in Oslo and then go on to Bergen.* I could not believe my ears. Bergen, the environs of Wittgenstein's real-life retreat. An innocent vacation was rapidly lurching into a business trip. I reverted to my most peremptory fashion: *So here's what I want. Photos. Simple, plain, small, isolated, wooden cabin. Ideally beside a lake or water of some kind. No people. And you're obviously going on a boat-trip up some fjords, right? Good. More photos. Water, mountains, ocean, forests. Beauty of nature, solitude, yes?* And Magda's response? *I will do my best.*

Regardless of the commanding nature of my demands I knew Magda would not be displeased. She is a talented amateur photographer—witness the Wit postcard—and I knew she would he happily snapping away anyway. My "assignment" in no way diverged from her own interests.

She certainly did not disappoint, arriving home with over a hundred photos. After leaving aside those of no use to us, there still remained dozens to consider. Every week or two we would go back to those photos, pulsating in the task of separating the most intense from the more common beauty, always striving for balance in both subject-matter (sea, mountains, trees, light) and colour (blue, green, white, gray, a bite of red).

Once we had finally reduced our list to the needed twelve, we attended to details: Where precisely was that hill to be cropped? Did this shadow need darkening? We also wanted to retain the grandeur of nature before the time of civilization so all electrical wires had to be Photoshopped out.

Our final step, before affixing the photos to the ceiling, was to decide their placement. The imposing 1000-watt naked light bulb at the centre had to be removed—it was far too significant an element in *The Observation*—and we replaced it with a sunset over mildly turbulent sea, all the other photos emanating from that dark centre in a widening circle, misty waters contrasting snow-flecked mountains with reds in opposing corners. The earlier decision to make every photograph the same size made the final to-scale design proceed smoothly. No hand-wringing here.

But why the ceiling? Disturbingly enough, towards the end of their meeting Wit's brother displays the razor-line scars on his inner forearms. He has ostensibly been "practicing his Schopenhauer." Wit excuses himself and retires to his hotel-room to mull things over: he knows that suicides often *do* carry through on their threats yet his brother is prone to playing narcissistic games.

At that point in the performance I suddenly crumple to the floor, lie on my back and mutter half-sentences. I segue back to Wit's brother's character by breathing the ghosts' words from *Richard III* (*Despair and die*) and during my catatonic state Magda, now *dea ex machina*, has turned the table-lamp's head to illuminate the ceiling. When I snap open my eyes, all I see is a fjord and then, shifting my eyes around, more of those familiar northern land- and seascapes—my siren-call of solitude in backlands Norway.

How satisfying was this overhead pictorial panorama? At run's end, the kitchen was restored to its original condition, knives removed from table, books returned to shelves. That huge bulb was screwed back in but the photos remain. I don't think a day passes without me tilting my head back for a minute and then gazing, wondering: *Will I ever pay a little homage to Wittgenstein and actually experience this magnificence myself?*

## Lights Blues

This is by far the most difficult aspect for me to write about for reasons that will become apparent soon enough. Mostly it lies in the fact I was not "present" at critical times due to unaccountable spasms of distress.

The bathroom was to contain the key lights source for the entire installation as well as one quarter of the audience who would be looking from there into the kitchen. We began by being confronted with a mostly-removed bathroom wall; the kitchen wall was dotted with small crude peep-holes, all residue of *Ember* (2006), a previous DNA show. Fortunately enough I had never gotten around to making the necessary repairs.

What kind of vantage point did we want to create for the bathroom-dwellers? Magda insisted the walls were to be different from each other. We had the bathroom wall's upper and lower parts re-built leaving a 30-inch-wide horizontal quadrangle running the width of the room. The vertical wooden beams naturally divided the space into four sections, one for each spectator.

Fashioning the kitchen wall to our desires proved considerably more laborious—we wanted, yes, another constellation, one of oval-shaped apertures, multi-sized, some upright, others on an angle or lying on their side, some as perfectly-shaped as possible, others unbalanced, wibberly-wobberly, none identical. Each quasi-egg-shape had also to be well-rounded and invitingly smooth inside, silently encouraging you to place your fingers in one for a grip. Were you to indeed succumb to this beckoning, your fingers would soon be coated with the chalky substance of the drywall's insides ...

Nothing to "design" here. All we needed was to enlarge those peep-holes, often joining adjacent ones to form the requisite shape, always making sure each quadrant had at least one large enough to allow a fine view, granted you might have to place your face quite close in order to peer through it. All this is so easy to describe but painstaking care went into plotting out and carving each sphere. When testing each potentially-grippable oval some part might crumble, dust would flare, necessitating re-smoothing. Day after day we found ourselves profusely thanking Seth for his persistence and forbearance.

Our first session with real lights was short as we experimented with a few colours and soon landed on a potent cerulean blue. I remember it being stressful, though. I did not at all like this light pointing at me in my chair. Steadily I deliquesced into despair. For whatever reason, this harmless little lights-test had smashed home the reality of the performance awaiting me. Yes, I had previously fallen prey to brief panic-attacks, reasonable expressions of anxiety for an ex-pianist who gave up that career due to an excessive number of memory-slips. But this was on a completely different scale. I could not wait to get out of that chair.

Seeing we had accomplished everything intended, Magda, empathetic as always, made me a drink and we went out on the porch. My ears were soon filled with words of comfort and encouragement, my spirits restored by assurances, declarations of her faith in me, her certainty I would be "just fine." Half an hour, two drinks and three cigarettes later I truly *was* "just fine."

In the ensuing days work continued as usual with nothing amiss—until Gord returned for the second session with three small but powerful fixtures which he proceeded to attach side-by-side to the bathroom's back wall, aiming them in a triangular direction through the ovals. I was told to sit in my performance-chair.

Magda was cheerful, perky—evidently relishing her first crack at designing lights. I was preoccupied, morose. The longer I sat in that chair the more engulfed I became by mounting forces of doubt. Magda was telling Gord to aim one light a bit higher: *What do you think, Hillar, is that better?* Me, distraught: *I don't know.* Then: *Look at the colour on the tablecloth, the reflection off the knife-blades! Isn't that great?* Me, mumbling: *Good.* Magda was delighted, she had found a new element to swim in: *I love the way the blue divides your face in two, one part Wit, the other part his brother, it's perfect, yes?* Me, barely audible: *OK.*

I had become terrorized, quaking with fear, reduced to mush amidst the stomach-churning, vomit-threatening, mind-paralyzing certainty of the collapse so clearly visible on the rapidly-advancing horizon. Magda's kindness was no longer able to penetrate. The only solution was to postpone the show, embarking me on a daily regimen of memorization so strict, so methodical, so relentless, from which the only conceivable emergence would be one of total assurance, unassailable confidence, victory.

Six weeks later? Close—but still a cigar.

Our final session with Gord, not long after my melt-down, was a breeze. We knew those fixtures were not perfectly placed and were determined to finalize ideal positions as well as angle each light in its optimum direction. We were both fully engaged, bustling about, studying every option, talking everything through. I had regained my opinionated decisive nature but ended up obeying a rule I was, at the time, not even conscious of : never sit in that chair for longer than a minute.

*** 

Irrespective of the suffering those blue lights caused me, I soon grew to love them. Their lability, their inherent instability became stimulating. They were all aimed at the bathroom-spectators' heads or backs, depending on their stature, and whenever bodies would move, the illumination would accordingly shift. It soon became impossible to distract me. The intensity of light was at a level my direct gaze could just tolerate. Over time I would become more aware of the light though I can't say I ever manipulated or used it for effect.

These lights clearly allowed the possibility of direct audience influence, even playfulness. I have no doubt there were those who, prizing their unobtrusiveness, made every attempt to stand rock-still. Similarly there were others who took pleasure in tilting to the right for a clearer view of my cheese-butchering, bending to the left to ascertain whether it really was glass I was scissoring, or—and of this I have no doubt—suddenly ducking just to see what would happen if my eyes were to get a direct blast of light. No one ever saw me flinch.

So in the end, Magda—as so often is the case—was right. Those continual shifts of illumination, gradual or abrupt but always vicissitudinal, dividing my face or body into equal or unequal halves was supremely apposite as I would continue to reveal disparate aspects of the brothers' contrasting, conflicting natures.

***

After making the first DNA shows some thirty years ago, I thought it might be a good idea to read a couple of books on theatre, just to get some perspective. I was untrained, unschooled—no doubt there was much for me to learn. Since the most famous innovative director at that time was Peter Brook, I purchased his *The Empty Space* and read it from cover to cover.

I found the book interesting, well-written, but cannot say it had any serious impact. Brook, despite being heralded for his imaginative stagings, is still at heart a man of the old school. There is much talk of acting techniques and different approaches to directing but my budding work with DNA had little to do with "character" and "plays."

However he did make a point about lighting that immediately struck me: white light is by far the most difficult medium with which to convey mood and emotion. I remember taking those words as a direct challenge and resolved henceforth to eschew lights of all colours.

Instinctively I knew that within "white" light there was a gamut of variety and there must be countless ingenious ways of using it. For some two decades there was nary a coloured light in any DNA work I directed.

I mention all this to illustrate what a radical move it was on our part to have the chief light be blue. Once started, I would not stop and pushed the issue: *How about avoiding white light altogether?* Magda saw no reason to object.

Soon the coffee/salt chest-of-drawers' corner had a small table-lamp with a proudly glowing blood-red bulb covered with a circular white shade—blue and red rapidly becoming WIT's defining colours—and we made sure to place our reddest photo almost directly overhead.

We turned on a gas burner on my stove and admired the flickering flames, constantly shifting shades of blue tinged with red. Alright, orange. I would turn on the burner every pre-show, adjust the flames' height, and leave it on for the duration of the performance. Seeing as it was directly behind a sitting audience member, it may well have cast more heat than light. Some were not even aware of its existence. One person noticed it only towards the end of the show, during my first cork-toss. He came to believe the cork hitting the bowl had triggered the burner's on-switch and later approached me, his voice revealing a sense of wonder: *How did you do that?*

Despite our new-found embrace of coloured lights we did not become crazed enough to try and fill in the entire spectrum. Nonetheless we did add a tinge of green by turning on the sound-system's receiver—though the speakers never emitted a sound—and then called a halt.

My desk-lamp created the biggest problem—we simply could not find a blue bulb that would provide sufficient light for me to draw my start-of-the-show sketch. And we needed enough light for *dea*'s photos-illumination. Thwarted in our quest for colours-exclusivity, we had no choice but to scrape off some of the bulb's blue casing—white light's jealousy and revenge.

## Wit's Brother's Identity Finally Revealed

One evening in early spring, Mike Hoolboom, erudite, sharp-principled, a wonderful writer and arguably Canada's most brilliant avant-garde filmmaker, was over for dinner. I mentioned working on a piece in which I would be playing both Wittgenstein and his brother. He thought out loud: *Wasn't his brother a pianist?*

That set off an irruption. First, it made me think that no wonder Gilbert, knowing my pianist background, had decided to model the brother after me. (I was wrong—Gilbert had not been aware of Wit's brother's pianistic fame.) Then the outpour: *Oh my god, wasn't his name Paul? Wasn't he the one who lost his right arm during the Great War? Wasn't he the one who commissioned Ravel's magnificent Piano Concerto for Left Hand?* Mike confirmed: *Yes, and he also* (news to me) *commissioned numerous compositions from other great composers.*

Soon after, Magda and I sat down and listened to much of that stunning concerto. (I avoided the last movement which I have never liked.) Magda agreed it was gorgeous. I asked: *What do you think about using it for* Wit? Two words: *No orchestra.*

I remember being taken aback by the severity of her pronouncement and I never questioned it. Perhaps I was too stunned by her response. This is atypical Magda, though she can, on rare occasion, be so direct and

forceful in expressing an opinion that it leaves no room
for argument. *No orchestra.* Nothing to discuss. And she
was right—we'll get to that in a moment.

Now, we always knew we wanted a musical component for *Wit* and suddenly we had a composer—Maurice
Ravel. I went to HMV and ordered CDs of his complete
piano works as played by Jean-Philippe Collard, little
known in our country but, in my opinion, one of the
great pianists of our time—and a Frenchman to boot.
The order would take at least two months to process.
Fine.

When the package finally did arrive, Magda and I,
on our own, listened to the two discs. I was prejudiced
from the start. Being familiar with most of Ravel's piano
compositions those CDs contained very little new for
me—but I had always had a special affinity for his exquisite, enigmatic *Gaspard de la nuit.* (When he wrote
the first of the three movements, *Ondine*, he set out to
compose the most technically difficult piano piece ever
written. He succeeded. It took a couple of decades for its
vicious complexities to be decidedly surpassed).

Happily enough, Magda shared my affection for this
piece. However she was also strongly attracted to the
spirited, exuberant first section of *Alborada del Gracioso*
from the suite *Miroirs*. This is a piece I had long enjoyed
and we had no difficulty incorporating both our favourites into *Wit*.

We arrived at a relatively simple conceit. Gilbert's
text refers to a student painting the floorboards in the hall
that leads to the kitchen. Well, we envisioned this student instead being in another room practicing the piano.
That made sense. He was most likely staying behind
to reinforce what he had been taught in a just-finished

lesson. (Never mind that later in the evening the brothers go upstairs to the bedroom where there is a piano and no one playing it. It is common for a pianist to have several pianos at home).

So what the audience heard was a series of stops and starts, repetitions, different stabs at specific passages as the student worked his way through *Gaspard*. And then the delicious interruption of *Alborada*, tossed off twice in a row—pure joy opposing hard labour—before his attack on the haunting *Scarbo*.

*No orchestra*? No kidding. Magda intuitively knew it was the right call.

## A Tale of Tails

Every once in a regular while Magda arrives at DNA and finds me in bed, drunk. Alright, perhaps only tipsy. This may be due to a particularly disturbing nightmare, despair over the stock markets, but most likely part of the ongoing saga of my insomnia. I will wake up ridiculously early, turn on the TV, take a wedge of sleeping pill, have a couple of shots of Dorlan and soon try to fall back asleep. Failing that, I repeat the process. Re-failing that, I once again repeat the process, a practice I learned from Fassbinder. Sleep still eluding me, Magda arrives.

On this occasion, however, I was simply fortifying myself—for courage. Now this is a curious admission as I really don't need bolstering in order to speak about *anything* with her. However this was the exception that probes the rule. I was concerned about broaching a topic excessively intimate. I will return to this feared transgression after setting the stage.

While in Estonia, making my one-and-only proscenium-arch show, Jäta Mu Hing Rahule (1995), I visited several second-hand stores and landed upon gorgeous tails—the highest-quality wool, impeccable classic cut, seemingly never worn. Knowing full well my piano-playing days were far behind me I could still not resist trying it on. This perfect fit was purchased for a mere verse of a song. Little did I know …

Having recently been reminded of Wit's brother's career as a pianist—no doubt here, as Wittgenstein's other ones had all committed suicide—I suggested the tails anchor my costume. Magda enthusiastically agreed: *Try it on.* For whatever reason I put it off for weeks until finally relenting. Flawlessly preserved, still a perfect fit, my body-shape not having changed in the ensuing years. Sweet. Yet I had my doubts. Something did not feel quite right. Was formal concert-garb an excessively obvious solution? Once my nagging fears had crystallized and I had found an intriguing new possibility, I knew I had to tell Magda something deeply personal.

Some ten years ago I decided one day, out of the blue, to derive an inkling of what it was like to be a girl. I realize it is preposterous to imagine gaining awareness of any aspect of girlhood by simply donning clothes, but there I was, once again, in Value Village, trying on various clothes before landing on the choicest item: a lovely pleated school-girl kilt which I combined with a pink frilly blouse, white knee-socks, bra, and ambi-sexual black flats. As it happened, I was scheduled, a day later, to see a show at Montreal's Festival des Amériques, and, after arriving, managed to quickly find not my ideal, but panties nonetheless.

How perfect was this? More than fifteen years had passed since DNA's performances at that very same festival; I had but few friends in the city; surely I could make my schoolgirl-debut unnoticed. Back in my hotel after the show, I carefully shaved off body hair, drank more than a few drinks, got gussied up and went out for a middle-of-the-night walk in downtown Montreal. Not that I was remotely "passable"—that was never my intent. It was a little scary, but I was not about to venture into any park where recent brutal attacks had occurred. I was not looking for sex, just a sensation.

The June air was warm with a touch of breeze and I felt wonderful and sexy, living out a possibly long-repressed fantasy as, years later, I had a memory-flash of my father doubled up in laughter one Hallowe'en as his eight-year-old son flounced about in my that-night-absent mother's lingerie and make-up. Today I can still remember feeling the delicious freshness of Montreal wind caressing my glabrous legs, the delightful kilt-taps on my thighs at each step as I walked the innocuous side-streets, finally venturing into the gay-hub section of Rue St-Catharine where I felt safe.

But just before that, a young woman in her backyard saw me and could not resist: *Peut-être que je ne devrais rien dire, mais tu as l'air tellement chic!* I turned towards her, made my best curtsey: *Merci.* Her remark I cherish to this day.

This—shall we call it a predilection?—continued to hold me in thrall and soon I decided I really must purchase a fine pair of girl-shoes, go to, say, Holt Renfrew, be fearless, spend a couple hundred dollars and then take religious care of them. Is it fate that intervened? Right after making that decision I found out about a female-shoe store that was closing, having a blow-out sale—and they were hoping to find big-footed customers, most females apparently being small-footed (ask the Chinese). I rushed over and tried on everything that appealed to me. At one point one of the owners said: *Are these for you?* With conviction, if not pride, I said: *Yes.* Hours later I emerged with seven exquisite Italian black-leather high-and-low-heeled shoes, among them two pairs of (single- and double-strapped) Mary Janes, my favourites.

I wonder now, as I remember telling Magda about this cross-dressing foray of mine, wherein lay the fear of transgression? It's not as though sex, for us, is a taboo topic. I know we share certain core beliefs about the total freedom of sexual expression: neither of us would look askance at any sexual practice between consenting adults. She is certainly aware of my "queer" nature just as well as I know that her curiosity—one of the defining aspects of Magda's character—does not extend to bi-sexuality. However we both have an ingrained respect of privacy and neither of us has even a remote interest in probing beneath the surface of the other's sexual interests. Was I stepping over a line here, was her mind cringing? *Hillar, please don't go there.*

Well, no, Magda was not distressed; she listened with interest and probable amusement—this is something I don't take all *that* seriously—yet at the same time she certainly was aware I was revealing something clearly in-timate, while no doubt wondering why I was even going down this road.

The answer lies in Wittgenstein's sexuality. He was gay—perhaps only vaguely so—and while there is no absolute proof, this presumption lies in inference and probability. Though for a time, early in life, he intended to marry a young Swiss girl, a look at some of his correspondence with certain boy-students leaves no doubt of his desires, if not undeniable confirmation of a certain degree of consummation. (When once asked whether his philosophy was affected by his homosexuality, he was angered and instantly responded in the negative).

Having digested these sexual clues, I had arrived at a conceit—perhaps he was attracted to girly-boys or being one himself. If my upper half reflected the elegant concert pianist, why couldn't the waist down be an imaginative expression of Wit's sexual fantasies? Magda's mind was nothing if not receptive.

No longer needing a drink, we went downstairs to a have a look. Over the course of time I had acquired more clothes and now, like any self-respecting girl, had several pleasing outfits though far from anything resembling a wardrobe. This underlines why I *had* to tell this story to Magda. We really don't hide things from each other. Had Magda gone with me to hunt for girl-clothes only to find out I had a selection in the basement, she would have been perplexed. So much of our relationship is based on the foundation of honesty and trust. She would have felt bewildered. *I don't understand. Why didn't you just tell me?*

Going through the kilts, it was effortless to decide upon the stylish blue-and-red one, and all we needed to add to the kneesocks and Mary Janes were red leg-warmers. Later, shopping for a fine white shirt, we agreed on the ideal one. I looked at the label—*H & M*—and was ecstatic. I had no idea an entire chain of clothing stores had been named after us!

The bottom half of the costume was not revealed until well into the show. While the audience entered, I was sitting in a chair behind the table and only when I stood fully up and opened the curtains hiding the Grand

Design was the kilt fully exposed. I do not remember any audible reaction, just a hint of *frisson*—but at that point we were at such a critical juncture in the piece, I believe most attention was directed at my explanation of the world's workings—revelations of considerably more import than my nether regions' covering.

This may sound like just a bit too much fun, indulgence on a high level. It is time now to disabuse you of this notion. Never for an instant did I derive anything even resembling sexual pleasure—either before, during, or after the performance. There were far too many other concerns to pincer my attention.

During the final days of the run I was feeling mild pain running up and down my left leg. It only got worse. After Closing I went to see my family doctor and as soon as he heard about the *Wit* footwear as well as me walking on pretty thick carpet, not ideal for balance and stability, the diagnosis was irritation of the sciatica nerve.

This discomfort did, however, lead to some amusement. That nerve troubled me for six weeks, but at least it had the courtesy to heal just before the Free Fall festival run. I had no desire for a repeat performance. As my regular doctor was away I had an appointment with a wonderful female physician in the same office. Perfect choice—she was a sciatica-sufferer herself. I had brought four of my shoes and asked her to examine them—pumps suddenly became the surrogate patients—and to put them in order of least- to most-likely to cause problems. This she did—goodbye Mary Janes—as well as giving me exercises to prevent re-occurrence. When I next saw my family doctor he gave me an arch look and read me the notes from that appointment, notes which suppressed her amusement until the final clarion call: *But the show must go on!*

## Walking away

This has been an exhaustive survey of what began as only a room and one would think it time to call a halt. Yet I am not quite ready to do so. Is this a classic case of monomania? Megalomania? Perhaps the only saving grace will be the brevity with which I manage to note the final, sly, touches.

Did you notice the butt plug calmly poking its cock-head out of the pens-holding coffee-mug? Did you smile when your eyes caught the pair of riding-crops hiding behind the pots and pans? Did you knowingly nod when you landed on Gilbert's laminated bathhouse bar-pass? What about his novella on the floor, the paperback you were not allowed to step on? Was that bookmark really the Norwegian flag? And that hunky roach sitting atop a cupboard, was it not appetizing? Surely before exiting you could have shared it with a few people. You certainly knew the sink-divider was the perfect place to butt it out.

Speaking of calling a halt, how did Magda and I know when to stop? What made it clear to us the installation was finished?

Recently I spent almost an hour sitting on the floor, staring at a large masterful Jackson Pollock painting (*Number 1A, 1948*). To some, no doubt, this is a chaotic mess but my admiration only grew amidst the austerity of his almost-exclusive use of white and black. Mere wisps of red, maroon, blue and yellow, scattered throughout the canvas, gave such a satisfying balance to the whole. This was not the case of, say, a landscape painter who could put away his brushes once everything in his chosen field of vision had been represented in the desired detail and colour. Here was pure abstraction, hundreds of superimposed ejaculatory gestures. How did Pollock know enough was enough?

I do not, of course, have the definitive answer to this question but I cannot help but feel that having started with some idea of what he wanted the painting to look like he could sense, at a certain point, that he was very close, it was time to circle it again and again, look at every square foot and then perhaps add something, perhaps not. The painting was finished when it *felt* right. And only he could know when it *did* feel right.

What I have just outlined—and some reading on Pollock confirms my conjectures—is a precise description of how Magda and I created both the disparate elements as well as the installation's unified whole. We started with certain key principles and stuck to them. Our vision evolved but did not stray. Every constellation developed rules which were obeyed and executed. One day there seemed nothing left to do. We stood together and let our eyes rove all over the room. We moved around and—closely—re-examined everything. After awhile I said: *It's all good.* Magda nodded: *We're done.* We turned off the lights, closed the door and walked away.

\*\*\*

Those blue tissue-boxes sidling up to the Atlantic Ocean smiling at the Blue Sapphire gin-bottle boasting to the blue pen pointing at the kilt flirting with the panties—reverberations all bathed in the light spilling from the ovals that, in turn, were beckoning to the eggs guarded by the scissor-heads hiding the spoon—a veritable echo-chamber.

The Grand Design's magisterial vase mirroring the coffee/salt amphora, both taunting the mug-handle that finds comfort in the wine-glass curves; the un-exploded entire world glowing with pride over all the pots, pans, bowls and glasses, all caroming off the lamp-shade, the celebrated whorls, the tissue-box circles, down to the knife-handle rivets—ricochet riches.

That soft red light imparting its hue to the Norwegian fishmongers' knives directing their glare at the scarlet tulips waving at my legwarmers encouraging the match-tips—a complexity of resonances.

The severity of straight lines contrasting gentle curves, the clutter of one table-half amiably neighbour-ing the purity of the other, the sharpness of the knives menacing the tulip-petals' softness, the disorder of book-stacks clashing with the calm neatness of the coffee/salt—a measured balance of yin and yang, the resolved conflicts of each constellation all submerged within the mysterious world of our installation.

***

Few questions remain: was *Wit* a fine installation? And who, exactly, is the judge of its quality: the audience, the critics, our peers?

The answers to both questions are simple. Yes, *Wit was* a marvellous installation. And the only *true* judges are Magda and myself. Everyone may have their own opinion, anyone can have their say. But the question's key lies in the word "true". For it is only the creator who knows what he set out to do, only she can outline the vision that was to be realized.

By now it must be clear we were both more than merely satisfied. We were, in fact, proud. Had we been dissatisfied, we would simply have continued plugging away. With Opening drawing near and the work falling short of our standards? We would have postponed the run. Had we come to the excruciating realization we were not up to the task, doomed to failure? The project would have been abandoned, the grant money returned, followed soon after by a long dinner focusing on one question: *How on earth could we have failed so miserably?*

Fortunately enough, such despair was not in our cards. In its stead was a deep sense of wonder. Entering my transformed kitchen—even in daylight—was always to be transported, awed, posing quite the opposite question: *How on earth did we manage to execute our vision so acutely?*

Beyond our own personal satisfaction, the compliments in the Guestbooks, the appreciative observations of friends who stayed behind for drinks, there was one more source of delight, something I never saw, but only heard.

When Magda was leading each group from the dark hallway she would open the door and, one by one, people would enter. At the time I was entirely focused on making my drawing and never looked up. Nevertheless I could sense the trepidation of slowly-moving bodies, the amazement, the discombobulation. But amidst the murmurs, most gratifying of all, was the occasional sudden involuntary gasp of astonishment: *Oh my God!*

# Women's Comedy of Resistance

## Ann Holloway

I wanted to be the voice of women's comedy of resistance in Canadian theatre; or at least a woman's voice in a theatre. My meeting Sky Gilbert was more like a rendezvous: two raucous comedy spirits courting and sparking onstage and off. As far as women having a voice in the theatre, any theatre, it would have remained a pipedream for many of us in the 80s and 90s if not for Sky, who stood out as a facilitator for innovative theatre voices, queer voices, voices of dissent. This piece is about the dream of being heard in a culture where women are silenced. I dreamed it so hard that I connected with Sky, an artistic director who was in a position to nurture my unique voice and who was similarly bent on vociferously opposing the ejaculatory propagandist rhetoric of the straight entitled male sex. I was beating the bushes for acting roles when I ambushed Sky and harassed him about casting me in one of his plays. Some people schmooze; I harass. It cuts through the red tape a lot faster.

In a heartbeat it seemed, I was cast in *Play Murder*, working with two hugely talented women theatre artists, Maggie Huculak and Anne Marie MacDonald. My character, Blanche Yurka, is Libby's acting coach; she is a con artist, a sham and social poseur whose grand gestures were trumped by her classically trained voice as she flagrantly disgorges her vowels with round tones. Blanche got laughs galore, many of them coming from Sky, who has a most distinguishable style of laughing: an ecstatic staccato seizure is the closest I can get; and of course he is always in the audience rooting for his actors. Soon after working with Sky as an actor, I was harassing him to give me feedback on my playwriting efforts. As many of you know, it's always a near excruciating experience handing over your first scripts, but Sky had no agenda when he either rejected or praised my work. Still, as a writer, I felt out of my depth in a way that I didn't as an actor; it took so much editing to get anything half decent I thought I was brain dead. Sky cheered on my overtly sexual (and by that I do not mean exhibitionistic) daring, witty, angry, poetic voice, formal considerations aside. The whole queer theatrical enterprise was a search for a non-formulaic structure stripped of convention. The absurdist playwright, Samuel Beckett, in an essay on Joyce, asserts that the work of art as a whole is its meaning; what is said in it is indissolubly linked with the manner in which it is said and cannot be said in any other way except with its ambiguities intact. It was co-founder of Buddies, Sue Golding, by Sky's admission, who turned his theatre head around about lesbian sex and its politics, and taught him that not all feminists are man haters just because we act out. Sue's sexual agency and unabashed pursuit of her sexual desire coupled with her proud bad girl stance introduced Sky to girls who were bending arcane puritanical/Victorian abusive strictures of sanctioned fornication still ghosting women's libido—submission-ary style with penetration inflicted in so many cases with violence. Ignoring a woman's orgasm is violence; trashing it is a declaration of war. Buddies accommodated and celebrated women's protesting voices, however raw and shocking, deployed in comedy to stage confrontations with our culture's endemic terror of woman's empowerment. The angry comic woman is disturbing whether she's blatantly sexual or not; but when she is, her figurations and reconfigurations of woman's eroticism, pleasure, desire as active urges to confound assigned gender roles. Needless to say, Buddies' discursive space, one that allows difference in by the front door, is anathema to the status quo. Like lesbian playwright Sonja Mills' protagonist, Frances, in *Dyke City*. Frances, Mills' thinly disguised self-parody played by the amazing Kathryn Haggis, embodies for her audience the monstrously incorrect dyke appetite for sexual passion. While other lesbians pussyfoot around new age sex, Frances' running commentary is rife with hedonistic, sexually carnivorous allusions; she is Dyke City's politically outspoken woman on top who emerges as a positive exemplar for women. We do not laugh *at* Frances. And even though she refers to a particular, exclusively lesbian society, everyone can relate to her. As much as the bawdy unruly woman is provocative, she is also the cradle of our being healing us by bestowing upon us the spasms of a hearty belly laugh releasing and releasing the waves of anxiety crashing against the shore of woman consciousness, tension that is carried in their bodies in the onslaught of vagina abuse as part of systemic misogyny; it is her bravado in sharing her story that reinvigorates society by breaking the rules. Frances' message of freedom of choice in the bedroom springs to life as a fleshed out comic everywoman.

Many of us artists at Buddies targeted the coercive significations that shore up the culture's totalizing phallocentric narrative. Realism and the proscenium arch were gone; artistic philosophy and practice became personal, enmeshed and coextensive with the artist's material life. The audience was mobilized into travelling around the space to the performers rather than being stuck in a one-dimensional fixed seating arrangement. Theorist Victor Turner maintains that "Carnival knows no footlights," and that "anything may go." (Bakhtin, 3) Buddies mirrored that topsy-turvy world unto itself, where the mingling of sensual sensibilities allowed for comic dissent like my theatricalized mock quest for the dream cock, where I fantasize having my cheesecake without having to eat it too by taking back, redesigning and re-feminizing erotica. The subtext of the piece alludes to the size of the woman protagonist's hoped for big orgasm. Penis size doesn't guarantee that he'll hit the Goddess Spot but she is desperate to find an answer to her prayers—an assisted big O. She is on her way to full sexual empowerment, however; when the male partner in the piece balks at cunnilingus, all bets are off and she does not settle; and most importantly, instead of blaming herself as the old sexist storyline goes, she discredits him in spite of his sexiness, and refuses to serve his desire to penetrate her. The message: don't trust anyone who throws crumbs at your hungry vagina, a name I use now with pride and authority. My vagina is hungry and deserves to be wined and dined to satiety, or I'll feast alone. No one but Sky would have accommodated this extreme parody of our culture's anxiety about vaginal orgasms and the raft of mystifying myths around women's libidos, like our supposed lack of sex drive unless chauffeured by a male. The piece was in the style of what Bakhtin calls the comic grotesque, a comedy genre designed to unseat social taboos around, in this case, loud, aggressive, forthright, lusty women of appetite. It is also interesting to note that I knew nothing of Rabelais and his world when I wrote it. The carnivalesque ideology is pro feminist and refutes the sexist claim that women are cursed with frigidity of the funny bone. The suppression of women's voices is an attempt to trivialize and demonize the Vaginal Orgasm or VO, in a strategy to downplay its archetypal status. Sexism-homophobia-misogyny is a covert shackling of the collective mindset using constant, univocal, desensitizing reiteration. Different laughter in a sexually diffuse oppositional context, where fixed identities and authoritarian dictates are thrown into disarray, re-sensitizes us and propels us forward. While draconian funding cuts were biting theatre on the ass hard in Canada, Sky's response was to party back just as hard. A particularly foul mouthed critic, Christina Blizzard, had her war paint on and soon appeared all crabby on Buddies' stage played by Sonja Mills in a wheelchair with a cast on her leg. This overt antagonism between queer theatre and cheap irate journalism was so refreshing I thought I was on a magic carpet ride out of the colonies. Yes, the theatre's name was proving all too prophetic: times were getting badder and badder in some ways; but the good news is: nothing is funnier than the tragedy of pea-brained rules that as Umberto Eco phrases it, we no longer wish to obey. Nothing bonds a diversity of folks more than laughing together at a common foe. I cannot stress enough how Sky's inclusion of women's voices of resistance on stage and behind the scenes at

Buddies, gave so many of us girls hope. We got paid and we got a space to experiment without patriarchal restrictions. Our comedy began to rumble with catharsis, the orgasm of the soul! Meanwhile, the commercial humour market, so mired in somnambulant stereotypes it looked like an episode from the *Walking Dead*, trudged on as queer laughter became a volatile force, disrupting ever so slowly but markedly a monopoly of male-authored sexist humour by undermining its claim of universal funniness. The Viva Vulva lesbian dance held in Tallulah's Cabaret at Buddies, is exemplary as a vanguard strategy of ironic re-naming that dismantles officialise and so undermines its truth claims. The Strange Sisters Com-Cab, for example, re-imagined theatre so that it resounded with cheering, hooting, whooping girls' voices. Listening to a near to all girl audience take the roof off the theatre was nothing less than thrilling. It gave me goose-bumps the first time I heard it. The solid bank of womens' laughter did sound strange indeed since it occurs so rarely in our culture; but there was something else, something unnameable; I can only say this burst of exuberance was there in my memory, only submerged for a long time. It was a welling up of a joy sisters once summoned up in congress in their own private temple rituals where comedy was used to mitigate cultural anxiety about the unknown mysteries of conception, birth, death and rebirth.

Meanwhile, outside the theatre's warm black curtain was a world gone insane. The entropic spiral down of the culture's values meant tax money being squeezed out of us to endorse killing fields for children; the testing of nuclear weapons on innocent civilians; discrimination in the workplace when one has to have money to survive and health care is threatening to disappear; the ongoing rape of our Native People; the trafficking of young girls and women sold as sex slaves; the Roman Catholic church's cover up of its rampant endemic sodomy of young boys; the orgies of gay bashing on our streets. The rug of certainty was jerked out from under our collective feet. This is the beginning of art. The kind of art that expands consciousness and awakens us to difference as an essential part of the social fabric. My hometown had one visible, and by that I do not mean out, homosexual in the 60s: a radio announcer by the name of Gerry Tinlin AKA Tingaling, need I say more. Gerry was also called Gerry the Fairy, who by the way never seemed all that fairyish to me, and who proved to be a vital link in my connection to Sky Gilbert. My town's one out lesbian was a biker in a black leather jacket with a large beer gut hanging over her studded belt and a disproportionately tiny head with stringy bleach blond hair from the wrong side of the tracks named Pearl LaSalle. Pearl was a cut-up; chain smoked Export A non-filter; and ran her own shoplifting ring. To say I was baffled by her is an understatement, because as strange as she seemed, she clearly had power in her world; nobody laughed at Pearl. As for Tingaling, it so happened, like Sky, he loved musical theatre (surprise surprise) and founded the Gananoque Tent Theatre with his partner, an adorable Italian pixie from New York named Lee Tommarello. The production was innovative for its time being that it was theatre in the round—not three quarters round—completely round with four ramps for exits and entrances. Blocking was a whole new science; imagine: staging that wasn't missionary position proscenium fucking arch!

I was cast in *Guys and Dolls* there, a great musical adapted from Brecht's *Happy End*, the greatest of all musicals in my humble opinion. I played a Hot Box girl, and that meant dancing and singing cabaret style. The following anecdote will render comprehensible my future collision with the theatrical spirit of Sky Gilbert and Buddies in Bad Times Theatre. It involves me in a choreographed dance number: Abigail's song of complaint to her fiancé, Nathan Detroit, who still hasn't come up with an engagement ring, entitled: *Take Back Your Mink.* All us Hot Box girls are in a stripper-esque chorus line and we've all peeled our long gloves off and whipped our pearls and mink stoles off while singing: "Take back your mink/ Take back your poils/ What made you think/ That I was one 'a those goils." We then launched into a rousing can can when suddenly I fell flat on my ass on the stage!! Without missing a beat the two girls on either side hooked their arms back through mine, hoisted me up, and we went right on high kicking. Sky and I coming together was a predestined meeting of two Hot Box girls with runs in our fishnet stockings (although Sky has the better legs). But there was another precognition. When I was around 15 years of age, I used to drive to Montreal with my girlfriend, Toni, who was 18 and had a license and a Volkswagen. Montreal was so much more cosmopolitan than Hogtown, and we discovered a bar called the Hawaiian Lounge where drag queens performed live. I was gobsmacked by these gorgeous creatures in elaborate femme wigs (this is mid 60s) lying in bathtubs and draped in feather boas lip syncing to pop tunes. I *love* feather boas and lip synching (only if done perfectly which is unfortunately rare) and even though drag was still embodiment then, I was fascinated by the transgression of masquerade. When I got to Buddies, drag had surpassed the Hawaiian Lounge fare and become politicized by the critique of parody or camp. Subverting erotophobia using gender parody was a trick of drag queen, David Bateman, whose parody of a parody of male effeminacy let the chest hair show through. One of my favourite camp images is David grinning with glee on his retro kitchen stage set wearing a red 50s frock and heels with a red turkey baster microphone. On the crisp white chef's apron is printed in big red letters: MAINLY BECAUSE OF THE MEAT. That pretty much says it all about Buddies' manifesto. Sky's Jane, with her hyperbolically fake boobs and platinum blonde wig spoofed not only the hooker cliché but the straight male paranoia behind her degradation. Lesbian comic, Deb Pierce, in her send up of Canadian songstress, Anne Murray, wore a beard to ridicule not the dykish manner of the closeted singing star, but rather the enforcement of the closet itself. These acts lay bare a tyrannical capitalist system intent on getting its queer ducks in a row by dunking them in the mainstream. Creating characters that couldn't be dampened down and co-opted became mandatory for queer artists. This calls for a dramaturgy of shock that cuts through the words and acts directly on the nervous system, as T.S. Eliot so aptly described the desired audience response.

All this was brewing in my head like I was on a crash course but I gravitated to black absurdist farce let's call it, the kind of humour that engenders horror laughter and makes you squirm a bit. Sky warned me about the contempt for explicitly lewd lippy women that still prevailed at the time even within comedy itself; but I had stories that I knew women could find themselves in. I had nothing to lose by mouthing off; I had burned my bridges on that score. Still, I was shy about exposing my as yet unseasoned literary/ dramatic voice. Luckily Ed Roy, Buddies' associate artist, who directed my first play, *Nothing from Nothing*, knew I was serious about writing comedy and hooked me up with Tarragon's playwright's unit chaired by Urjo Kareda, artistic director of Tarragon which was the good old boy academy to Buddies alternative theatre, and I had a healthy suspicion of its elitism, as did Sky; but I wanted to be heard, and Urjo was respected as a dramaturg. I already knew he could be weirdly reactive, so I stepped into the bear's den only to get mauled. We got off to a bad start when Urjo stated at our first meeting that he knew within the first seven lines of a script if the artist had a voice. I don't take kindly to such arrogance. The play I developed in the unit was a raw look into women phone sex workers scraping out a living talking dirty. I saw the whole phone sex industry, which was brand new at the time, as a metaphor for all capitalist enterprise where women are positioned as the abject; but the girls I knew and wrote about were rebellious and hostile, wickedly funny and bitterly sardonic (when they weren't on the nod, that is). They were not stupid or uneducated; they were just addicted, and in all cases victims of sexual abuse. I was intrigued by the perceived safety of phone sex, where there is after all no risk of physical harm. I felt the rage my characters felt being shut down by a bunch of male hypocrites in denial about their animal side; what place does this have in theatre? I knew I didn't have total control over the rage in my art yet, but nothing prepared me for the day Urjo screamed, in response to my first draft: "What audience wants to see a play about a bunch of lowlifes?" I only wish I'd had the wherewithal to scream back: *What signifies a low life exactly! You mean a sex trade worker? You mean a drug addict? Then say that! Say it say it say it!!* The following dramaturgical note would have nicely sufficed: rage spread on a bit thick. I gave the play to Sky and he said basically that. A technical note I can work with; it was high time to let the male Theatrical Guru die. Still, it was grist for the resistance mill and Sky and I clicked and whistled along whenever we bitched about pontificators like Urjo, who was after all in the closet. How open could he be about sexuality and passion? It was ludicrous, this intellectualizing of drama, the homophobia, and the deep anxiety about women's desire raging through the performing artist community! Sexually adventurous women were still slutty, but big-mouth women were absent. Fortunately for me, Sky writes rebellious, non-stereotypical women characters who live outside traditional male representation; women who trumpet their desire to fly out of their pigeon-holes. This unruly woman figure is at the heart of current feminist carnivalesque theory, such as the work of Natalie Davies and Mary Russo, who see her as part of a comedy matrilineage for women speaking out today in order to forge new social subjectivities. However, Russo warns, transposing her into our current theatre context risks recalling the scold, a traditional stock comic figure authored and played by men as the butt of the joke in conservative forms of carnival. Russo problematizes recuperating the unruly woman on top into our world view; at the same time risking it chances altering that world view. My process of arrogating a carnivalesque voice to myself, which I just thought of as my brash, no holds barred irreverence and silliness was nurtured by playing the transgressive women characters in Sky's plays and movies but also informed them. Which brings me to the deliciously touchy subject of Sky's mother. Soon after we became friends, he began regaling me with stories about his non nurturing hypochondriac money-hoarding society girl mother who evaded her son's homosexuality in spite of the fact that he was running around town in a sequined mini dress, spike heels, platinum blonde wig and fake boobs staging protests as Jane. Being a published author, he had given his mother one of his provocative books as a gift, which she proudly displayed on her sitting room bookcase. But sadly, upon his return visit, he spotted the book on top of the fridge in behind some stuff. I grew up upper middle class like Sky, and was all too familiar with the reception of one's work as half pride/half horror. To our progenitors/self-appointed arbiters our original artwork is, after all, if nothing else Canadian; so how good can it be? What loosey-goosey, coked-up literary critic would allow this creation to pass muster, they must wonder. Sky's mother was monstrous when she wanted to be and I loved that about her. She was a hoarder of family money, and a passive aggressive complainer who once moaned for months about having cancer until it turned out to be constipation. I might venture to say that never is Sky funnier than on the subject of his mother. She is the ambiguous: an older lady of a certain class but tough as nails; an emotional blackmailer, but witty; and much more self-involved than anyone's mother should be, but attractive and rarely boring. Sky marries his mother with other cold fish mothers to create the mother figures I portrayed in his work. Here is an analysis of three characters written specifically for me.

## *Jim Dandy: A Play with no Plot or Meaning.*

Marsha from *Jim Dandy* is a non-mother: an uncensored, over the top portrait of a white trash woman gone stir crazy from her repressed sexist society. Her spirit of crude subversive sexuality and vulgar laughter was an inspiration for me, particularly because the pain that underpinned her brazen wisecracks is all too familiar. Marsha is the walking wounded/trickster desperate to turn her drab reality into something like feeling alive while trapped in a wretched job as a waitress at the Bit and Bite no less, where her boss, Mr. Chanagwa pinches her on the ass whenever his gonads move him. But on this day, Chanagwa has pushed Marsha too far, and she reacts like the hothead she is by taking off early. It's a hot humid mid-afternoon. As the scene opens, Marsha comes through the door in her garish tangerine waitress uniform which she is already unbuttoning. Marsha flings her Bit and Bite hat over her shoulder, goes directly to the fridge, takes out two beers, downs one in a split second, sits at the kitchen table now wearing only her slip and cooks up a scheme to shock her girlfriend and win a fifty dollar bet that she can't get her own son, Marlboro, to get her off sexually. Marsha leaves the phone off the hook and starts working on her teenage son Marlboro as soon as he comes through the door. She tongue in cheek seduces him while letting him in on the prank with the girlfriend eavesdropping all the while; and knowing how much beer fifty bucks'll buy, Marlboro pretends to eat Marsha out. The writing was spot on, navigating its way through teasing wordplay touching on the testy terrain of mother/son incest: spanking the monkey type of thing. What surprised me most was that many of the cast members' middle aged parents came and they thought it was funny as hell. At one point in the simulated act of cunnilingus, Marsha cries out to her son: "It's the hole you came from!" That line so defined Sky's ouvre that the cast and crew including Franco Boni who dramaturged the play could not stop saying it: it's the hole you came from; it's the hole you came from.

Anyway, as far as acting style goes there wasn't one. My one affectation was my working class Ontario accent, eh. The script stated that I was an actor playing Marsha the waitress; so in true postmodern style, I was Ann-as-Marsha skylarking with my son Michael McMurtry-as-Marlboro. We both pulled on our masks in the wings and came out and played the scene like it was tiddlywinks and I loved that. There was no pretence of meaningful emoting; we just tossed the absurdist dialogue back and forth and then we went straight to the bar.

## The Bewitching of Max Gunter

This dark comedy was written in response to the spate of deadly serious plays about AIDS through the eighties and nineties. Once again, Sky showed his talent for terrific casting by hiring Mark Christman, Gil Garret and the awesome Tracy Wright. I played Anne the prototype mother reacting badly to her son's AIDS condition, Max's repressed mother, a witless woman who has no empathy for her bedridden son who is dying on a hospital ward. It's no wonder Max calls his mother the monster behind her back. Anne is a brooding hulk of a woman: myopic, menopausal, straight laced and passive aggressive, with a case of selective blindness and an imaginary pain in her hand that she deploys like an uncontrollable tic to rankle everyone within earshot. Anne affects coke bottle thick, black, horn-rimmed glasses, and a too large mannish black overcoat with shoulder pads, clunky orthopaedic shoes and prop cane. Her sole mission in life is to nag her son about producing an offspring, even though she has not a nurturing bone in her body. Add to this the fact that her son, Max Gunter, is a dyed in the wool homosexual in love with a man and is clearly on his deathbed. This miracle birth event that Max's mother fetishizes is rendered more incongruous as we attempt to envision the monster as a granny holding a baby in her rocking chair. Anne is the last person on earth you'd leave your baby with and the last woman on earth you would picture fucking the devil. But she Gilbert makes it plausible somehow, Anne not just fucking the devil, fucking the dark lord with wild abandon and thrilling vocals. The Monster's running commentary of the sexual encounter as it progresses begins as an hysterical reaction, but Anne soon boards Satan's fast train to unfettered passion where not even the poo on the end of his dick dissuades her: "Is it shit!? Is it shit!?" she cries undaunted while thrashing in ecstasy unrestrained.

Just as we had all chanted: "It's the hole you came from!" in Jim Dandy, the phrase: "Is it shit? Is it shit?" became our mantra. Somehow the vision of transmigrating faeces cracked Anne's addled brain like a walnut and lovely soft flesh appeared. The erstwhile monster has an epiphany and marries herself; the play ends with Anne slow dancing romantically with the handsome black gay stage manager/candy striper. My character actually had an arc in this piece; it was a dance from alienation through an abrupt transition to awakening. Just for stage business alone *Max Gunter* was hysterically funny. Pretending the devil was fucking me was a riot, and I earned my one and only Dora nomination for fucking the devil. If that doesn't sum up being a woman in Canadian alternative theatre I don't know what does. My favourite part of Max Gunter was a transition moment onstage where all the characters say in unison: Gay gay gay gay gay, as if we were up to our eyeballs in gay, and we were. Making jokes about AIDS is risky business, but comedy of resistance must expose the explosive chaos beneath the floorboards of society. This outrageous bedevilment scene is classic Gilbert and no one else could have pulled it off.

## Bad Acting Teachers

This character stymied me; I could not figure out how to make her funny for myself. She didn't turn me on, this uncreative, neurotic, boring bully with no voice of her own reciting the male acting manifesto like a martinet. Even the monster had the guts and passion to break through her ignorance, and Marsha spoke back to her oppression with utter irreverence. Marsha and Anne rise above their entrapment albeit in unorthodox ways as part of their journey; and these acts, however coarse, dignify them as women. But this character goes nowhere. She doesn't have the juice or wit to redeem herself from being the butt of the joke. I discovered that I am not good at making a repressed character funny the way Gavin Crawford can for example; unmitigated repression is a zone of emotional distress for me. Take the bit at the end, where I scream at the top of my lungs: "All men are rapists!" I resisted the reverse misogyny instead of going for it and blowing it up and baring my gums and lolling my tongue out. I also had menopause memory and for the first time ever I was near paralyzed with OCD over remembering my lines.

Having said all that, I loved the premise of the play and Sky's nightmare vision of washed-up ego freaks posing as therapists, and revelled in the scathing criticism of the highly suspect profession of teaching acting. I found the other two scenes hilarious because it was attacking egomaniacal male actors. Jason Cadieux's flip-out is one of the highlights of Canadian comedy for me, not to mention the adorable Gavin who was of course a dream onstage and off and hysterically funny. I felt vindicated by the play. I loathe the idea of teaching acting like in Lee Strasburg's studio; students jerking off in a studio while some charlatan rants on about the method. What method? Everybody knows that in the end you just do it. Like the Brits. Send the poetic images and the propagandist messages of the play out to the audience. Lee Strasberg commercialized and misappropriated Stanislavsky's method as a bizarre interiorizing of real emotion as if the actor disappears into her ribcage and is subsumed by the character. Stanislavsky was not seeking total integration between role and player but rather a more naturalistic style of acting than the stiff, declamatory one of his time. Acting in the west had long been cursed with stock wooden gestures taken from a manual for the deaf; Hamlet in his address to the players called such mechanical histrionics sawing the air. As for crying real tears, some actors can turn on the waterworks; for the rest of us, there's onions. You see the elitism being constructed here; when in actuality acting revolves around vocal technique: tenor and projection and articulation, because the function of theatre is to make the audience react; and for this they need to hear the playwright's dialogue, no matter the character's dialect or inherent eccentricities of speech, loud and clear. Acting class is now over. In the end, it was both Sky's solid encouragement and Urjo Kareda's biased criticism that sustained me as a struggling writer; but mostly it's because of all the girls at Buddies who came out and laughed at my comedy written for them, that could not have existed without them.

## Works Cited

Bakhtin, Mikhail. *Rabelais and His World*. Bloomington, IN: Indiana University Press, 1984

# Rope Enough

## Sarah Garton Stanley

*How sad that what is melodramatic is often true.*
(Bobbi to Cecilia, *Rope Enough,* 16)

I used to be the Artistic Director of Buddies in Bad Times Theatre. It still amazes me and I grapple with this fact of my past on a regular basis. What to do? Determine my needs. I needed to understand. I needed an MA. I needed to look at failure. I needed to get over myself. (I have accomplished the middle two). Plus I needed to put in a good amount of time to be able to see more clearly, or perhaps, to feel more deeply. During my tenure at Buddies in Bad Times Theatre I did not program any of Sky's plays. I believe this makes me not only the only woman to have run the company (but really, after all this time—and Judith Butler—am I still hung up on such essentialist identification? Yes. Yes I am) but also the only Artistic Director to not program Sky's work. I was not in the job for long. Don't get me wrong (although if you do, my hunch is that Ichabod Malframe would most heartily endorse it). My leaving Buddies had nothing specific to do with this historically accurate programming reality. But ruminating now on a love song to fog (aka *Rope Enough*) I have a sense that my leave-taking was in part connected to it. Or—to be Ichabodian about it—not.

Why would anyone choose to hang?

As part of my recent education I came across all manner of intellectual framing that did a few things. In the first instance, it forced me to look at a set of academic writings that coincided with my time at Buddies. As to the work that actually looked directly at Buddies In Bad Times during that time, I was shocked as to how completely inaccurate it was. How—I wondered—could peer review allow for these gross inaccuracies? And therefore to extend outward, what does this mean about the balance of academic writing in general? Is it all steeped in a kind of "I hope I get away with it" brew? Second, I was invited into an academic club of queer consideration(s) that helped frame my time at Buddies in ways that—almost 15 years later—I am just now starting to unpack. And lastly, it introduced me to the book I would have loved to write but instead I just re-read and refer to with alarming regularity. I am speaking here of Judith (Jack) Halberstam's *The Queer Art of Failure*.

> Failing is something queers do and have always done exceptionally well. (Halberstam, 14)

In the winter of 2012 I climbed aboard the stage at Buddies in Bad Times Theatre during the Rhubarb Festival. This was the first time I had performed anything at the theatre since my resignation in late 1999. The show was called *The Failure Show or: a 13-point manifesto for the consideration of failure*. In it I did many things, shared my manifesto, drew analogies between me and Detroit, and asked the audience if it was possible to hold failure. As it turns out audiences agreed that they could hold it, and I was the recipient of some great hugs every night. But at the play's centre was an apology for letting the ideas of a time, my time as artistic leader at BIBT, down. This was one of the more frightening things I have done onstage and, therefore, one of the most rewarding.

Things come to us, as they will. The plan exists only as a result of a backward glance, how when looking back, we can see how we got to the "now". This rumination is written on the heels of losing my dear friend Patrick Conner who passed away December 7, 2012. It also comes at a moment when, having finished a new degree in my education I am able to comprehend (if not understand) Sky Gilbert's writing in a whole new light.

## Inconsistent Calculus

The above mathematical discovery was introduced to me in Sky Gilbert's *Rope Enough*.

In 2012, I was in Vancouver in my capacity as Associate Artistic Director of English Theatre at Canada's National Arts Centre. We were there to hold general auditions for our acting ensemble. In walked a young hopeful. He sat down and launched into a speech. No introduction as to who the playwright was, but a surprising and engaging interpretation of Ichabod Malframe's speech about Cecilia Wainscott's misunderstanding of everything ensued. I recognized the writing, the voice, and the approach: it was Sky Gilbert's *Rope Enough*. And in an instant I was struck by a set of things.

First up: This was the first Sky Gilbert monologue I had encountered in a general audition. I am not exaggerating by saying that I have seen well over 1500 auditions in my career. But I might be lying (albeit not on purpose) about *never having witnessed another Sky Gilbert monologue in an audition.* Regardless this is my sense of things.

Inconsistent Calculus.

Next up: Gossip starts the play when Cecilia Wainscott speaks the opening lines about her friend Bobbi Lacrème. In the 2005 premiere, my dear friend, and oft-collaborator, Patrick Conner, played the role of Bobbi. Here is how Cecilia Wainscott (Played by Catherine McNally) opens the show:

*I worry about Bobbi.*

This sets the tone for a play that aims to reveal the enduring hypocrisies of the mainstream impulse to sub-jugate its citizens through restrictive definitions.

Patrick is now gone. Given what we learn about Bobbi, it is possible to surmise that Patrick's days may also have been numbered. But I never worried about Patrick, and I don't worry about Bobbi. Yet I can see why Cecilia would. I was taught that understanding was the answer to all. I have since learned that it (understanding) sits in equal measure to many other factors. And that love (for me) holds a far greater value than understanding. But this is with hindsight. Cecilia's perspective lives in me, a desire to harness or possess that which is different, under the guise of "understanding," and against this impulse I must remain vigilant.

Online I found this review of the text, it is likely five years old and it was summed up with these closing remarks:

> ... with *Rope Enough* he's content to preach to an
> LGBT audience that will shake its collective head at
> well-meaning but clueless straights like Cecilia, while
> appreciating Ichabod's attitude that, if society is going
> to paint homosexuals as evil, you might as well play
> the stereotype to the hilt. Ichabod and Dylan get the
> last laugh, but it's the hollow laugh of defeat. After a
> career spent fighting to have queer life understood, I
> hope that doesn't suggest Gilbert is ready to throw in
> the towel. (*Martin Morrow*, Books in Canada)

Recently, at the 2013 launch for the largest Toronto-based performance festival (if we are to judge the size by the budget and we will) Jorn Weisbrodt (married to Rufus Wainwright), said the following:

> Great art does not need to be understood it needs to
> be experienced (Quoted in Terauds, "Jorn Weisbrodt's
> eclectic 2013 Luminato festival crosses disciplines,
> highlights collaborations," April 16, 2013)

Finally up at bat:

Ichabod Malframe is a master of inconsistency and this notion links to a set of queer thinkers that I "met" recently in my return to school: First among them is Gayle Rubin's, *Thinking Sex*. In this groundbreaking article she classifies types of people according to mainstream phobic response potential. She suggests and—I believe negates its actual validity—a kind of sexual essentialism. I connected too to thinkers such as Foucault, Butler and Sedgwick and then on through to Halberstam.

> For queers failure can be a style, to cite Quentin
> Crisp, or a way of life, to cite Foucault, and it can
> stand in contrast to the grim scenarios of success.
> (Halberstam 14)

Ichabod Malframe says very little about failure but the character says a lot about representing varying points of view in order to present a "person" as inconsistent as the mathematics theories he so brilliantly penned. Any opportunity to affix an identity will be foiled by a principle of inconsistency. So did he and his lover do it? It doesn't really matter. There is *Rope Enough* for them to hang—regardless of their "innocence" but then again there is *Rope Enough* to have "our" (our being the mainstream audience member to whom this appears to be speaking) chains yanked for believing anything definitive about these two men.

And this same inconsistency pertains to Bobbi. Why would la crème de la crème wish to endanger both his health and social standing by practicing unsafe sex in bathhouses? What could possibly motivate this kind of a choice? Gilbert's argument is not—I think—about the character's motivation, so much as it is the misplaced desire of the straight privileged woman, Cecilia, to understand. She never can.

Throughout my tenure at Buddies, I felt that there were so many things happening that I did not understand, and that all I could do was trust in the experience. However, not unlike Cecilia I chose the mainstream fear-based response, to fight to understand. I was incapable of fully *experiencing the unknown* that leading a Queer organization in the 1990s was bound by. And in this regard, like each of the characters in Sky's play, I feel that I too was provided with—well—*Rope Enough*.

This young actor who showed up for a general audition in Vancouver taught me all of this. He taught me that now, after studying failure and experiencing it too, that I might have enough life understanding to be able to experience more fully the work of Sky Gilbert. *Rope Enough* is a really fun play. But it is also a play that demonstrates real concern for all of its characters and, I believe, for its audience too. It also opens with one of the sexiest scenes you are likely to see on a stage anywhere. A scene where an undercover cop gets off on the details of the crime he is allegedly investigating, while the two "criminals" give him the best night of sex he is likely ever to have received while in the line of duty.

Inconsistent Calculus.

This play was written and produced several years after I left my position at Buddies. Notwithstanding any of the above I am fiercely proud of my time there, although I remain quizzical about so much of it. But I close with these four thoughts: I lost my dearest, dearest friend, whose demise was foretold in Sky's play. But I doubt very much that Patrick's life had all that much in common with Bobbi Lacrème. And yet, he is gone. Sky remains provocative and fearless as ever and Buddies thrives with a leader that can and does galvanize both action and art. And yet they struggle to fill their houses with audiences in a consistent manner. And, as I write, a new Sky Gilbert play is set to open at Buddies.1 And finally that love is as unknowable and as trustworthy as anything else in this world. And so as melodramatic as I am sure this sounds:

I am so grateful that a young actor taught me how to consider love again, and that the consequence of this was to grapple with *Rope Enough* by Sky Gilbert, and that as a direct result of all of this grappling I have come to recognize the difference between comprehension, understanding and experience. Ichabod Malframe is a great teacher, mal-framed though he may be, and Oscar

Wilde (who Sky quotes in the opening pages of the play) understood the need for fog because, I warrant, he knew how to experience it.

## Endnote

1. It did open and Gavin Crawford who played Ichabod Malframe in *Rope Enough,* was awarded a Dora Mavor Moore Award for Sky's play *A Few Brittle Leaves.*

## Works Cited

Gilbert, Sky. *Rope Enough.* Playwrights Canada Press, 2006. http://www.amazon.ca/Rope-Enough-Sky-Gilbert/dp/0887548725.

Halbertam, Judith (Jack). *The Queer Art of Failure.* Duke University Press, 2011.

Terauds, John. "Jorn Weisbrodt's eclectic 2013 Luminato festival crosses disciplines, highlights collaborations," *Musical Toronto* April 16, 2013. http://www.musicaltoronto.org/2013/04/16/jorn-weisbrodts-eclectic-2013-luminato-festival-crosses-disciplines-highlights-collaborations/

# Interviews

# The Genius of Sky Gilbert: An interview with Ellen-Ray Hennessy

## Moynan King

Moynan King: You've performed in eighteen plays by Sky Gilbert over the past twenty-five years. One of the first would have been *Theatre Life*, is that right?

Ellen-Ray Hennessy: Oh my god, yes, but don't forget, he was infamous to me before I even met him. In grade eleven at Martin Grove Collegiate, we had a teacher, this crazy guy, and he brought in these shows for us to do. There was a show called *Love is a Many Splendored Orange* and the name of the writer was Sky Gilbert, and I thought that he had the coolest name: Sky Gilbert. *Theatre Life* was at the old, old Theatre Centre—I don't know if anybody remembers that but it was this phenomenally experimental company. Anyway, I don't remember auditioning for *Theatre Life*.

MK: While Sky does sometimes audition actors he often uses actors he knows and he writes for them—you are certainly one of those actors.

ERH: Oh my god, he's written stuff for me, and even when he was writing the play he'd say: "Oh Ellen I've got a play for you." *Theatre Life* he said was written for me. He had seen me in something else.

MK: I've done two of his plays as an actor, and one as choreographer, and the way it works is you just get a call (or an email now) and he's so humble. It'll be like: "I don't know if you want to do this, I don't know if it's of any interest to you." And you're like: "Sky, of course I'm interested." It's such an honour, and you feel so respected. And then you go into rehearsal and, well, can you talk a bit about what it's like to rehearse with Sky?

ERH: There's no rehearsal. (Moynan laughs) There's no rehearsal, there's no rehearsal.

MK: Ha! He knows what he wants, that's for sure, and he doesn't drag rehearsal out.

ERH: He hires you because he believes you know what you're doing. He stays out of your way. He may say one thing, or say "great," and he'll be chewing on his pencil. I've worked with other performers who aren't used to his methods. You can't freak out or be worried because you think you need more rehearsal, and think: "I don't know what I'm doing." He likes that you don't really know what the hell you're doing.

MK: It's deliberate …

ERH: Oh, I think so.

MK: It's visionary. His method is clear. "I've written this play, you're talented and you're right for it so I'm going put you in it and then I'm going to let it happen and not mess it up."

ERH: It's like Sky's writing, he doesn't do rewrites—he writes. As the years have gone on he writes more and more naturalistically, so it's all colloquial, with lots of weird jargon, really natural, and you want to be really honest to the writing, and oh my god, memorizing is just lunacy.

When Sky sails is when he takes people that have existed. His best scripts for me are the ones that are based on incidences of specific people. He captures something that is great I think, and he's done it a lot.

MK: Like Ayn Rand in *The Emotionalists*.

ERH: I loved playing Ayn Rand, Elsa Lanchester, Libby Holman, Tatum O'Neil, Virginia Woolf—these are/ were *all* living women who Sky gave voice to. And they inhabited my being—I had nights whilst playing each of these characters that they invaded me and literally took over while I, as the actor, had to take a backseat and watch the show.

MK: His real life characters are all slightly fictionalized.

ERH: Yeah they all are. And sometimes with Sky you might think he overstates his resolve—like particularly in the climax—when it's in like debate land. But that's all clearly "in case you didn't hear it the first time," or the second time.

MK: Or just in case there's any chance that there's any doubt in your mind that you don't think he's saying something as radical and sexual as he is.

ERH: And I don't think you or myself as safe actors, you know. I played Heliogabalus' mother (in *Heliogabalus*) and they had an incestuous relationship—probably one of the hardest things I have ever had to do on stage. I had to do a monologue while the actor playing my son preformed cunnilingus on me, and I had to orgasm, then commanded him to leave me. The audience froze! Sky tends to create moments like that in *all* his shows—freezing due to fear and disbelief, or due to an opening of the spirit and mind, where truth and delight flood in like a rain shower on the desert. What you feed grows and I believe that Sky Gilbert feeds his students, actors, writers, audiences with possibilities, a key to risk-taking and discovery.

MK: Yes, and all of those people feed him. He's always on the go, always searching, questioning, and commenting simultaneously. This is a quality of his life and his plays.

ERH: And there is always a hairpin turn that will always happen somewhere with the characters I play. I never let my audience get ahead of me, I don't want anyone ever thinking they get it before they get it. There is a lot of empathy towards the female characters I've played. They're always broken. Heliogabalus' mother—broken; the heroin addict on dancing with the stars married to Agassi—broken. Even Charles Laughton's wife. All these incredibly kind of larger than life people … the rocks in her pocket writer what's her name.

MK: (laughs) Virginia Woolf, rocks in her pocket.

ERH: Struggling to keep her head above water—really beautiful stuff where you just go ooooh.

MK: And Sky has a sense for recognizing actors who can go the distance with him.

ERH: And he laughs at everything, and it makes you feel as though you're capable of it. He said to me once: "You astound me as a performer because just when I think you're this larger-than-life wild doyenne you turn around and you go like (she twists her fingers)." The hairpin.

MK: Maybe that's part of what makes his female characters so compelling.

ERH: I'm always an extension of Sky's mother. Having met her I knew her quite well, she shared qualities with my own mother. I understood that partially the female matriarch in his mind was always his mother.

MK: Yes, not to get too psychoanalytic but yes, I see what you are saying. We fear her and we respect her. And even though she's a bit aggressive, and loopy, the audience will always come to empathize with her.

ERH: I will be that old crone who sits there and says: "I was Sky Gilbert's muse."

MK: And do you think his work has influenced you as an artist?

ERH: I made very specific choices. I was warned not to do a Sky Gilbert play, I was warned that I would get pigeon-holed for doing queer work. Form those who were in the know, you know. Finally I turned down the Shaw Festival. I did two seasons. It wasn't me. I wanted to do new works and Sky's work was what really interested me. It set the tone for my career.

MK: You share a sensibility with Sky, a tenacity as an a artist. He has been completely blasted and disavowed at times. He's not impervious, you know, he's fragile and …

ERH: Sky is such a dichotomy of a human being. You know there is such a little boy in him. There is like a playful wildly free young boy in him and there is a frightened unworthy boy too. People will say to me: "Why is he so mean to me? He didn't even say hi to me." And I say: "You don't understand, he is struggling to be present." Because I do believe he is a genius.

MK: What's a genius? I think Ralph Waldo Emerson said something about genius being the god within—and letting that god speak.

ERH: A genius is someone who lives brilliantly apart and holds the integrity of thought they believe in.

MK: Right, and is only ever acknowledged in retrospect. Because they are not marketing themselves, they are listening to their own inspiration.

ERH: Maybe genius comes from being "other than," and upholding that.

MK: And incidentally, he brings out the genius in others.

ERH: He brings out the genius in me.

MK: Yes. And really the way I think Sky perceives the world is something I aspire to. To not concern myself with how my work is perceived but to keep trying to get it right, to keep saying what I feel I have to say. That's what I want as an artist: to keep trying to say what I mean to say. Sky has always inspired that in me.

ERH: What really matters to Sky is that "I created a story and I have those who can tell it … I have a story and those who can tell it."

He is courageous and yet strangely humble. He feeds us with ourselves—the good, bad and unquestionable—the forces that can move solid rock. He blasts us with a sense of our own largess and the infinite characters that make up human landscape. He feeds us community and in that, we find our humanness. I will never say no to a Sky Gilbert play—I would starve.

# "The Control of the Camera is Fascinating": Sky Gilbert on his feature films — A conversation with RM Vaughan

## RM Vaughan

No discussion of Sky Gilbert's extensive theatrical and literary output can be complete without an exploration of his sudden, and too brief, venture into feature film making. In the 1990s, Gilbert produced, directed and wrote a handful of features, all starring members of his loosely knit theatre "company"—including Daniel MacIvor, Tracy Wright, Ann Holloway, Ellen-Ray Hennessy, Caroline Gillis, and Clinton Walker—films that feel and present as extensions of his theatre practice, and not merely because of the familiar faces.

As in a Gilbert play, characters in Gilbert's features (*My Addiction*, 1993; *My Summer Vacation*, 1995; *I Am The Camera Dying*, 1998, plus the short *Film/Fill 'em*, 1991) chatter relentlessly, (arguing the fine points of everything from the sex trade and S/M to queer separatism and economics to theories of aesthetics), are witnessed performing in styles that range from high Naturalism to cabaret charade (Gilbert frequently filled the smaller parts with Toronto-based drag artists, comedians, and performance artists), and speak directly to the lens/audience, thus disrupting the illusion of audience passivity.

Filmed on micro-budgets (by feature film standards, at least) and shot on 16mm, the films have a grainy, vaguely seedy look, entirely cultivated, that harkens back to mid-century porn and art cinema—again, in parallel with Gilbert's minimalist, raw approach to stage decoration. Costumes are kept simple, vernacular (and likely were owned by the actors), sets, such as they are, are borrowed spaces, not constructed ones, and the lighting, when not natural, is blunt and searching, alternating between flattering and lyrical and peering and invasive (much like his light plans for the stage).

During a Gilbert film, one is always aware that one is watching a filmed proceeding, yet one is quickly seduced by the prevailing arguments of each scene. The traditional Gilbert double whammy, wherein one is made aware of the artificialities of the stage (or screen) and yet one is constantly engaged by the dynamics contained within that artificial system, are thus replicated on film. You cannot view a Sky Gilbert film passively, and yet you can only, of course, sit still and watch the film unfold.

Gilbert wields his camera in the same way he directs action on stage. He shows a scene, allows the viewer to recognize the inherently manipulative strategy of "showing," presents dilemmas to be unpacked (and one does unpack them, one does take sides, has moments of illusive "identification" with particular characters) and then moves on to the next scene, repeating the passive/active game play.

Critics often responded to Gilbert's features with the pat argument that his films were "just like plays"—but that was never the point for Gilbert, despite the obvious similarities (see above! Perhaps I am doing it too?). Yes, the films were "like plays" in that they, as actor/writer David Roche once described theatre, were essentially "[p]eople being rude in a room."

However, Gilbert's films ought to be read as *extensions* of his theatrical practice, not celluloid copies of same. With each film, Gilbert's view grows wider, more encompassing, and the boundaries of the stage are readily, then confidently, challenged, met, and surmounted. What critics never recognized when they made the easy parallel with Gilbert's plays was how Gilbert sought to create, via the mobility of film, a more generous version of his already established theatrical view.

The films, though talky as a drunken whore, are never still, never stilted, never flat. It's as if Gilbert sought to document, permanently and in a somewhat journalistic fashion (at least visually, although certainly not performatively) the demimonde his plays had, and continue to, celebrate: the lousy apartments, grimy bars and cafes, the outdoor sexual cruising spots, the public toilets, the bleak, dank alleyways. All the best parts of town!

Looking at these films today, one sees not only an emerging filmic style coming into its own, but also a Toronto that no longer exists: the Toronto of the early to mid 90s, a city recovering from a wrenching recession and coming to terms with its new global status, as absorbed, lived, and endured by its various outsiders (sexual, economic, artistic, and just plain crazy). Gilbert's films were hardly "filmed plays" (is there any more damning label for a movie?) but can arguably be read as crafted, scripted docu-dramas that relied on, and sought to capture forever, the idiosyncrasies of a generation of accomplished theatre artists.

In the summer of 2011, I met with Gilbert to talk about his feature films, his processes, and why he ultimately abandoned filmmaking. To my happy surprise, Gilbert revealed he is working on a new feature, a "family reunion" (his words), that will update viewers on the fractured lives of his recurring, interconnected characters, on the perpetually trying city they continue to inhabit, and the core struggles and questions yet, if ever, to be resolved.

At the centre of each of Gilbert's features rests a simple imponderable: how to live as one wants? I can't wait to see the progress, or, more likely, antic regress, made by Gilbert's beloved, madcap ensemble.

RMV: Why did you stop making feature films?

Sky Gilbert: Because I wasn't getting any funding. I wrote a couple of other films, and I submitted them, and I got rejected twice, and then told I couldn't apply any more, by the Canada Council. When they told me that, I shrugged filmmaking off. It was my only way of funding them. I was also at one of those points where I was doing so many things in my life, and I thought: Something's got to go.

RMV: Like many filmmakers, you decided early on to work with a core troupe of actors.

SG: I've always had a troupe around, absolutely. I was writing for a group of people—that was one of the things I loved about making films, was that I was able to work with theatre actors that I knew, and worked with before, but also ones that I admired, but had never worked with or hardly worked with at all, for whatever reasons.

RMV: Talk about your blending of performers and actors.

SG: One of them was even my ex-boyfriend! A lot of my friends turn up in my films too, because I was looking for volunteers! Ha! These were people I would not normally put in a play, because they were not professional actors—but that doesn't mean they were not great on film. That's the thing, I got people to be in the films and wrote parts for them that were basically copies of who they were anyway—there's a certain kind of strength when you use performers that way. And they all worked great.

RMV: Here's the ten buck question—how does directing a film vary from directing a play?

SG: Hmmm, well, hmmm—for one thing, I can't really claim to be a film person. I'm not, generally, very visual. I think my films are valuable, I hope, because of the actors. I'm not a big fan of contemporary cinema. My films are kind of antithetical to the way movies have turned. They hark back to Warhol, they hark back to a time when movies were all about faces and personalities. And, I mean, in general, you don't usually rehearse in movies, or not very much. The camera is doing a lot of the work too, doing a lot of the attitude in acting—except in my films, where the camera really doesn't do much at all! All the camera has to do is make the film. Plus, in film, people pretty well know what they are doing when they show up. It's not like a play, with weeks of rehearsal.

RMV: You made four films in a very short time, and then stopped. What would you say you learned from filmmaking that you later applied to your plays?

SG: Basically, filmmaking made me think about Naturalism, which is one of the reasons I started making the films in the first place. I'm interested in Naturalism, yet a lot of my plays have fantastical elements to them, so I've been doing a lot of work in the last few years that mixes very naturalistic things with not naturalistic things. I think I have an affinity for Naturalism, I can write naturalistic dialogue quite well, but then, in between those scenes, I'm inserting other elements. What I learned from my movies is that I actually like writing scenes for real people, about real people. Movies are generally about Naturalism, and theatre is not. Theatre always has some sort of frame. What people like about movies, even fantastical films, people love the fact that it looks real. Film is about detail, about close ups. On another front, film is not inherently conservative, but because there is money involved, it tends to be. However, you can't make money from theatre, so that's what makes theatre wonderful! But I don't accept the argument that theatre is inherently more avant-garde than movies. Henry Jaglom's films are as full of questions, even the ones where very little is happening in front of a stable camera, as any theatre piece.

I think the play of mine that came closest to being "like a film" is *Jim Dandy*, this crazy play, a huge flop. There were scenes of that play that were videotaped while it was being performed, and I still have this film that somebody made during the filming … funny, I forget about that play … it was a total intersection for me, of film and theatre. I wrote these naturalistic scenes that were introduced and sort of presented on stage by this crazy, totally un-naturalistic narrator, who framed the play. But I guess it was just the wrong play at the wrong time. It may be more interesting than I knew at the time.

RMV: Would you consider blending film and theatre again?

SG: Here's a weird thing I've noticed: when you do Naturalism in a film, nobody is threatened, but when you do it in the theatre, people find it unnerving—Oh, oh! Those people are having sex really close to me! Oh no, those actors are going to talk to me! The control of the camera is fascinating, how it gives power to the viewer and takes power away. But I think people should always distrust the point of view, in film or theatre.

I love it when people say: "I'm not sure what Sky wants me to think about this play." And it's not as easy to get that response in a film, because people trust film more.

# Sky Gilbert: Criticism, Vomit, Sex and Greatness: an interview with Hillar Liitoja

## Mike Hoolboom

Hillar: All right, what do you want to know?

Mike: Why don't I give you the first half of a sentence, and you can fill in the rest? I've been thinking a lot about this upcoming interview on Sky Gilbert. And I've decided there's one thing about Sky that I really can't divulge, and that's when …

Hillar: You're working on a false premise because there is almost nothing that I can't speak with him about. However you have hit upon a very interesting point because there is the *almost*. And the *almost* is … now maybe this isn't finishing the sentence properly, but it's a springboard to a completely different point. Sky is not good about taking criticism. In fact, I had the experience of Sky telling me exactly what to say if I didn't like his last book. I wasn't allowed to say: "Well Sky, the weakness of this book lies primarily with the main character who doesn't really come across. I also found the London park sequence weak, it didn't stimulate me." You cannot say that to Sky. He told me: "So Hillar, if you didn't like it, then what you say is: 'You know Sky, this piece wasn't really for me.'" And so I said to him: "You know Sky, this piece wasn't really for me." And then he said: "OK," and we moved right on. It's true. He will actually put The Words into your mouth. He will tell you The Right Thing To Say, so that his feelings are not hurt, and he's not offended. It's definitely about him not wanting to know the specific grounds of your discontent.

Mike: That makes me wonder about Sky playing Claudius in your 8-hour production of *Hamlet*. It was a large and difficult role, and one that likely generated some director's notes.

Hillar: There was a ritual during the course of that never-ending performance whereby an entire roast chicken would be delivered, complete with potatoes and carrots. If I were playing that role, I would eat a leg of chicken, I might have a taste of the breast. Good. If I was feeling particularly hungry I would also have a wing. Sky would work through the entire chicken. He was still onstage, but he didn't have another cue for 30 or 40 minutes. I remember looking on with amazement as he calmly chomped his way through that chicken at every performance.

I should make something clear. What I just said about his aversion to criticism does not apply to him as a performer. You're totally OK to ask: "Could you say this louder or softer, or with more feeling, or move slower when you offer him the knife?" He's great at following direction, that's not criticism. What I'm talking about is a poem, play or novel that he wrote. We can sit here and argue that his acting is also a form of creating, but I think he draws a really clear line between being under the iron hand of the director …

Mike: That would be you.

Hillar: That would be me.

Mike: Mr. Iron Man.

Hillar: We're talking basically when he's written a play. I was going to say when he's directed a play, but I can't remember the last time he directed a play that wasn't his own. You cannot criticize his direction or his text. In fact, I think I know why that is. It's a tricky kind of thing. You don't mind if I smoke?

Mike: No.

Hillar: If it gets unpleasant we'll open the door, there's several things we can do. You see, I think what happened with Sky is that early in his career, I guess in the early 80s, he was part of a thing at Tarragon. I don't know what it was officially called, but it was like a writer's workshop. There was a group of four or five writers, and the idea was that they would write, and then their work would be critiqued by the dramaturges at Tarragon. I'm pretty sure it was Tarragon. I don't recall a specific Sky and Hillar conversation on this topic but I have heard it from others, and maybe Sky has actually spoken to me about this. What happened at Tarragon was that the dramaturges tried to shape his theatrical writing to fit into a norm, conforming to the currently "correct" style of writing. He actually submitted to that criticism, and then wound up not only disliking the final product but also feeling that his creative integrity had been violated. I think that he's never really gotten over that. To this day he feels criticism as an attack on himself, an affront to his artistic essence. And if he does feel that way, I don't blame him for repelling criticism of all sorts. Yet there are times when I wish he would not categorically repulse all suggestions. That he might view them as genuine attempts to bring greater clarity or focus to his own vision.

This is something I've also discussed with Gregory Nixon, who is the president of DNA Theatre, and a friend. Gregory takes a slightly different view on the matter. Gregory feels that Sky's whole take is primary expression: I'm going to write what I feel right now and there is a truth, purity and validity in that. There is no point in going back to alter anything or ... what is the expression? To polish.

Mike: First thought, best thought.

Hillar: According to Gregory, Sky would say: maybe this would be clearer if I would change a line or two. However that would be fighting the essence and truth of the original impulse. There is a perfection in the ... I want to say vomit, and I don't mean that at all in a bad sense. I just mean that when you vomit, it all comes out at once, and it's perfect. It's a perfect cleansing, it's all there. No, I'm not going to go back and airbrush those phrases to make them more powerful, that would be destroying the integrity of the origin.

Mike: Your last play was based on Sky's novel about Wittgenstein, *Wit in Love*. How did that come about?

Hillar: I was in Costa Rica when I received an email from Sky saying he'd written a new book that would be published soon. He'd loosely based one of the characters on me, and asked if I could read through it and make sure that he wasn't overstepping any boundaries. I wrote him back and said: No, I'm not going to read it. You can write whatever you want, bring me a copy when it's published. So he did, and I read it, and then months later he came over for dinner. I thought the evening was coming to its close when all of a sudden he brought up *Wit in Love*. What did I think of it? How did I feel about the portrayal of my character? Oh my god, I'd completely forgotten about that. It was nearly Christmas and I'd read it in August so it was not at all in the forefront of my mind. But it was very clear to me where he was completely stretching the truth, and where I could recognize myself. And then the miraculous thing happened. I went into the studio and got the novel, came back into the kitchen, opened it up to the chapter that dealt with me, and began reading out loud. Very soon Sky was laughing, and the more I read the more he laughed. I was laughing too, it seemed that nothing came out of my mouth without it sounding very funny. I had the thought that maybe it could be a performance, and Sky was enthusiastic and that's really how it all got started. I only got two pages into the text, by that point I was a combination of drunk and stoned and my brain was just freewheeling. I was just so excited at the thought that there might be something there. Two weeks later I realized that not a single day had passed without me thinking about the potential of doing a performance/installation.

Mike: Can you say describe the novel?

Hillar: The book was fine, it's not one of my favourites of
his. It's basically about Wittgenstein, though there's a lot
of Sky in Sky's version of Wittgenstein. I don't think it's
a coincidence that Sky is now a university professor and
Wittgenstein was a professor of philosophy at Cambridge.
And I don't think it's a coincidence that Wittgenstein
was gay, as much as he denied it. He definitely had this
homosexual impulse and of course that's something that
would deeply interest Sky. Particularly when it was not
overt, where there is a struggle in a human being to accept his or her homosexuality. And on top of that, there's
also the struggle of coming out of the closet and how do I
do that, and will I be rejected by everyone? Wittgenstein
never admitted his gayness, God only knows if he ever
*did* have sex with a guy.

Mike: Why would that be of particular interest to Sky?

Hillar: Number one, it's just more interesting. It's more
complex than: I'm six years old and I know I'm gay. When
I get into puberty all of my sexual fantasies are about
boys. I want to touch them and I want them to touch me
in the most special places and in the most special ways.
It's much more interesting to have that conflict because
we've got to remember … what are we now, 2011? It's
only been in the last 40 years that homosexuality in most
of the western world is not considered an aberration, a
mental illness even. We've come so far in the past couple
of decades that it's often hard to remember that. The
other point I would make is, hello? Sky had a girlfriend,

at least one. So therefore he was living a heterosexual way of life. Obviously something happened to make him ... transgress? (laughs) Would you throw in the mushrooms, and a little bit of oil and stir it?

Mike: Can you talk specifically about your chapter in the context of the book?

Hillar: In the context of the book which I read only once, a year and a half ago? When Wit is unsure of what his next move is, or when he's facing the proverbial brick wall, the idea is to go to his brother and talk it out. The text describes it as psychic purging. As irritating as his brother might be, he is able to bring out of Wit some different way of seeing things, suggesting how he might extricate himself from a particular mess. And that's exactly what happens. After seeing his brother, he goes back to his hotel and decides to return to Norway, alone. It's time to extricate himself from the situation in Cambridge.

Mike: The chapter in the book is largely set in a kitchen that is modelled after your kitchen, and you reflected that by staging the play right here in your kitchen.

Hillar: How much more convenient could that be? The bulk of the chapter does take place in the kitchen and the bulk of ...

Mike: ... your life happens here.

Hillar: Yeah, a really big part does happen here. I was very fortunate that he cast it in my home, and in this kitchen.

Mike: Imagine this scene. There's a shopper in a book-store surrounded by a horizon of beautiful covers. Oh look at this handsome, it's about Sky Gilbert. Never heard of him. Our shopper picks up the book and opens it somewhere in the middle. He doesn't want to know anything about this guy, he wants to find a way to make new sentences. Go ahead librarian, make my day. So this Gilbert makes plays. I don't care. Queer? I'm over that. Can you lay down a Sky moment that might speak to this feckless bookstore stranger?

Hillar: I'm not very good with moments. But I think we've already hit upon one thing that defines Sky's essence. The sense of his artistic integrity. What else? Part of it has got to be sex. Do you know of a more sexual person than Sky? You could argue that all of us are sexually motivated to a certain degree. I find you really attractive or I do not find you attractive. I want to have sex with you. No, I don't want to have sex with you. That's still a sexual way of thinking. As opposed to: I'd like you to cut my hair because I love the way your wave curls. I think that's a really important element of Sky, his sexual being, and the fact that he is so willing to talk about it. His willingness to try anything. OK. We're lovers, we've been lovers for four months, and one day you come here and say: "Oh Hillar, I've just been thinking about pissing on you. I would love to get you dressed up as Peter Pan and pee all over you. And ideally you would also gasp so I could pee in your mouth." Now, for a lot of people that would be disgusting and revolting.

Mike: The Peter Pan part you mean?

Hillar: I should have proposed Alice in Wonderland? Sky would say: "Sure, absolutely. We'll try it." I'm not at all suggesting that Sky would allow that again and again if he didn't like it, or if there wasn't any pleasure in it. Or if there wasn't a balance of: "OK, I'm not really enjoying it, but he loves this, so I'll continue doing it. It's not like I hate it, I don't really care for this, but you're so turned on by it that of course I'll do it again." That's how I see Sky, as totally willing. I'm using the word open to mean two different things. One kind of open is that we can talk about any aspect of my sex life, you can ask me anything about sex. But a completely different thing is that I'm open to every kind of sexual suggestion you might have. I'm totally willing to try it once, at the very least. There is no such thing as taboo for Sky. Though I'm not going to the extremes of OK, Sky, what would be really interesting is if I were to take my knife and cut off your cock, and then stick it in your bum. I don't think that Sky would go that far. Because that's mutilation, that's castration, and that would destroy a big chunk of Sky's sex life. I'm not talking about something as transgressive as that, but essentially, yeah, you'd like to pee on me while dragging me by the hair? Sure, let's try it. In that sense, he is a totally extraordinary human being. I'm going to make another point about that. I have a feeling that his willingness to be so open about sexuality and sexual practices is a reflection of his openness in terms of theatre, in terms of art, in terms of accepting or giving a chance to anything that is wild, wacky, strange, unheard of. And I'm going to be really clear about this. It's not that Sky is in favour of anything just because it's way out there. It's not that being crazy makes something good. The point is that there is a greatness in his humanity that allows him to be able to accept all kinds of possibilities, whether they are sexual or artistic. There is a greatness about Sky. Although it doesn't extend to culinary matters.

Mike: Culinary matters?

Hillar: Yes, Sky's taste in foods is very … parochial, not at all adventurous. I remember being at one of those post-opening receptions at Buddies where they recently adopted the formula of ordering a bunch of pizzas with different toppings. I was standing beside Sky, who was talking with someone, and saw him absentmindedly reach out and take a slice. I instantly grabbed his arm and said: "Don't." He looked at me bewildered. I said: "Anchovies," and took the slice from his hand. Sky gave me this big smile and said: "Thank you. Thank you so much." I beamed, I had made his night. I couldn't help but feel that my saving him from the dreaded anchovies might have meant more to him than the success of his play.

Mike: The Iron Hand again.

Hillar: Yes.

Mike: But back to sex, do you feel like he pushed you sexually?

Hillar: As far as sexual transgression goes, I don't need any pushing, OK? It's not like accounts of his adventures made me think, oh yeah, that's also possible. I think I have enough of a creative imagination myself, call it perversion if you want. So I don't feel that Sky has influenced me in that sense. But, now here's an interesting thing. Let me think about this for a moment. When I was in the early stages of doing my girl thing, my trans ... what is it called? It's not transgender. I guess it's called transvestite, when you dress up as a girl. Sky was one of the first people I ever spoke to about it. He would never condemn anyone for any kind of consensual sexual practice, or any kind of sexual intuition, or sexual proclivity. You would only get encouragement from him. And I think this goes back to how difficult it was to be gay 40 years ago, and I'm sure for many people how difficult it is to be gay right now. Putting myself in the shoes of that 16-year-old boy who is wondering about being attracted to guys, it's the loveliest thing to find someone who is supportive, and not condemning. How encouraging and interested he was when I talked to him about that. Sky didn't precisely dress me up but said try this on, try that on.

Maybe criticizing a play of Sky's is equal to criticizing his sexuality. That makes a lot of sense because of the way he defines himself. I think he would say: "I'm an artist" and then: "I'm a sexual being," more or less in the same breath. Those are the two most important things in his life. Why can't they be linked? You attack one, you're very possibly attacking the other. And you cannot attack my sexuality therefore you cannot attack my art. By the way, did you add oil when you put in the mushrooms? Could you? Because they love it, they soak it up. That's perfect. And stir it. And if they're getting mushy then just kill the heat. You know what? They're going to be heated up again when we add the rice, so why don't you just put the lid on and kill the heat? We're going to eat well tonight.

# Bob Wiseman Intro Before Lyric
# From http://backtotheworld.net/,
# Followed by Bob Wiseman Lyric

## Introduction by Carl Wilson

And one title plays on the fact that this is also the syntax of email: mothface@yahoo.ca, the address of the Toronto actor Tracy Wright (previously discussed here), who broke many of our hearts when she died at age 50 in 2010 of pancreatic cancer.

The song tells the story of a time in the 1980s when Wiseman agreed to act in a play Wright wrote "that made no sense" because he figured no one "in their right mind" would put it on, but then theatre artist Sky Gilbert signed on to produce it in his Rhubarb experimental-theatre festival. As a result, Wiseman sings: "I always knew that I had nothing in common with Sky Gilbert." The line is repeated over and over, anthemically, in harmony.

Hearing it first at last week's launch concert at the Tranzac Club in Toronto, it started annoying me: Who outside a small Toronto arts circle gives a shit how Bob Wiseman feels about Sky Gilbert? Why write a song picking on Gilbert anyway?

Then the lyrics cross-cut to Wright's memorial, when Gilbert got up and said just what Wiseman was feeling and thinking about her, and moved him to tears. It turned out the two had something in common after all: "the love of you." And I came close to tears myself.

I wondered whether other people, who hadn't known Wright or who Gilbert is, would be so touched. Would they even keep listening up to the final twist? It made me ask, too, if the electricity of the launch, where many members of the local music community were renewing frayed connections, would come across to an outsider, and whether that mattered.

These are questions Wiseman's album prods: the effects of reference, and specificity versus so-called universality.

*About the memorial for friend Tracy Wright who died too young.*

**lyrics**
*Bob Wiseman*

I always knew that I had nothing in common with Sky Gilbert
I always knew that I had nothing in common with Sky Gilbert

When my performance art girlfriend
Wrote a play in the 80s
That made no sense at all
She asked me to act in it
I said yes because I knew
No one in their right mind would produce it

But then Sky and his friends unanimously agreed
To put it on at the Rhubarb festival

I always knew that I had nothing in common with Sky Gilbert
I always knew that I had nothing in common with that guy

But then I saw him standing at the podium
At your memorial
And he said everything I felt inside
He said everything that I thought about you and
He made me cry that guy
Now I stand corrected
I have something in common now with Sky Gilbert
 … the love of you

# Two Reviews

## David Bateman

## CANADIAN SHEEN

April 16 2011 http://batemanreviews.blogspot.ca/

Charlie Sheen and Sky Gilbert have a lot in common. They're not afraid to say what's on their mind, and they don't care if it pisses a lot of people off when they say it. This past week Toronto was treated to brilliant extended tirades from both of these maverick celebrities in an age of rampant moralism and self-righteous Sheen bashing.

Charlie's two-night stint at Massey Hall was a spectacle to behold, second only to the voracious voyeurism we have been treated to by the likes of Oprah Winfrey and Jerry Springer over the years. A queer theory professor once said to me that there is a fine line between Winfrey and Springer. I agreed at the time, but now I don't believe there is a fine line at all. They do the same thing, in different ways. They do what Sheen is doing. They bring trouble onto the stage and screen and they let us become titillated by it and they get paid hefty sums to do so. The difference between Oprah, Jerry, and Charlie is that Charlie does it to himself. Winfrey and Springer do it to other people and play high priestess slash lofty chaperone to the fugitives and the dispossessed.

I was in the second row centre for Sheen's torpedo tour and two women to my left could not get enough of hearing themselves howl in support of Charlie's sex crazed drug induced escapades, and they clearly loved both pastimes themselves. They had to be restrained by security guards at one point. Later in the show another woman screamed from the balcony: "Charlie will you go down on me?" Charlie, in a sense, took the moral high road by saying that of course he would never do a thing like that in public, and then played devil's advocate by asking the woman what she would actually do if he were to take her up on her seemingly preposterous proposal. Moderator Russell Peters intervened by jokingly suggesting a live sex show, but was overshadowed by the two screaming crack loving sex goddesses to my left who yelled out, loud and clear: "You would spread her legs and eat her Charlie. That's what you'd do!!!" Wow!!! I was loving every distasteful minute of this horny night in Canada. My own past forays into booze, sex, cock and roll were being pandered to and it felt good—in a strange, uncomfortable and totally satisfying way.

The spectacle at Massey Hall last week was not primarily about Mr. Sheen. It was all about me, and you, and the ways in which we, as a viewing public, play voyeurs to so many acts that we may not want to always take part in ourselves, but many of us love seeing them enacted within the framework of television, film, theatre, what have you. But when it steps outside of those safe, comfortable confines some among us tend to moralize and begin to loathe the same people we loved when they were just pretending. Charlie Sheen never really pretended. As a character named Charlie on *Two and a Half Men*, where he continually battles with strong, complex, sexy women who frequently demolish his testosterone ridden ways, it is clear that he is playing a version of himself.

If Sheen, in 'real' life, chooses to take part in what some people (not me) consider a grave illness that needs to be disavowed, then so be it. I'm not condoning or damning any of his behaviour. I'm devouring it. Clearly some of his behaviour will be up to the courts to judge. But in the final analysis, Sheen is just capitalizing on something that has been going on culturally for a very long time, and whether he knows it or not, he has decided to be one of many glorious sex positive metaphoric pricks attempting to burst our self righteous little bubbles regarding the fine line between art and life—sometimes they are the very same thing.

On the second day of his Toronto visit Sheen publicized a walk from the Ritz Carlton to Massey Hall, and invited anyone who cared to join him to make the trek with him in support of people struggling with bi-polar disorder, something Sheen has been recently diagnosed with. I was otherwise occupied and not feeling terribly bi-po that day. But if circumstances had been different, who knows, I might have joined the crowd of 200 groupies who graciously accepted his invitation.

And as if that was not enough gorgeous, over the top, sentimentality on Sheen's part—at the end of the evening when I was at Massey Hall, Sheen invited a Toronto woman onstage who had publicly declared her severe depression over her husband's sudden death two years ago. She revealed that she had mourned for a year by staying in bed and finding profound comfort in watching *Two and a Half Men* episodes every single day. Apparently she had sent Sheen a letter asking if it might be possible for him to christen her husband's ashes onstage during his Toronto visit in order to help her lovingly let the legacy of her hard drinking hubby rest in peace. Her honest disclosure and subsequent ritual were a wonderful testament to the healing powers of televised, hilarious, syndicated mayhem. Charlie and his torpedo team could not have asked for a better finale. It was outrageous and it was moving and I tried not to shed a tear. But I failed, miserably, succumbing to sentimentality in the same way I cry at the end of *Extreme Home Makeover* or during an especially harrowing episode of *The Young and the Restless*.

And how does any of this relate to Toronto playwright Sky Gilbert? Well, go to see his current play *The Situationists* at Buddies in Bad Times Theatre and find out for yourself. It sparkles and shines with fabulous vulgarity, glamour and a particular brand of Canadian sheen that Gilbert has become famous for. It is an exhilarating and intellectually stimulating two hours (one intermission) in the theatre with a brilliant cast lead by the magnificent Gavin Crawford sporting a French accent that competes with the comedic genius of Peter Sellers' memorable Inspector Clouseau.

Basically, Gilbert's play does what Sheen is doing, in a different way. It rips the veil off of polite, moralistic discourse and implicates the audience in a complex web of farcical antics that cross sensitive political lines, exposing cultural, social, sexual, and intellectual play as complex social constructs to be reckoned with. The only thing it lacked, and certainly didn't need, was a running commentary by Russell Peters, the wonderful Canadian comic who came to Charlie's rescue last week and fended off potential hecklers with his impeccable brand of self mocking, reverse racialized humour that is simultaneously dangerous, uncomfortable, and absolutely hilarious. So if you missed Charlie and Russell, and prefer your farce a little less "reality based," then there is still time to catch the frightening and delightful antics of Gilbert's play, running until April 24th at Buddies In Bad Times Theatre.

What a week! I think I need theatre rehab!!!!

## PRANCING, DANCING QUEEN

**Monday, April 23, 2012**

> *You're a teaser, you turn 'em on*
> *Leave them burning and then you're gone*
> *Looking out for another, anyone will do*
> *You're in the mood for a dance*
> *And when you get the chance …*
>
> *You can dance, you can jive, having the time of your life*
> *See that girl, watch that scene, diggin' the dancing queen*
> *                    —ABBA*

Are we ever really happy if we don't hear ABBA's *Dancing Queen*, or at least read the lyrics online, at least once a week? Perhaps this is an unanswerable, unethical "gay" query, given the much needed mode of omni-sexual identity that embraces everything from gay to lesbian, trans, bi, metro, and even the odd straight acting straight looking straight man who likes to dress up every now and then and promptly return to the suburbs without a frock in sight. But how does any of this relate to Sky Gilbert's latest funfest on the nature of love, romance and post-modern queer entanglements? Not much. But it is divinely relevant to the essential premise of the ABBA lyric, "having the time of your life!!!!"

*Dancing Queen*, currently running at Buddies In Bad Times Theatre, and lusciously choreographed by the ever fabulous Keith Cole, is a beautifully strident and cunningly intricate piece of dramaturgy-cum-dance that borrows from old film scores and classic dance sequences in order to create entertaining and thought-provoking glimpses of gay relationships as they reach out toward a world of youth, clubs, dancing, drugs, and non-monogamous desire.

Gilbert's knack for edgy fast paced dialogue, and his directorial prowess as an artist keenly aware of the detailed nuances of brilliantly physicalized conversation, shines in this production. He is blessed with a three-tiered cast that delivers his heart tugging conversational whimsy with the speed of light, coupled with a very insightful and moving look at three fags in search of a brand of romance that allows for fun and loyalty among the unfaithful.

As Alan, the neophyte newcomer, Nick Green's witty, enthusiastic performance seamlessly presents passionate speeches about how "real" relationships don't allow for the kind of promiscuity that the some gay couplings embody. David-Benjamin Tomlinson as Bart is able to counter these pleas with a cool, convincing subtlety that makes him a very appealing, provocative, and sympathetic character despite the non-traditional sexual equation he lives by.

As Calder, Ryan Kelly crafts an incredibly nuanced performance both physically and emotionally. His writer character runs the gamut from Alan's fumbling neurotic would-be paramour, to the compromised, love struck wise old fag baffled by a variety of internal conflicts. Bart's career as a mathematician, Calder's role as an author, and Nick's desire to write, conspire to construct a metaphoric sub-narrative on the creativity and common sense that lasting relationships often rely upon.

As a vastly entertaining and comical adjunct to the script, Keith Cole's choreography has the cast engaging, between dialogues, in silent, scored arrangements that strike one as a cross between vaudeville, musical comedy, and a Busby Berkeley extravaganza—except everyone has balls and there are no gowns or high heels, just men in boaters and summery clothing (beautifully designed by Sheree Tams) enacting everything they have been denied for decades by conservative elements of impolite hetero-normative culture. A sweeping staircase and a variety of clever props by Andy Moro complete the dance sequences with iconic finesse.

Gilbert hits upon a diverse array of social and polit-ical issues around queerness without ever really making the script into a "gay play"—whatever that is. And this is perhaps the beauty of a show and a piece of writing for the theatre that strikes home in a queer'ish world where the specifics of sexuality are being subsumed under the cloudy horizon of an all-embracing form of queerness. All of the sexual equations he devises end up representing very wise, empowered, and "normal" living strategies that grapple with big life questions around romance, fidelity, longevity, and ways in which we might consider including multiple love interests as part of our individual lexicons of sexual and romantic abandonment. What the play ends up giving us, in movement and conversation, is a lovely, warm-hearted, sexy tale about fear, love, and the pursuit of every body we desire.

Ultimately this two hour, one intermission piece of pure theatrical delight drives home the point that, paradoxically enough, we are as different and as similar to normative conjugal union as we allow ourselves to be. Gilbert deftly lays bare the structures we have been denied, and have sometimes resisted (i.e. same sex marriage), showing us that all of our lives can include all of the sublime, the ridiculous, and the joyful offerings anyone in search of a night on the town, in pursuit of the ideal dancing queen, has ever desired.

# Sky Email From Palm Springs

## Sky Gilbert

## David

I might as well reply now as I am sitting in Palm Springs waiting to go to the pool. Just torturing you … Anyway, to answer you question, I would say that my ideas about AIDS have been consistently radical and sceptical of the medical establishment. The throughline from the beginning has been that I see no reason to believe that the medical establishment, like everything else, is not infected with homophobia, and that AIDS has been, from the beginning, more of a mindset than a disease. But what is a disease, but a mindset? I have 'arthritis' for instance, but on probing the doctors, it's just their dumb name for any joint problem. In other words 'arthritis' could be caused by any number of things, and could manifest itself in thousands of ways, and is very different with every person who has it, all they share is their aching joints. Of course I get arthritis in my eye—which is always shocking to people, and shows that there are LOTS of different kinds of arthritis, so to talk about 'arthritis' is misleading. This is also related to AIDS as I was once diagnosed with AIDS by an eye doctor when I had 'eyeritis' which is the funny name for arthritis of the eye. He looked at my eye inflammation, asked me if I was a homosexual, and when I said yes told me I probably had AIDs. This anecdote forms the basis for some scenes in *Ban This Show* where Mapplethorpe is diagnosed with AIDS by an eye doctor—of course there I was making the link between a diseased eye (of the photographer) and his 'diseased' mind.

In *Drag Queens On Trial* I wrote about AIDS for the third time (*The Dressing Gown* has a big illness as the result of drugs and sex in it, a kind of precursor of AIDS writing—but it's a very moralistic play that I don't really like now … *Theatrelife* has a whole funny and dark thing about AIDS, very *Angels in America*, we find out that the boy with HIV thinks he is dying of 'love' and that ends the play …). The idea is that Lana's disease is part of her otherness and she embraces it, in a way. She is 'proud' in a way to have AIDS. I think this is oddly prescient. Nowadays, gay men are watching *Treasure Island* videos that extol unsafe sex and let me tell you, being in Palm Springs, it's all about flirting with getting the disease through unsafe sex. Taking that cum up your asshole is a badge of bravery and pride for some.

Anyway, that was DQOT [Drag Queens On Trial], since we were being accused of being dirty filthy unGodly homos and we deserved our AIDS, Lana was pulling a Genet and saying yes, and I love being an outlaw and I love my outlaw status and my disease (not surprisingly, as I mentioned before, The Glines in NYC wanted the play but NOT that sentiment, so I wouldn't let them do it—they finally produced it in NYC in the late eighties).

In the mid nineties just as I was leaving Buddies I got involved with HEAL and AIDS radicalism through the influence of Carl Strygg (still around) and Rob Johnston (who unfortunately died). Both were on the fringe of the arts, Rob as a bon-vivant of sorts and party creator, and Carl as the possessor of a beautiful countertenor voice, but who has trouble in the industry because people are afraid of effeminate countertenors. Anyway I believed in the notion that HEAL puts forth that AIDS was a construct and that we shouldn't trust the medical establishment completely. This got me into a lot of trouble with the gay community. Of course they ARE DUMB PEOPLE and thought I was saying that if AIDS was a construct then ... *Well what are you saying, that my lover didn't die of anything? Are you saying he didn't suffer? Are you trying to take all pain and suffering and my victim status away? Etc.*

No no. I was trying to relieve suffering as was the rest of HEAL by saying for instance don't just take all that AZT. Of course we were right. AZT was toxic and killed more people I would venture to say, than it saved. HEAL was basically a naturopathic organization which was what scared many.

But then of course they came up with the magic "cocktail" which at first doctors were prescribing like crazy but finally when they got the dosage right it only hurts your liver SLOWLY, and keeps the "AIDS" at bay.

Do I think that AIDS is caused ONLY by the AIDS virus? Ummm ... no. Think about it. How come lots of people have the AIDS virus and live normal or quasi normal lives without drugs? We know people like that. It's like cancer, it's like any disease, it works differently in different people, and the medical establishment made a lot of money through pharma by deciding it was caused by one thing.

What are young gay men dying of now? I would say drugs more than unsafe sex (crystal meth anyone? It's epidemic here in Palm Springs, but no one talks about it) tho the two go hand in hand. I think that it's all about self hatred, which we try and pretend is gone, and THAT kills us.

This was the message behind the man Casper Schmidt, who was a hero for me in the late nineties. I wrote a play and a novel *I Am Kaspar Klotz* about him. He was a real psychotherapist in the USA who died of AIDS but who had a theory that AIDS was masked depression, and basically a form of mass hysteria. I agree there is some truth in what he says.

How can we get better and grow old if we hate ourselves so much and think we deserve to die. Did you see the picture of the twin babies with their arms around each other? The one baby saved his brother by touching him. But no … people get AIDS … but don't touch them! No wonder so many men died in the early 80s! I still believe all this but the fact that cocktails do seem to work for some people now, and then Rob Johnston died, and then everyone HATED me for being a part of HEAL, I toned down my public and personal involvement.

The play *Casper Schmidt* is a kind of deification of Schmidt, I use the name because I thought the real Casper Schmidt was an AIDS visionary, so in the play it is used as a name for the baby they will have that will (as I remember ) be HIV positive but cured and redeem them all—I have to go back and look at the play but that's what I remember of it. My novel about Schmidt was about a man who WAS the AIDS virus … he is on trial but I think found innocent … which of course refers to the medical establishment's fascism around AIDS causes, and unwillingness to see the homophobia involved in their diagnosis.

By the way, when I was diagnosed with Maria Spondylitis Arthritis, which is what I have, the weird doctor (because I had been too frank upon admission to the hospital) said to the intern: "This is Sky Gilbert, he is a promiscuous homosexual with arthritis." I know what goes on with doctors …

*I Have Aids* was an attempt to move beyond by AIDS radicalism and speak about AIDS while referring to my own radical ideas but moving beyond them. In it I tried another tactic. Fags just don't want to have the idea of AIDS challenged because for many they have their whole identity wrapped up in it (this was what I was trying to say with the character with the monologue at the end—there are people whose entire identity revolves around AIDS) so instead I wanted to just look at AIDS as a manageable disease, like arthritis … which it is these days. That, though is very radical for straights, and even for gays who refuse to release their victim status. The play also tries to deal with unsafe sex and drug use, but of course the fags just thought that part of the play funny, and mildly shocking as it actually reflects their lives.

Being here in Palm Springs and looking at the end-less unsafe sex and meth … I fear for our future and that all of the nice fags are so hell bent on only seeing us as married and adopting children that they cannot see the self hatred out there that is so connected with AIDS and a greater part of AIDS I think than some microbe.

xx

Sky

# Conclusions

# To Myself at 28

## Sky Gilbert

**Me**: I have these papers now. I need to read from papers. Shuffle them around. I spend a lot of time with papers … but the papers are on computer so in order to make it theatrical I thought I would just shuffle papers around here like this. (*He shuffles them, then turns to younger self*) So what I would say to you is this: when you are 60 years old you will find out that you have no cartilage in your right hip and it will be very difficult for you to walk without a full hip replacement.

**Myself** (pause): So?

**Me**: I want you to think about that.

**Myself**: Oh yeah right that sounds 'very wise.'

**Me:** I didn't say it was wise.

**Myself**: Well what the fuck am I supposed to do about that.

**Me**: I didn't say you had to do anything about it. I said you should think about it.

**Myself**: Again. That sounds very 'wise.'

**Me**: Are you suggesting I'm condescending to you?

**Myself**: Duh.

**Me**: Okay, let me spell it out for you. When you get to be 60 years old you will find that your body fails you. You will get old and you will not be able to do the things you did when you were 28.

**Myself**: Can I ask you something?

**Me**: Sure.

**Myself**: Why do old people always think that saying things like that has an effect on young people?

**Me**: Well why wouldn't it?

**Myself**: It doesn't. All I can think about is the possibilities. I just came out for Chrisssakes. I want to create beautiful art. I want to fall in love. Are there things you did that now you think you shouldn't have done so that maybe ... you wouldn't end up with a bum leg?

**Me**: No.

**Myself**: Then what the fuck are you jawing on about, old man?

(*blackout. Lights up*)

**Me**: I think there are two things going on here. First, I don't think we should be getting automatic grants or anything. Just because we're old. Chateaubriand says that it used to be an honour to be old, now it is just a nuisance, or something like that. This is when they are carrying his grandmother into the garden on a litter. Anyway, I'm not saying that the young should be carrying me in on a litter. But why should it automatically be assumed that it's time for me to go on the shelf just because I have a limp and I am not as sexually attractive as I used to be? Just because I'm old, does it mean that I have nothing of importance to say? Or that I'm just talking about old things that are of no interest to the young?

**Myself**: Well that's a perfect example of a complete load of bullshit.

**Me**: Meaning?

**Myself**: No one cares about your whining. You're old, that's one thing, but don't whine.

**Me**: Can I give you some advice?

**Myself**: Okay.

**Me**: It would make a lot of sense for you to skip the first gay hating years of your gay life.

**Myself**: Meaning?

**Me**: Meaning, this is what's going to happen to you. You are going to spend a whole year looking for love. But no one will even kiss you. Why? Because you're just so fucking intent on it.

**Myself**: I don't know how NOT to be intent.

**Me**: Okay, but much worse is what happens AFTER that.

**Myself**: Which is?

**Me**: You're going to fall in love with Glenn—two n's—and it's going to completely fuck up your life.

**Myself** (*standing up, eager*): Who's Glenn? Where is he?

**Me**: Sit down. Calm down.

**Myself**: Fuck the first year of not being kissed—I can't handle that—I want to meet him now.

**Me**: But you can't. Because you don't just want to get laid, like any sensible person. The problem is you're looking for true love, you're looking for the whole DAMN thing.

**Myself**: Well what's wrong with the whole damn thing?

**Me**: Well you can never find it.

**Myself**: Why not?

**Me**: Okay. We learn about love from movies, or TV, or the internet or whatever disguises itself as something else but is really mass entertainment now. And we learn from mass entertainment that there is someone out there who we should and will become co-dependent with. That person will fulfil all of our needs and will love us forever and will be beautiful and sexy and kind and smart and when we meet them our life will be solved. But that's not true. It never happens that way.

**Myself**: So you've given up on romance then?

**Me**: No. I'm very much in love with my boyfriend.

**Myself**: So you've got a boyfriend.

**Me**: Yes.

**Myself**: Thank God.

**Me**: Thank God what.

**Myself**: I'm so afraid I'll end up alone.

**Me**: But you will.

**Myself**: I thought you said you had a boyfriend.

**Me**: I do.

**Myself**: But then you said—

**Me**: We all end up alone. Okay? Unless we do a suicide pact with our lover but even then the person we are committing suicide with can't get inside our head and experience death the way we experience it.

**Myself:** Okay okay we all die alone Mr. Morbid but there's a lot of time before that—

**Me:** And you will spend a lot of that alone too. Do you think your boyfriend is going to be your babysitter or your mother? He has his own life too, and that's part of why you're in love with him.

**Myself:** But at least you have great sex with your partner—

**Me:** I don't like the word partner and I have better sex with other people—

**Myself:** You have great sex with other people NOT with your boyfriend? (*He turns to the audience*) How fucked up is that? (*to* ME) Do you still have sex with your boyfriend?

**Me:** That's none of your business.

**Myself:** That means 'no.' (*to audience*) How sad is that?

**Me:** Did I say you could do asides to the audience?

**Myself:** I'm only doing what's in the script. (*He picks up one of the old man's papers*)

**Me:** Yes, of course I forgot. I guess I just didn't think it would hurt so much.

**Myself:** To have me trash you to the audience?

**Me:** Yes.

**Myself**: Well most of them are young. They need someone to identify with.

**Me** (*looking out*): I see old people.

**Myself**: Whatever. (*to the audience*) He still thinks stepping out of character and being metatheatrical is 'innovative.'

**Me**: Anyway ...

**Myself**: Anyway ...

**Me**: Anyway ... I just think it would be better if you figured out even before you meet Glenn that he will never be your life partner and just enjoy him for the sex and fun you can get out of it.

**Myself**: Describe Glenn.

**Me**: Tall, seventeen, curly hair, round furry butt, Greek looks, Scottish background, wants to be a writer.

**Myself**: WHERE THE FUCK IS HE!

**Me**: Calm down—

**Myself**: I WANT HIM NOW ...

**Me**: I'm telling you, he's ultimately not right for you. He hurts you very much.

**Myself**: Why?

**Me**: He falls in love with a skinny dumb no ass blond named Ricky and ditches you.

**Myself**: (*disbelief*) No.

**Me**: Yes.

**Myself** (anger): No.

**Me**: Yes.

**Myself**: I can MAKE him love me!

**Me**: Look at how tragic you are.

**Myself**: I know I can make him love me. I KNOW IT. (*blackout*)

**Me** (*in the dark*): Well at least you'll get a couple of good plays out of the whole tragic mess. (*Tragic music plays in the dark. After a few seconds of this, lights up on MYSELF. He strips off his shirt and pants and is wearing nothing but a pair of fetching underpants so we can admire his lithe youthful body. He does an interpretive dance.*)

**Myself** (*after a few minutes of dancing*): Fuck this.

**Me**: What?

**Myself**: I said fuck this.

**Me**: What's the problem?

**Myself**: I don't want to do this.

**Me**: What, the show?

**Myself**: I'm talking about this stupid interpretative dance. I mean first of all, there's a major lie going on here, one that I think I have to confront.

**Me**: Which is?

**Myself**: You have chosen somebody to play yourself who is like one hundred times more attractive than you EVER were.

**Me**: Untrue.

**Myself**: Oh like come on you were always pudgy and your face is … round.

**Me**: I was lovely.

**Myself**: You were never lovely. You were always, passable, doable, fetish material—

**Me**: Fetish material?

**Myself**: Well you have no hair on your body.

**Me**: That's a fetish for some people?

**Myself**: Of course. And why should it take your young self to tell you that? Anyway, it's typically hypocritical of an old guy like you doing a show like this to pick someone unbearably hot like me to play your young self when you yourself were never unbearably hot. It's kind of sad really.

**Me**: There's that word again.

**Myself**: Well I call a spade a spade. Speaking of which, I also wish to point out that the whole idea of me doing a dance to show off my 'lithe young body'—to quote the script—is completely offensive and inaccurate.

**Me**: What are you talking about?

**Myself**: Here. (He picks up the pile of papers) It says here: "He strips off his shirt and pants and is wearing nothing but a pair of fetching underpants so we can admire his lithe youthful body. He does an interpretive dance ..." You were NEVER lithe.

**Me**: When I was at York University I weighed 160 pounds.

**Myself**: For one month. And even then you were NEVER lithe.

**Me**: Lithe is ... in the eye of the beholder ...

**Myself**: No. It's definitely not. And don't you think it's kind of weird and a little perverted that you want me to do an interpretative dance in my underwear? I think you're getting off on this. Do you find me sexually attractive?

**Me**: Yes, in fact, I do.

**Myself**: That's sick.

**Me**: I think it's healthy that I find my youthful self appealing.

**Myself**: But I'm not you. I'm an actor you hired to play you.

**Me**: Here (*going over and collecting a bunch of papers from the pile*).

**Myself**: What's that?

**Me**: It's a copy of a photo that was taken of Glenn and me many years ago. I want people to have a look at it. (*He starts to hand it out to the audience*).

**Myself**: Let me see. (*Gives him one*) What's this supposed to prove?

**Me**: It proves that I was attractive. Did you know that when I took this photo I thought that I wasn't as attractive as Glenn, that in fact he was beautiful and I was ugly?

**Myself**: You love going on about that. (*He looks at it*) I think you're both pretty gross.

**Me** (handing out photos): Why are you being deliberately cruel?

**Myself**: I'm just being honest. Do you know how sad this is, you handing out pictures of your young ordinary looking self to the audience?

**Me**: STOP SAYING I'M SAD! YOU OBVIOUSLY THINK OLD PEOPLE ARE ALL SAD. YOU ARE GOING TO HAVE A TERRIBLE TIME AGING!!!

**Myself**: I rest my case. (MYSELF *goes to the side of the stage and picks up a curly brunette wig and puts it on his head.*) This is what you really looked like when you were young.

**Me**: I cut my hair.

**Myself**: But this is your real hair. Why are you ashamed of your real hair?

**Me**: That's not … a good look for me.

**Myself**: Why—do you want to hide who you really are.

**Me**: I'm NOT HIDING. I'm the OUTEST PERSON IN TORONTO for Chrissakes. I'm practically the outest person in the whole FUCKING WORLD.

**Myself**: I'm not talking about being out. Being out is easy. I'm talking about being yourself.

**Me**: Excuse us, for a minute, will you? (*Blackout. Pleasant music plays for a few seconds. Then the lights come up on the two of them.* ME *sits calmly in a chair.* MYSELF *is lying on the floor tied up, in his underwear, writhing about.*) I apologise for having to do this but myself just got out of hand. So this is the situation as I see it. This play is called "To My 28 year Old Self" and the subtitle is "Sky Gilbert talks to his younger self." The idea was that I would have the opportunity to impart some knowledge to my younger self, wisdom that was the result of age. (*He kicks* MYSELF *who is making too much noise*). Sorry. And on that note this is what I wanted to say. (*He searches for a place in the paper and reads.*) The problem with you Sky is that you care too much what other people think. This is something that comes from your ambitious parents but there's no point in talking about that, is there? Basically your parents taught you to live in fear of the judgment of others just as you lived in fear of the judgment of your parents as a child, so you have spent your life trying to please other people, and worrying about what they think. You have to nip this in the bud right now. Because you did and said radical things you could fool yourself into believing that you don't care what other people think, but in fact, every bad review wounded you, every disapproving comment upset you, when you wrote your plays you wanted people to enjoy them, you wanted to make people laugh. It's abandonment issues (MYSELF *makes a big groan and is kicked by* ME *again*) which is stupid and boring to talk about but the point is that you don't have to prove yourself all the time. All the good things in your life are NOT going to suddenly disappear if you are not CONSTANTLY being told that you are wonderful. And that means really not caring what other people think of you. Okay. So could you try that? Before it's too late, maybe? (*He throws the paper down and sits in the chair. Blackout. Music. Lights up on* MYSELF *who has put his clothes back on. He is walking around a chair that* ME *is seated in.* ME *is tied to the chair. Fully clothed of course, but his mouth is not covered yet).* How did you do that so quickly?

**Myself**: It's the magic of theatre. (ME *struggles for a minute*) I hope you don't find this sexually exciting.

**Me**: I do actually. I enjoy very much being tied up my a young, effeminate male.

**Myself**: Oh Jesus.

**Me**: You're not quite effeminate enough, actually.

**Myself** (*fey*): Mercy me.

**Me**: It also reminds me of that scene in that James Bond movie where Daniel Craig is tied to a chair and the villain tortures his balls.

**Myself**: I'm not going to torture your balls.

**Me** (*disappointed*): No?

**Myself**: It might be a little too much fun for you.

**Me**: But you actually might find that it opens up some new avenues of (MYSELF *takes a piece of tape and puts it around* ME's *mouth.* ME *just wriggles.*) I guess I'm pretty disappointed about how you ended up being an old letch. So many hopes … dreams … as I remember it, you once wanted to be a world famous writer. You thought that you would write bestselling books that would be in demand everywhere—they would laud you in the *New Yorker* and the *New York Times*. That hasn't happened. You are a minor Canadian playwright, the one they invite on the panel when the can't get Daniel MacIvor, or Brad Fraser. Nobody reads your novels. Nobody CARES Sky. Friends … umm …. theatre friends. Nuf said? I mean sure they LIKE you in their WAY, they like you on stage but do they really want to spend a lot of time with you? No. You're lonely Sky. You're sixty years old and you're lonely. Your lover well … your lover says he loves you very much, but he also says you're a big disappointment as a boyfriend. You don't listen to him, you don't care enough and you're just ultimately … not very supportive. You're not very good at loving so how can you expect to be loved back? And are you happy? Can you really say you are happy, Sky, when the only time you experience true pleasure anymore is when you are writing a play … a play that probably no one will come to see and no one will ever want to read? Isn't that just … narcissism? Oh yes … and sex … what about sex … the 'right' that you fought for, you campaigned about, the thing that you wrote about so passionately as being so important … well as far as I can tell, you can't even get it up. (ME *makes noises*) I know … I know. You like to say that you don't need to get hard because you're a gay man after all and you can always get fucked. But the truth is, you don't LIKE to get fucked Sky. Aye there's the rub. So I'd say you haven't really got much left. Your Dad is deaf and has a pacemaker, and your mother died of alcoholism … so that's what's in store for you. And right now you're already … you're a cripple Sky what life has in store for you is a future as an old crippled deaf, alcoholic. I'd like to use nice words like … disabled or handicapped but the fact is you're a good old-fashioned cripple and you know what people are saying ... they're saying ... wow did you see Sky Gilbert hobbling around? It's so very sad ... but you know that Sky Gilbert had a lot of fun once, you know, when he was young ... I guess he's paying for it now. (*pause*) Is this how you wanted it to end, Sky? Is this how you expected it to be? I always think about what it might be like when I get old, you know, and the one thing I fear, is this image I have of a lonely old man sitting at a table in a rented room with nothing but a single candle. That's my biggest fear. And you know what, Sky? ... it's come true. I don't know how to tell you this. But you're my worst nightmare.

(ME *has been struggling all through this ending.* MYSELF *rips the tape off his mouth.* SKY *gasps and writhes, but says nothing. blackout. Dream music. Letters come up on a project* DREAM SEQUENCE. *The lights come up.* ME *has escaped and is running up the stairs of the audience*).

**Me**: HELP! LET ME OUT!

**Myself**: Hey what's wrong?

**Me**: You know what's wrong.

**Myself**: No, I don't , honestly.

**Me**: You've just embarrassed me very much in front of everyone. That was okay when we did this play the last time but now it's just ... it's just too horrible to handle because ... well when we did the play first at Videofag last February the audience was mostly friends and queer people.

**Myself**: So.

**Me**: So it was okay for me to humiliate myself in front of people who know how fabulous I am.

**Myself**: How fabulous are you?

**Me**: YOU KNOW WHAT I MEAN! LET ME OUT OF HERE!!!! (*He bangs doors.*)

**Myself**: I'm just kidding. Maybe, the problem is, you didn't go far enough.

**Me** (*sits down and puts his head in his hands*): What do you mean.

**Myself** (*sitting down too*): What I mean is … maybe you have to go all the way into the heart of darkness before you can come out the other side. Just think about Joseph Conrad in the *Heart of Darkness*, you know that book—

**Me**: Yes I know that book, I'm a fucking English teacher—

**Myself**: Okay, so you know if the hero in that book if he didn't go all the WAY into the depths of the jungle to see KURTZ and you know, confront the horror.

**Me/Myself**: The horror.

**Myself**: Well if you just go part way there—then you'll never understand the actual full horror of yourself, and it's only if you understand the real horror that you can return to the real.

**Me**: You mean I have to go back to the time when Glenn broke up with me?

**Myself**: Yes.

**Me**: How do you know that's my horror of horrors?

**Myself**: We're in a dream sequence. I'm no longer your young self. I have all sorts of insights because I'm the actor and writer Spencer Charles Smith. So let's do that traumatic incident when Glenn, your first 17-year-old lover, dumped you for a skinny blonde so many years ago.

**Me**: Okay. (*They both stand up*).

**Myself**: Follow me. (*They walk down the stairs and stand on stage. When they do, the words DREAM SEQUENCE change to an image of Sky and Glenn standing beside each other in the photograph. The two actors walk into the photograph, so that the photograph is projected on them*).

**Me**: So Glenn.

**Myself**: Yes.

**Me**: What's up?

**Myself**: Well, I have to tell you something.

**Me**: Oh no. What are you going to tell me?

**Myself**: You don't know yet, so why are you getting upset?

**Me**: Because when people say they have to tell you something it's always something horrible.

**Myself**: Well it's not horrible.

**Me**: Well … what is it.

**Myself**: I think we should stop having sex.

**Me**: What? Why?

**Myself**: Because, I just think it would be better.

**Me**: I don't understand.

**Myself**: There's nothing much to understand, it's just—

**Me**: No, you can't do that. I won't let you—it's impossible, you can't—

**Myself**: And … I'm moving in with Ricky.

**Me**: You're—how can you do that.

**Myself**: I am.

**Me**: Are you in love with him?

**Myself**: I love him very much yes.

**Me**: And you don't love me?

**Myself**: I didn't say that—

**Me** (steps out of the picture): This isn't working—

**Myself** (stepping out of the picture): Why?

**Me**: Because that was exactly the stupid conversation that we had and he never told me the real reason he left me so what good does it do to go over it again?

**Myself**: I'll fix it—

**Me**: But how—

**Myself**: Keep going. I'll fix it. (*They step back into the picture*) You want to know why I think we should stop having sex?

**Me**: Yes.

**Myself**: Because I'm not sexually attracted to you.

**Me**: I knew it. I KNEW IT. I KNEW I WAS UGLY. YOU'VE JUST CONFIRMED THAT FOREVER!!!! I'LL NEVER THINK I'M ATTRACTIVE EVER AGAIN BECAUSE OF YOU. AND I'LL NEVER THINK THAT I CAN HAVE A BEAUTIFUL BOYFRIEND OR A SMART BOYFRIEND AND I'LL NEVER THINK THAT YOU REALLY LOVED ME EVER!

This is too much I have to get out of the heart of darkness.

**Myself**: You can leave at any time. You've always been free to leave.

**Me**: How am I supposed to leave? ... Do I just tap my ruby red slippers together?

**Myself**: Sky. It's you who've locked yourself in. What made Glenn fall in love with you—and he was in love with you by the way—were things about you that were fabulous and wonderful. And those fabulous and wonderful things about you THEY DON'T GO AWAY. When people desert you, they don't take the good stuff with them. The good stuff stays with you buster—so you can go on to create the next wonderful phase of your life.

**Me** (pause): Wow. How come you're so perfect?

**Myself**: I'm not perfect. (*pause*) And if you want to know the truth, I'm especially insecure about doing this dream sequence where I'm just being myself, the very insightful and precocious Spencer Charles Smith a young playwright and your protégé.

**Me**: Why?

**Myself**: Well it's hard to be Sky Gilbert's protégé. Don't you think I might end up carrying that mark for life? Are all the people who hate you now going to hate me? What if being your protégé is the only thing people ever remember about me?

**Me**: This is getting way too complicated. Can the Dream Sequence be over now?

**Myself**: You wrote the damn thing.

**Me**: I guess you're right. (*Blackout. Music. Lights on. A candle is lit.* ME and MYSELF *sit on the floor*)

**Me**: I remember …

**Myself**: Bad start …

**Me**: No, I think you remember it too. It's from when we were a teenager.

**Myself**: What.

**Me**: It was the last day of high school and me and Dan Hill and someone else … some girl …

**Myself**: That' is SO BAD … some girl …

**Me**: I can't remember what her name was or anything about her, I just remember Dan Hill, I guess I was in love with him a little bit and he wrote the song for my high school play and went on to be Dan Hill, you know … "sometimes when we touch" Dan Hill and I went on to be well … me …

**Myself** (with a sigh, leans back): Yeah … well, them's the breaks …

**Me**: And the three of us, after that last day of school in high school we sat on a hill in the park in summer and just talked all thru the night.

**Myself**: What did you talk about?

**Me**: Hopes ... dreams ... the kind of things you talk about when you're that age, all the things we were going to do and how we were going to change the world ... and life was bright and ... it was just so bright ... even though we were in the heart of darkness darkness ... (*he makes a growling sound*) Ahh ahh!

**Myself** (*laughs, feeling bad, trying to say something nice*): You're funny, you know that?

**Me**: You think so?

**Myself**: I really think you're funny.

**Me**: Well I'm glad someone thinks so.

**Myself**: And you (*searching again*) ... don't have a lot of wrinkles.

**Me**: No. I have skin tags.

**Myself**: What the hell are skin tags ...

**Me**: I mean a doctor told me once that when people get old they either get wrinkles or skin tags. If you have dry skin you get wrinkles and if you have greasy skin you have skin tags. But everyone gets something.

**Myself**: That makes sense.

**Me**: No one escapes life ... unharmed.

**Myself** (pause he lies down, comfortably): And you're smart too.

**Me**: Oh … you're nice. You think so?

**Myself**: Yes. I really think you're smart.

**Me** (*after a pause*): Now you're trying to make me feel better after you eviscerated me before.

**Myself**: Am I?

**Me**: I think you are.

**Myself** (after a pause): You mentioned what happened after the last day of high school but you didn't mention what happened after the last day of grade six.

**Me**: What happened?

**Myself**: That's the point. Nothing.

**Me** (sadly): Oh yeah.

**Myself**: Remember? There was a big party at Cathy Marletty's house, a pool party, and Jeff Rubach, who I was secretly in love with, would have been there. And I wasn't invited. I mean I think that would be your 'rosebud'. That would be why you did everything—like Orson Welles, who you unfortunately, resemble—in *Citizen Kane*. Because after grade 6 I was never invited to the popular party, and so I'm going to go on and create

Buddies in Bad Times Theatre, everything so I can be the centre of attention.

**Me**: Sad.

**Myself**: Hey—that's my line.

**Me**: I thought I'd say it before you did. (*Good natured pause. Then*) Can I say something?

**Myself** (sits up): Sure.

**Me**: You don't have to sit up.

**Myself**: I want to, sounds important.

**Me**: Well it is sort of important, what I want to tell you. Which is … basically … why I can't have a happy gay life.

**Myself**: Well if you can't have a happy gay life then I won't have one either.

**Me**: That's right.

**Myself**: So it would be pretty important for me to understand that.

**Me**: The reason I can't have a happy gay life is … because there are no happy gays.

**Myself**: Oh here we go again—

**Me**: Well—

**Myself**: Are you going to say—

**Me**: Yes I'm going to say the word. Homophobia. Because of homophobia. It's impossible to be a happy gay man because it's impossible to imagine a happy gay man because there are so few happy gay stories out there ... only sad ones. How can you be something that you can't even imagine? So OF COURSE you think I'm sad—

**Myself**: Please, not that tired old—

**Me**: When you were having your little ... fun when I was tied up, and yes I would have preferred ball torture, you talked about your fear of an old gay man all alone and a single candle—well that's ... homophobia. That's a homophobic nightmare ... can't you see that we have it drilled into each of us, each one of us, that we are sad—all of society does that to us, because no matter what we do, our how much we achieve in the 'arts' or culture' or how many smiling families we manufacture to be a part of for all to see ... so many people STILL disapprove of us ... and there are so many laws still ... against us ... and so much ... disgust ...

**Myself**: What about the things I said in my speech. I feel bad about saying them now. But they were true ... weren't they?

**Me**: I want to ask you some more questions.

**Myself**: Okay.

**Me**: What are you dreams ... what do you want out of life? What do you dream for and wish for?

**Myself**: Well—

**Me**: No lay back, relax, think about it.

**Myself** (lays back): Umm ... well ... I want to find my true love ...

**Me**: And who is your ... true love ...

**Myself**: Well I guess not Glenn ...

**Me**: No. I guess not. So who then?

**Myself**: I guess ... my soulmate.

**Me**: Okay. Your soulmate. (*pause*) Well I've found my soulmate.

**Myself**: But I thought you said your partner—

**Me**: Boyfriend.

**Myself**: Your boyfriend—says that you're a lousy boyfriend and YOU EVEN SAID that you have better sex with other people than you do with him.

**Me**: But he's my soulmate.

**Myself**: How do you know that?

**Me**: Who's going to know that better than me?

**Myself**: Well I guess … I guess nobody.

**Me**: Okay. What else? What else do you dream for and wish for?

**Myself**: Well most of all … most of all … I want to be a great writer.

**Me** (after a pause): I am.

**Myself**: You are?

**Me**: Yes.

**Myself**: But Brad Fraser and Daniel MacIvor are the ones that get asked on panels.

**Me**: True.

**Myself**: So …

**Me**: So what?

**Myself**: So how can you say you are a great writer?

**Me**: I'm a great writer because I think I am.

**Myself**: Isn't that delusional?

**Me**: Maybe.

**Myself**: Well you keep telling yourself that if it makes you happy.

**Me**: I will. It does. (*pause*) What else is there?

**Myself**: You mean ...

**Me**: What other hopes and dreams ...?

**Myself**: Oh, well ... I hope I don't end up alone.

**Me**: You've expressed that particular hope and dream in the form of a negative.

**Myself**: It's MY hope and MY dream so I get to express it any way I want.

**Me** (*pause*): Well I'm not alone.

**Myself**: I thought you said we all die alone.

**Me**: We do. But right now I have ... I have a very few friends but they are good friends. And a man with a few good friends is richer in friendship than a man who has many many friends who are not true.

**Myself**: Who said that?

**Me**: I did.

**Myself**: Oh well, it must be true then.

**Me** (*sitting up, emphatic*): That's one thing you could really start doing now, is start listening to your own opinion of yourself and not other people's. It would be a good start.

**Myself**: Start of what.

**Me**: A good start on the rest of your life.

**Myself** (sitting up, too): You know I'm glad we had this time together. (*He takes the candle to the washroom*)

**Me** (singing): Just to have a laugh and sing a song! (MYSELF *returns and looks at him quizzically*) You know. (*He shakes his ear*)

**Myself**: What the fuck are you going on about?

**Me**: Carol Burnett?

**Myself**: Sky, I'm Spencer. I've never even HEARD of Carol Burnett.

**Me**: Oh, I guess that means the play's over. (*pause*) Did you learn anything?

**Myself**: Not really. I mean it's not like I'm going to take advice from you. What do you know.

**Me**: Nothing, absolutely nothing.

**Myself**: So, I'm in the mood for a drink. (*He blows the candle out. The lights go up to full and they stand up.*) Do you wanna come?

**Me**: I hardly ever say no to a drink.

**Myself**: Where should we go?

**Me**: Woody's?

**Myself** (in disbelief): Woody's? Are you serious, Woody's? You want to go to Woody's?

**Me**: Why not?

**Myself**: Even I'm too old for Woody's. They must run for the hills when you hobble in there.

**Me**: They do, but I don't care. Watching all that panic in the young, is kind of sexy. Well … where do you want to go?

**Myself**: I don't know. (*pause*) The Gladstone?

**Me**: The Gladstone? Is that even a gay bar?

**Myself**: Well it is and it isn't.

**Me**: That means a bunch of trendy fags who don't look gay because they have beards and glasses hanging around with straight people trying to pretend they are straight.

**Myself** (Sigh): Do we have to go to a GAY bar—

**Me**: Hey I thought I was talking to my young self, my young self would always want to go to a gay bar …

**Myself**: Not when you first came out, when you first came out, you were looking for love ... remember? ... And I want to go to the Gladstone ...

**Me**: You're not going to find love at the fucking Gladstone. (*pause*) What about The Beaver?

**Myself**: Okay.

**Me**: At least The Beaver is actually gay.

**Myself**: I'm fine with The Beaver.

**Me**: And you might fuck the bartender or a member of some band that's playing there in the washroom to make up for not finding true love.

**Myself**: ...Whatever ...

**Myself** (*as they go out the door*): Are you going to desert me for the bathhouse later?

**Me**: Probably sooner than later.

**Myself**: That's so sad ...

**Me**: Sad is in the eye of the beholder Buddy ...

**Myself**: Is it? I'm not so sure ...

The End

# The AIDS Plays, Or "oranges are not the only fruit"

## David Bateman

*These cultural events provide the means for memorializing the dead, mobilizing the living, and sustaining hope and survival. Equally as important, AIDS theatre and perform- ance create new ways of imagining community in the face of crisis. If we are now to resist the banalization of AIDS, and if we are to continue the cultural work necessary so that we do not abandon hope, we will need to draw upon the historical legacy of AIDS performance and activism. When we do so, we both recover a record of our past and seek to secure the future of our communities. These efforts ... are the acts of intervention that we must continue to produce in the ongoing struggles against AIDS.*[1]

*—Román, 284*

Sky Gilbert's work has consistently addressed the AIDS pandemic in startling liberationist ways. Rather than delving into the complex often polemically driven nar- ratives embraced by playwrights such as Larry Kramer in his formative AIDS narrative, *The Normal Heart*, Gilbert first began[2] by locating the issue surrounding AIDS within a broader realm that embraces one of his

favourite topics, effeminacy. In a 2009 letter of support
for my application to the Chalmer's Fellowship program,
Dr. Gilbert located the idea of femininity in a gay male
body within the larger context of an AIDS narrative he
had seen me perform:

> It is my belief that the key to queer politics is the
> exploration of male femininity, and this has been the
> focus of David's work for years. The idea is not of
> course to suggest that all gay men are feminine, but
> to look at gayness through the lens of femininity,
> valuing effeminacy and the redemptive qualities it
> has for our culture.

At the risk—as delightful and attractive as it may
seem to me—of inserting too much of my own creative
strategies into an essay about Sky Gilbert's AIDS plays,
it is interesting to me as an HIV/AIDS artist of sorts to
look at the ways in which Sky has been able to see a variety of styles and impulses within a single area. His talent
for multi-narrative diversity within what could become
a narrow didacticism in the hands of a less insightful
playwright, can be a startling and satisfying spectatorial
experience that may seem both baffling and enlightening
at the same time.

When he described my first AIDS monologue as
"a particularly successful example of [my] style which
combines poetry, performance and politics into a witty
mélange which in this case challenges some of our fundamental ideas about HIV and AIDS," I was of course
flattered and yet taken aback by something I was fully
aware of. My own femininity has inspired much of my
autobiographical work, which of course is like saying
that the life of an orange is about being orange. To hear

someone else tell me that in a letter of support is another matter entirely.

But apart from my own biopic tendencies, I was struck by the ways in which Sky was able to traverse a variety of styles and creative strategies that he sees within a particularly "gay" context. His historicization of the term "euphuism"—a particularly feminized term historically—was my first introduction to the term and his immense interest in it as a distinct writing style:

> When I saw David's piece at Rhubarb! I was struck by it's similarly to the Euphuist style (an early modern poetic style which is attributed to John Lyly). Euphuism took the simile and stretched the form to an almost ridiculous baroque extreme—which is what David has always done in his work. David's Euphuistic style is very suitable to a performance piece that is focused on endless similes. This kind of work is the literary equivalent of mannerism in visual art, and is in my view connected with the gay camp sensibility of "too too"—too much. This overflowing deluge of words and images reflects the gay experience of a world in which we are often excluded from traditional relationships and societal institutions and through our work become hysterical describers of it.

Although Sky doesn't take part in the Euphuist tradition on a regular basis, it is fair to say that the repetition of a powerful AIDS narrative within his body of work, attaching itself to a variety of seemingly disparate issues, sheds a strong light upon a kind of cultural euphuism whereby words and language in general take on particular decorative characteristics in order to perform particular effects. This is the essence of performativity, and relates specifically to the courtroom scene J. Paul Halferty insightfully refers to in his opening essay.

The juridical nature of certain forms of performative speech were first outlined by J.L. Austin in his 1960's book *How to do Things with Words*, and provided a diverse breeding ground for a substantial amount of queer theory to refract from in the following decades. Some forms of queer theory, in the hands of writers such as Judith Butler, Eve Kosofsky Sedgwick, and D.A. Miller, to name only a few, exhibit a kind of decorative approach to language indirectly akin to a euphuistic style.

The at times "decorative" performativity of any given Gilbert play, and the AIDS plays specifically, illustrates how marginalized situations located within the realm of sexuality and all of its "messy parts" can become about more than one thing. Lana's courtroom speech, already cited in Halferty's essay, drives home a significant point about illness and femininity in a single blow from the point of view of a memorable character who has, in all likelihood, given and perhaps been given many many blowjobs. Let's not quibble about specific sexual acts. Undoubtedly she puts the promise back into promiscuity in her own wilful and celebratory self-defence.

> LANA: And who are you, who is anyone to judge? Yes, I am a drag queen and yes I am dying of AIDS. Perhaps I have made choices many would not agree with but I followed my heart [...] I have not been afraid to look inside myself, to live on the edge of morality, society, of the world itself and if I must die for it, so be it. And to all the little boys out there who don't want to wear their blue booties but pick out pink ones, to all the little girls who would rather wear army boots than spike heals, to anyone who

has ever challenged authority because they lived by
their own lights I say don't turn back. Don't give up.
It was worth it. (78–79)

Much later in Sky's work, a speech by a central character echoes Lana's words with a familiar yet fresh ring
of AIDS liberationist rhythmic celebration. When Ron
stands proud in *I Have AIDS*, at the end of an extended
monologue representing a call to young homosexual men
from all walks of life who may be confronting illness from
within an isolated environment, we have a startling and
moving tribute to perseverance and hopefulness much
like Lana's narrative thrust in her courtroom monologue.

> You have to learn to embrace adversity. That's what
> I've tried to do. I'm proud to have AIDS. AIDS is
> part of who I am. I have a wonderful supportive
> community around me and it's made my life a lot
> better than it ever was. And I'm not afraid to say it.
> That's what I want to tell you. (57)

By navigating his way through a lengthy autobiographical journey the character of Don, played with a
beautiful and powerful passivity and grace by Ryan Kelly,
Gilbert's AIDS character in *I Have AIDS* proclaims his
brave compulsion. When he clearly states—"That's what
I wanted to tell you"—he uses his voice in order to make
his stance on his pathology very clear. He locates his illness within a lifetime of oppression and marginalization.
By doing so his voice becomes a radiant and radiating net-
work of experience that has led him to a particular point
in his life. Like Lana in *Drag Queens In Outer Space* Ron
has seen his way through a sometimes harrowing series of
life events. The events of Lana's life are decidedly more
performance oriented and surrounded by the diverse

degrees of glamour found within the world of drag. And yet, Lana and Ron are not such very queer bedfellows from within the overall lexicon of Gilbert's AIDS dramedies. They are cut from the same cloth and reveal the diversity and texture of a rich dramaturgical fabric.

Another Gilbert play, situated between *Drag Queens In Outer Space* and *I Have AIDS*, reveals a similar compulsion for the construction of a somewhat compulsive character caught between the slices of a delicious heterosexual sandwich—a triangular aperitif of sorts—to call out to a world of AIDS hysteria with a message of hope and revision. In a *Theatre Journal* review in 2000, seven years before my own diagnosis as HIV positive, I cited the significance of Sky Gilbert's revisionist plea imagined through the words of a truly memorable character.

> By giving his central character the opportunity to create a kind of comic soapbox upon which to perform his social and sexual identity, Gilbert creates a sophisticated brand of didactic political comedy. The inclusion of excerpts from Casper G. Schmidt's theories in Howard's final monologue adds an elegiac quality to the play. Howard prophesies that John and Mandy's child will be born with AIDS but will live and love happily and "disease free" to a ripe old age without endangering the lives of others. By sharing his dream for Mandy and John's unborn baby, Howard asks the audience to consider a revisionist version of an all too familiar tragic scenario. He names the baby Casper as homage to Schmidt's plea to reevaluate the cause of AIDS.

*Theatre Journal,* Johns Hopkins Press, Volume 52, Number 1, March 2000 pp. 125-126 | 10.1353/tj.2000.0002.

The above speech, and the title of the play *The Birth of Casper G. Schmidt* reveals both the hopeful revisionism and that astute and timely historicization Gilbert's AIDS related plays have consistently possessed. Birth becomes a resistant signifier toward the idea of imminent death that has been projected onto the bodies of HIV/AIDS survivors from the very beginning. The naming of a significant historical figure, Casper G. Schmidt, in the title points to well born documentation of the struggle to re-define AIDS for the living—and to honour the dead—and to give it a less damning and negative cultural pathology as it plays itself out in the lives of millions of victims of what—despite profound medical advance-ment—remains a mysterious pathology that acts and reacts differently depending upon its host. Gilbert's work hosts many possibilities within these AIDS inflected realms and provides an amazing trajectory for audiences and readers interested in the ways in which one queer Canadian artist has intervened and resisted "the banaliza-tion of AIDS," (Román, 284) by continuing to do "the cultural work necessary so that we do not abandon hope … to draw upon the historical legacy of AIDS perform-ance and activism … When we do so, we both recover a record of our past and seek to secure the future of our communities." (Román, ibid 284)

When I die of AIDS, or some related physical fuckup, sometime over the next several centuries, I will always have the memory of the first time I saw the title of Sky's most recent AIDS narrative on a poster, and how I recoiled at the thought of something so bold. Thinking to myself: "Oh no, what is he going to say about this!?" There is jealousy and there is love. I am jealous of Sky's plays for one simple reason. Because I love them. I love their compulsions, their distortions, their relentless refusal to accept the banal stereotypes frequently thrown onto the raging fire of queer representation, and his refusal to let any political question that occurs to him go unanswered.

> I don't know how to answer. I know what I think, but words in the head are like voices underwater. They are distorted.

> —Jeanette Winterson

Sky knows that oranges are not the only fruit, but he continues to write about the lives of fruits relentlessly, often raising the same issues over and over again in grand reiterative ways that simultaneously distort (a necessary and innate distortion) and sharpen social and cultural perceptions of what it is to be alive, gay, feminine, masculine, and many other disparate things that have become the intersecting frequently euphuistic cornerstones of his work specifically, and gay liberation in general, from the very beginning. His plays serve to enlighten and entertain audiences about significant political issues that rise from the compulsion of his relentless reiterative and rewarding creative imagination.

Compulsion, among other things, is his muse.

## Endnotes

1. Ròman, David, Acts of Intervention: Performance, Gay Culture, and AIDS (Unnatural Acts: Theorizing the Performative), Indiana University Press, 1998
2. See the J. Paul Halferty essay in this collection.

# Bibliography

## Books by Sky Gilbert

*The Mommiad*. Toronto: Plawrights Canada Press, 2012. (poetry)

*Come Back* .Toronto: ECW Press, 2012. (novel)

*I Have AIDS*. Toronto: Playwrights Canada Press, 2010. (play)

*A Nice Place to Visit*. Toronto: ECW Press, 2009. (poetry collection)

*Wit in Love*. Toronto. Quattro Books. 2008. (novella)

*Bad Acting Teachers*. Toronto: Playwrights Canada Press, 2006. (play)

*Brother Dumb*. Toronto: ECW Press, 2007. (novel)

*Rope Enough*. Toronto: Playwrights Canada Press, 2006. (play)

*An English Gentleman*. Toronto: Cormorant Books, 2004. (novel)

*Temptations for a Juvenile Delinquent*. Toronto: ECW Press 2003. (poetry)

*Coupable*. Paris: H&O Editions, 2002. (French translation of *Guilty*)

*I Am Kaspar Klotz*. Toronto: ECW Press, 2001. (novel)

*Avoidance Tactics*. Fredericton: Broken Jaw Press, 2001. (plays)

*Ejaculations from the Charm Factory*. Toronto: ECW Press 2000. (memoir)

*The Emotionalists*. Winnipeg: Blizzard Publishing, 2000. (play)

*St. Stephens.* Insomniac Press, 1999. (novel)

*Guilty.* Toronto: Insomniac Press, 1998. (novel)

*Digressions of a Naked Party Girl.* Toronto: ECW Press, 1998. (poetry)

*Painted, Tainted, Sainted: Four Plays by Sky Gilbert.* Toronto: Playwright's Canada Press, 1996. (plays)

*This Unknown Flesh: a selection of plays by Sky Gilbert.* Coach House Press, 1995. (plays)

*Playmurder.* Winnipeg: Blizzard Publishing, 1995. (plays)

*The Dressing Gown.* Toronto: Playwright's Canada Press, 1984. (play)

## (Selected) Plays written and directed by Sky Gilbert

2013   *An Evening With Lucky Jim LaCroix.* Artword Artbar, Hamilton.

2013   *To Myself at 28.* Summerworks, Toronto.

2013   *A Few Brittle Leaves.* Buddies, Toronto.

2012   *Naked Hamilton.* Artword Artbar, Hamilton.

2012   *Dancing Queen.* Buddies, Toronto.

2011   *Backstage.* James Street North Theatre, Hamilton.

2011   *The Situationists* Buddies, Toronto.

2010   *Hamilton Bus Stop.* Artword Artbar, Hamilton.

2010   *Reconciliation.* Buddies, Toronto.

2009   *Why We Tortured Him.* James Street North Theatre, Hamilton.

2009   *Steven and Chris Design Your Mind.* Pearl Company, Hamilton.

2008 *Ladylike.* Tranzac Club (part of the 2008 Fringe), Toronto.

2008 *Happy: A Very Gay Little Musical.* Buddies in Bad Times.

2007 *Will the Real J.T. LeRoy Please Stand Up?* Buddies in Bad Times.

2007 *Crack.* James Street North Theatre, Hamilton (workshop).

2006 *The Dreadnought Hoax.* Buddies, Toronto (workshop).

2006 *Bad Acting Teachers.* Buddies in Bad Times Theatre, Toronto.

2005 *Rope Enough.* Buddies in Bad Times Theatre, Toronto.

2004 *The Secret Life of Haddon MacKenzie.* The Theatre Centre, Toronto.

2003 *Heliogabalus, A Love Story.* The Theatre Centre, Toronto.

2002 *The Boy Jones.* Studio Glen Morris, Toronto.

2001 *The Bewitching of Max Gunter.* Theatre Passe Muraille Backspace, Toronto.

2000 *The Emotionalists.* The Music Gallery, Toronto.

1999 *The Birth of Casper G. Schmidt.* Tarragon Theatre, Toronto.

1994 *More Divine.* Buddies in Bad Times, Toronto.

1993 *Playmurder.* Buddies in Bad Times, Toronto.

1992 *An Investigation into the Strange Case of the Wildboy.* Buddies in Bad Times, Toronto.

1992   *My Night With Tennessee*. Buddies in Bad
       Times Theatre, Toronto.

1991   *In Which Pier Paolo Pasolini Sees His Own
       Death In The Face Of A Boy*. Buddies in Bad
       Times Theatre, Toronto.

1991   *Suzie Goo: Private Secretary*. Buddies in Bad
       Times Theatre, Toronto.

1990   *Capote At Yaddo*. Factory Studio Cafe,
       Toronto.

1990   *Ban This Show*. Beaver Hall, Toronto.

1988   *Lola Starr Builds Her Dream Home*. Edmonton
       Fringe, Edmonton.

1987   *TheatreLife*. The Theatre Centre, Toronto.

1986   *Drag Queens in Outer Space*. Lee's Palace,
       Toronto.

1985   *Drag Queens on Trial*. Metro Theatre, Toronto.

1984   *The Dressing Gown*. Poor Alex Theatre,
       Toronto.

1984   *Lacey or Tropicsnows*. Theatre Centre, Toronto.

1984   *Dark Glasses*. Young Peoples Theatre, Toronto.

1983   *Pasolini/Pelosi*. The Theatre Centre, Toronto.

1980   *Lana Turner Has Collapsed!* The Theatre
       Centre, Toronto.

1980   *Art Rat*. The Revue Cinema, Toronto.

1979   *Torch/ Song*. Toronto Free Theatre, Toronto.

1979   *Angels in Underwear*. The Dream Factory,
       Toronto.

1978   *Paris Spleen*. Factory Theatre, Toronto.

# Performances of Gilbert's plays by others

2010   *The Emotionalists*. Summerworks.

2008   *Theatrelife*. Toto Too Theatre, Ottawa.

2001   *Lola Starr Builds Her Dream Home*. Denver
       Civic Theatre, Denver Colorado.

1998   *In Which Pier Paolo Pasolini Sees His Own
       Death In The Face Of A Boy*. New York Fringe,
       New York City New York.

1997   *Lola Starr Builds Her Dream Home*. Windsor
       Theatre, Sackville New Brunswick.

1997   *TheatreLife*. Black Hole Theatre Company,
       Winnipeg Manitoba.

1996   *Drag Queens in Outer Space*. Houston Texas.

1994   *Capote At Yaddo*. Studio Theatre, Washington.
       D.C.

1994   *Drag Queens on Trial*. The Glines, New York
       City New York.

1994   *Ten Ruminations on an Elegy Attributed to
       William Shakespeare*. Riverside Studios,
       London England.

1990   *Drag Queens In Outer Space*. Theatre
       Rhinoceros, San Francisco California.

1989   *Lola Starr Builds Her Dream Home*. Live Bait
       Theatre, Sackville New Brunswick.

1985   *The Postman Rings Once*. Alberta Theatre
       Projects, Calgary Alberta.

## Fiction and Theatre Awards

2010   Shortlisted for the Relit Award for *A Nice Place to Visit*

2008   Longlisted for the ReLit Award for *Brother Dumb*

2007   Shortlisted for the Rogers Writer's Trust Fiction Prize for *Brother Dumb*

2005   ReLit Award for *An English Gentleman*

2005   Silver Ticket Award (Dora Mavor Moore Award) bestowed upon an individual who has excelled in their own career while also nurturing the development of Canadian theatre

2004   Margot Bindhardt Award (Toronto Arts council Foundation) presented to a Toronto artist whose leadership and vision, whether through creative work or cultural activism, have had a significant impact on the arts in Toronto

2004   Notables Award (Writers Notes Magazine Book Awards) for *Temptations for a Juvenile Delinquent*

2002   The John Glines Award (Columbus National Gay and Lesbian Theatre Festival) for Best Director for *The Birth of Casper G. Schmidt* (2002)

2002   The Tosos Award (Columbus National Gay and Lesbian Theatre Festival) for Best Ensemble Play Script for *The Birth of Casper G. Schmidt*

1991   Dora Mavor Moore Award for Best Production for *Suzie Goo: Private Secretary*

1990    Dora Mavor Moore Award for Best New Play
        for *The Whore's Revenge*

1987    Nominated for a Dora as best supporting
        actor for portraying Maurice Sachs in the
        Nightwood Theatre production *The Edge of
        the Earth is Too Near, Violette, Leduc*

1985    Pauline McGibbon Award for Directing

## Chapters in books

Booth, David, and Gallagher Kathleen, eds. *How Theatre
    Educates.* Toronto, University of Toronto Press,
    2003. 182–188

Golding, Sue, ed. *Eight Technologies of Otherness.* London:
    Routledge, 1997. 156–158

Heble, Ajay (and class) eds. *Guelph Speaks: A Community
    Anthology.* Guelph Narratives Collection, 2007.
    32–34

Kerr, Rosalind ed. *Queer Theatre in Canada.* Toronto:
    Playwrights Canada Press, 2007. 256–264

Labonte, Richard and Lawrence Schimel eds. *2nd Person
    Queer.* Vancouver: Arsenal Pulp Press, 2009. 64–67

Labonte, Richard and Lawrence Schimel eds. *I Like it
    Like That* Vancouver: Arsenal Pulp Press, 2009.
    70–73

Labonte, Richard and Lawrence Schimel eds. *First Person
    Queer.* Vancouver: Arsenal Pulp Press, 2007.

Wharton, Greg, ed. *The Love That Dare Not Speak Its
    Name.* San Francisco: Boheme Press, 2003.

Whittall, Zoe, ed. *Geeks, Misfits and Outlaws.* Toronto:
    McGilligan Books, 2003.

## Articles (by date)

"A Sparrow Falls: Olivier's Feminine Hamlet." *Brief Chronicles: An Interdisciplinary Journal of Authorship Studies* Vol 1 2009 (237–252)

"Crack." (play published with autobiographical commentary). *Canadian Theatre Review,* Spring 2008 (58–67)

"Canadian Actor's Equity: Recognize What is 'Canadian' about Theatre Practice in This Country." *Canadian Theatre Review* (Summer 2005) 15–18

"Rand as Guru." *The Journal of Ayn Rand Studies* (Spring 2004): 479–483

"Political Theatre: Because We Must." *Canadian Theatre Review* (Winter 2004): 25–28

"Steal Well: racial and ethnic diversity in the Club Queen World." *Canadian Theatre Review* (Summer 2000): 28– 31

"In Review: Insomnia by Daniel Brooks." *Canadian Theatre Review* (Spring 1999)

"Dramaturgy for a radical theatre: Buddies in Bad Times." *Canadian Theatre Review* (Summer 1996): 25–27

"Ken McDougall: we always listened." *Canadian Theatre Review* (Fall 1994): 151–2

"Towards a director-centred theatre." *Canadian Theatre Review* (Fall 1993): 59–60

"Scenography of Hillar Liitoja: Childish glee." *Canadian Theatre Review* (Spring 1993): 27–28

"Closet Plays: an exclusive dramaturgy at work (Edward Albee's Who's Afraid of Virginia Woolf)." *Canadian Theatre Review* (Summer 1989): 55–58

"Drag and Popular Culture." *Canadian Theatre Review* (Spring 1989): 42–44

## Editorial or bibliographical work

*Gay Monologues and Scenes.* Toronto: Playwrights' Canada
     Press (editor, expected publication September 2007)
*Perfectly Abnormal: Seven Gay Plays.* Toronto: Playwrights'
     Canada Press, 2006 (editor)

## Plays in collections

Filewod, Alan, ed. *The CTR Anthology.* Toronto: U of T
     Press, 1993. 532–572
Wallace, Robert, ed. *Making Out.* Toronto: Coach
     House, 1990. 94–188
Wasserman, Jerry, ed. *Modern Canadian Plays.* Vancouver:
     Talonbooks, 2000. 403–428

## Poetry in collections

Barton, John and Nickerson, Billeh. (eds.) *Seminal: The
     Anthology of Canada's Gay Male Poets.* Vancouver:
     Arsenal Pulp Press, 2007. 220–223
Brooks, Carellin and Brett Josef Grubisic, eds. *Carnal
     Nation.* Vancouver: Arsenal Pulp Press, 2000. 244–246
Cabico, Regie and Todd Swift, eds. Poetry Nation.
     Montreal: Vehicule, 1998. 236–237
Connor, Michael, ed. *Desire, High Heels, Red Wine.*
     Toronto: Insomniac Press, 1995. 22–46
Crosbie, Lynn, and Michael Holmes, eds. *Plush.* Toronto:
     Coach House Press, 1996. 11–34
Denisoff, Denis, ed. *Queeries.* Vancouver: Arsenal Pulp
     Press 1993.
Holmes, Michael, ed. *The Last Word.* Toronto: Insomniac
     Press, 1996. 27–29

mclennan, rob, ed. *Written on the Skin*. Toronto: Insomniac, 1998. 32–33

McPhee, Peter, ed. *Carnival.* Toronto: Insomniac Press, 1996. 167–169

Moramarco, Fred and Al Zolnas, eds. *The Poetry of Men's Lives: An International Anthology*. Athens: University of Georgia Press, 2004.

## Journalism

2010  "Greatness Forsaken" *Xtra Magazine* (Toronto)

2009  "Yes, Hamilton is a Real City" *View Magazine* (Hamilton)

2009  "If that's what it means to be gay I quit" *Globe and Mail* (Toronto)

2009  "HIV Stigma Radiates from Behind the Bench" *Xtra Magazine* (Toronto)

2009  "Hamilton's Biting Bac," *Xtra Magazine* (Toronto)

2008  "The portrayal of gay men in Mark A. Wainberg's July 26 Three for Thought about HIV/AIDS" *Globe and Mail* (Toronto)

2008  "The Promise of Gardasil" *Xtra Magazine* (Toronto)

2008  "Class and Sexuality" *View Magazine* (Hamilton)

2008  "Our Neutered Lifestyle Hosts" *fab magazine* (Toronto)

2007  "Lit Types" (quarterly column). *Mayday Magazine* (Hamilton)

2007 "Lit Types" (quarterly column). *Mayday Magazine* (Hamilton)

2007 "R.I.P. Gay Fiction" *fab magazine* (Toronto)

2007 "Come On Mr. Copper Get Over It" *View Magazine* (Hamilton)

2007 "Lit Types" (quarterly column). *Mayday Magazine* (Hamilton)

2007 "Notes on Another Scandal" *Xtra Magazine* (Toronto)

2006 "Diary of Jaunty James St Walk" *View Magazine* (Hamilton)

2006 "It's a Beautiful Day in my Neighborhood" *View* (Hamilton)

2005 "What's the Future of Church Street?" *Xtra Magazine* (Toronto)

## Films written, directed and produced by Sky Gilbert

1997 *I Am The Camera, Dying* (1/2 hour short 16 mm black and white) starring Tracy Wright, Peter Lynch, Ellen-Ray Hennessy, Ann Holloway, Darren O'Donnell, Shaun O'Mara and Caroline Gillis. Screenings: Vancouver International Film Festival 1998; Inside Out Lesbian and Gay Film and Video Festival of Toronto 1998

1995   *My Summer Vacation* (feature length, black
       and white and color 16 mm film) starring
       Tracy Wright, Ellen-Ray Hennessy, Daniel
       Mac Ivor, Ann Holloway, Clinton Walker,
       Sonja Mills, Caroline Gillis, Shaun O'Mara
       and Christofer Williamson. Screenings:
       Melbourne Queer Film Festival (Canberra,
       Darwin, Perth, Tasmania) 1996; San Francisco
       International Gay and Lesbian Film Festival
       1996; L.A. Lesbian and Gay Video and Film
       Festival 1996; Philadelphia Lesbian and Gay
       Film Festival 1996

1993   *My Addiction* (an hour long black and white
       16 mm film) starring Tracy Wright, Ellen-Ray
       Hennessy, Daniel Mac Ivor, Caroline Gillis
       and Shaun O'Mara. Screenings: San Francisco
       International Lesbian and Gay Film Festival
       1994; Pacific Cinematheque 1994; Five Days
       of Independent Film (Cinq Jours du Cinema
       Independant) 1994; Lesbian and Gay Film
       and Video Festival of Toronto 1994; Virtual
       Cinema (John Spotton, Toronto) 1994

1991   *Film/Fill'em* (a 45 minute long 16 mm
       black and white cinéma vérité film) star-
       ring Caroline Gillis and Shaun O'Mara.
       Screenings: Hong Kong Lesbian and Gay Film
       Festival 1992; London Lesbian and Gay Film
       Festival 1992

# Contributors' Notes

**David Bateman** is a performance poet, literature and creative writing instructor, journalist, and visual artist living and working in Toronto.

**Keith Cole** is an independent scholar whose research explores gossip, hearsay, rumours, theft, speculation, and appropriation within contemporary art. He also advocates for the forcible dismantling of civilization

**Sky Gilbert** is a writer, director, teacher, and drag queen extraordinaire. He was co-founder and artistic director of Toronto's Buddies in Bad Times Theatre for 17 years.

**J. Paul Halferty** completed his Ph.D. dissertation, a history of gay performance in Toronto from 1967 to 1985, at the University of Toronto in 2013. His work has been published in *Theatre Research in Canada*, *Canadian Theatre Review*, and in the anthology *Queer Theatre in Canada*, published by Playwrights Canada Press.

**Ann Holloway** is a playwright and performer who has originated roles in the plays of Judith Thompson and Sky Gilbert.

**Mike Hoolboom** is a fringe media archaeologist who lives at www.mikehoolboom.com.

**Ian Jarvis** is a graduate of OCAD. He is the Technical Coordinator for Centre3 for Print and Media. His many films have been shown on television and at festivals around the world. His long-term partner of 15+ years is Sky Gilbert.

**Moynan King** is a Toronto-based theatre artist, feminist, and scholar who likes to write about, and do, queer and/or feminist art things.

**Hillar Liitoja** has done some reading, some writing, some directing and is now engaged in a continual, though futile, struggle to avoid reaching twenty-five words.

**Sarah Garton Stanley** makes new work, directs plays, and works dramaturgically in most things. She is the Associate Artistic Director of English Theatre at Canada's National Arts Centre and co-director of selfconscious theatre.

**Hope Thompson** is a playwright, screenwriter and film director whose work focuses on queer mystery, melo-drama and comedy. Her award-winning films have been screened internationally.

**RM Vaughan** is a Canadian writer and video artist the author of many books and contributes articles on. His short videos play in festivals and galleries across internationally. He is currently between countries.

**Wendy White**—co-creator Empress Productions (1989–1991) with Diane Flacks & Victoria Ward (Sky invite to Rhubarb!); costume & set design (8 Dora nominations with 2 Sky play wins!); high school teacher ("Jane" hosts annual school "Drag Day"!).

RECYCLED
Paper made from
recycled material
FSC® C100212

Printed in June 2014
by Gauvin Press,
Gatineau, Québec